CATECHESIS

and

RELIGIOUS EDUCATION

in a

PLURALIST SOCIETY

CATECHESIS

and

RELIGIOUS EDUCATION

in a

PLURALIST SOCIETY

by

R. M. RUMMERY

Preface by

NINIAN SMART

Professor of Religious Studies

University of Lancaster

Distributed by
T. Shand Publications
221 Golders Green Road,
London, NW11   01-203 1057

First published 1975

E. J. Dwyer (Australia) Pty. Ltd.

Sydney, Australia

Copyright © E. J. Dwyer (Australia) Pty. Ltd.

ISBN 0 85574 297 6

Acknowledgement

THE DOCUMENTS OF VATICAN II (Abbott edition) reprinted with permission of © America Press, Inc., 106 West 56th Street, New York, N.Y. 10019. 1965.

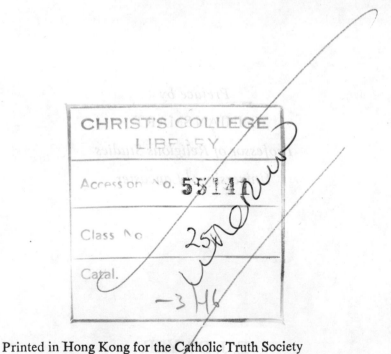
Printed in Hong Kong for the Catholic Truth Society

Preface

Religious education has undergone some revolutions lately, and though too much novelty can be dangerous, there is no doubt that religious education is about the most exciting field of educational thought at the present time. Naturally various traditions need to re-think their approaches.

Roman Catholic catechesis has a strong past; and it is moving into a new future. Brother Rummery's book will contribute to this movement, for it is a rigorous, systematic and open account not only of the implications of Vatican II for religious education, but also of the various changes and ideas in modern religious education outside that context.

Also the book succeeds in clarifying, for the Christian and more particularly for the Roman Catholic believer, the theological commitments and insights which may be behind the refreshingly new approach argued in this work. Brother Rummery sees something of a convergence between the traditional principles of the Christian faith and the modern secular and plural drive of religious education in contemporary democratic societies.

This is important, for it gives the teacher a new hope of reconciliation between his confessional and professional commitments, always otherwise a continuing problem for the Christian teacher in only a partly Christian society.

It so happens that Brother Rummery worked with the Department of Religious Studies here in Lancaster, England. It was certainly a happy thing that we could have an interplay between a Catholic theology of religious education and the secular principles which necessarily a state system of education espouses.

I commend this book for its system, detail, clarity and sympathy.

Ninian Smart

Introduction

Anyone acquainted at first hand with the teaching of religion in schools today is aware of the controversy which has accompanied the introduction of new methods and new texts or the retention of the old. Of the situation in Great Britain Joseph Rhymer wrote in the January/ February 1973 copy of "Catholic Education Today":

> "So far the debate in this country has been marred by an anger and rudeness which have made it impossible for the problems to be examined calmly and profitably. The very idea of anyone being a specialist in catechetics awakens public denigration, and 'expert' has become a term of abuse."

The argument of this book is that much of the confusion arises from a failure to appreciate the important distinctions which exist between the concept of catechesis as such and the concept of religious education as it is variously interpreted in the English-speaking world. Catechesis, in particular, has been so strongly linked with the locale in which it has been principally exercised viz. the separate Catholic school system in which it had a privileged position, that objective inquiry into its nature and methods has been difficult to pursue without encountering the "anger and rudeness" already referred to. Yet, it is possible to note in the past twenty-five years or so the increasing use of the term "religious education" in contexts where Roman Catholics would previously have used the term "religious knowledge" or "catechetics" or "catechism". In the United Kingdom, the wording of the 1944 Butler Act included the term "religious instruction" but recent writings have supported the term "religious education" as a more apt description for the only compulsory subject in Britain's schools. Such changes, it will be argued, are those very changes in language which are an indication of a different way of perceiving reality. So too, minority groups have deepened their understanding of what it is to be an integral part of a pluralist society, not so much as jealous and somewhat suspicious guardians of their isolated position nor, on the other hand, as strangers anxious to submerge their uniqueness to some lowest common multiple, but rather, as contributors to the richness and diversity of a pluralist society based on the ideal of respect for freedom. Behind such large scale changes, there is a complex array of forces—sociological certainly, but also theological, philosophical, educational and, in the broadest sense, political.

For these reasons, a word needs to be said about the approach taken throughout this work. Although the method followed is primarily analytical and philosophical, the very nature of the investigation involves considerations which are variously theological, sociological, historical and educational, for catechesis and religious education are influenced by these disciplines. To the extent that an analysis can take account of the interplay of such separate disciplines, it may become possible to do some bridge-building between groups at present polarized, if only because analysis may remove some of the confusion at a conceptual level which results in mis-understanding and mis-representation of an apparently contrary position. Hence, it is central to the method of this work to consider closely changes in language and terminology.

To establish a common background of ideas, it seems necessary to begin by offering what might be called an analysis of the catechetical movement of the past forty years or so. To launch into such an analysis without first paying attention to exact definition and an explanation of terminology has its own dangers, but it seems more important to try to establish a common background against which such clarifications as are necessary can be attempted subsequently. Hence the importance of the diagram in Chapter 1 which, in attempting to make an analysis of the modern catechetical movement viewed in terms of certain criteria, offers the opportunity not only for an evaluation of the past but also for the recognition and discussion of those permanent factors which help to afford some perspective towards the future.

The opening chapter, therefore, having presented an overall interpretation of the recent past and present, is basic to the three chapters which follow it, each of which takes up and amplifies something mentioned or described in the original analysis. Thus, the second chapter concentrates on the historical evolution and a detailed evaluation of the traditional catechetical model, the third chapter deals with the principal theological influences of recent years and the fourth chapter describes and explains the special character of the contemporary catechetical model known as "the education of the faith".

The second part of this book begins specifically with an analysis of the concept of religious education, paying attention both to theoretical considerations resulting from an analysis of the traditional terminology as well as to the kind of teaching models which can be found in English-speaking societies. This forms the basis for a comparison with the model of catechesis, "the education of faith", derived earlier, and leads in a third section to the discussion of some theoretical and practical implications resulting from this study.

To substantiate the viewpoint that changes in language are simply an indication of changes in the reality which language describes, there is an appendix which traces in outline, at least, the origin and meaning of much of the terminology associated with the modern catechetical movement. But for our present purposes, it is sufficient to indicate the general contemporary sense of "catechesis" or "catechism" or "catechetics" within the following statements:

"Catechesis refers to religious instruction given in a school setting or in a church grouping apart from worship, to young people of school age, generally by means of a basic text or catechism. Such instruction is usually associated with a pedagogical method of question and answer with some emphasis on committing answers to memory. The term is frequently used in a strong sense as a description of traditional Roman Catholic religious education."

Contents

Part One

Chapter One

THE MODERN CATECHETICAL MOVEMENT

INTRODUCTION

The following chapter is best thought of as a selective analysis of the changing relationships between educational, sociological and theological factors in the catechetical movement which was highlighted by the Munich Congress of 1928 and which has continued to the present. To place the movement between important seminal works, it is the period included by the publication of J.A. Jungmann's *Die Frohbotschaft und unsere Glaubensverkundigung*[1] in 1936 and the decade following the event of the Second Vatican Council and the publication and study of its documents i.e. into the 1970's. The broad lines of this same period as regards religious instruction under the provisions of the 1944 Butler Act in England have been well drawn in a number of books, articles and reports,[2] but it is generally true that specifically Roman Catholic religious instruction developed in a manner quite distinct from the national tendencies during this period. Hence this chapter is initially concerned with developments which originated with Roman Catholic thought in European countries and which, with a certain time-lag, influenced most countries where Roman Catholic schools were conducted.

The point needs to be made that this was not simply the continuation of the traditional catechetical activity of the Roman Catholic Church; it was a resurgence and in many ways, an innovation. This is evident in the foundation or growth of specifically catechetical institutes such as the *Lumen Vitae* Centre in Brussels, the catechetical Institutes in Paris, Lyons and Strasbourg, the Higher Catechetical Institutes of Nijmegen and Munich and many others less well known internationally. Associated with the foundation or growth of these centres was the publication and support of explicitly catechetical journals such as *Vérité et Vie, Catéchèse, Catéchistes, Lumen Vitae, Verbum* and many others, all of which are still being published. It corresponded also with the publication of new national catechisms (over thirty such were reviewed or mentioned in *Lumen Vitae* between 1948 and 1962), and with the holding in various parts of the world of explicitly catechetical Congresses.

The analysis of such a period runs the risk of distortion especially when, as in the following, the nature of the inquiry is restricted by the framework of the diagram used. But within its own limits, it does offer an overall view which makes it possible to trace the links between educational, sociological and theological factors.

---

1. Published by Pustet, Regensburg, 1936.

2. For example, **Revolution in Religious Education**, by H. F. Mathews, Religious Education Press, 1966; **The Fourth R: the Durham Report on Religious Education**, Chapter 1.

AN ANALYSIS OF FIVE

1930

APPROACH	TRADITIONAL	PEDAGOGICAL
1. Keynote	Magisterial Authority of the teacher was most important single factor.	Application to teaching of increased knowledge of factors, psychological & sociological to teaching and learning.
2. Relationship of participants	Master & pupils.	Teacher & pupils; role of catechist as guide.
3. Model of teaching	'teaching that...'	Aiding pupils in 'learning that.'
4. Starting point	The lesson in the catechism.	Reflections on life-situations often by use of "themes" leading to catechism answers.
5. Content	Truths of *the faith* to be known; Syllabus of Creed/ Commandments/Sacraments; much learning by heart.	Syllabus to be taught in an interesting fashion but often in sequence and emphasis as before & attention to catechism.
6. Motivation	Duties as members of the One & True church to learn the truths of *the faith*.	Interest roused by good teaching methods to ensure learning of truths of *the faith*.
7. Expectations of parents & teachers	Knowledge (and understanding) of catechism to lead to living of one's Christian duties.	Knowledge and understanding of the truth of the catechism as basis of Christian living.
8. Dimensions of religion emphasised (in order)	Doctrinal & moral. Liturgical mainly in sense of obligation of Mass attendance.	Doctrinal and moral as before. Better preparation for Sunday liturgy as of obligation.
9. Role of texts catechism & Bible	Catechism as authoritative statement of truths to be known; Bible history & some New Testament.	Teaching material — projects & activities leading to catechism; Bible history and New Testament.
10. View of Revelation and of the church	Revealed truths of the faith were taught by the church and were to be known and believed.	Revealed truths summarized in catechism were to be known & believed on authority of church.

2

TAGES OF DEVELOPMENT
- 1970

KERYGMATIC	LIFE-CENTRED & SITUATIONAL	GROUP-CENTRED
'Christo-centric' in emphasis; content stressed rather than method; theme of 'salvation history.'	Human development precedes & accompanies catechesis; in part reaction to 'historical' by emphasising present.	Dynamics of groups — often non-directive in extra-class or non-formal religious teaching in camps, week-ends.
The "apostle" and his followers; the 'herald' or witness and his listeners.	Leader of a 'faith-community & his followers; catechist in role of 'prophet.'	A community of faith but in a non-hierarchical way; role of service to others.
Proclaiming *what* God has done for *us!*	Teaching/learning *how* by reflection and discussion.	Teaching/learning *how* & *why* in group situations.
Encountering the *good News* in Bible/Liturgy/Doctrine/Witness.	Real life situations and use of thematic approaches.	Reflection on life & the group experience; open ended.
Salvation history often in a chronological sequence via the Bible; reflection on Bible leading to 'predetermined' applications to life; key role of word of God: liturgy and para-liturgy. German and Australian catechisms.	Human situations studied more along lines of curriculum and its development rather than use of set syllabus.	Reflection on the life and experience of the group in their present situation; as before — curriculum rather than syllabus.
Joyful message of the Good News brought by Christ; duty of Christians to witness to this and spread it.	Growth in discovery of the relationships between faith & life; freedom in response to God's call; importance of deeds.	Example & influence of group in exploring meaning of life for the Christian.
Understanding & appreciation of Salvation history and the coming of Christ for our lives.	Personal and vicarious experience of life as aid to a Christian commitment.	Development in group situation of personal concern for others and perception of Christian view to life.
Morality as Christian response; Doctrine as traditional means of expressing faith; liturgy in its social aspect of an encounter with God's word.	Experiential — both social & liturgical as prelude to examination of doctrinal & moral aspects.	Similar to preceding but primacy of group experience of liturgy; practical living of doctrinal & moral beliefs through group participation.
Importance of the Bible as Word of God and as text for personal & liturgical use. Catechisms in spirit of kerygma.	Documents & audio-visual material of life situations; Bible *one* of sources used.	Documents and audio/visual material to promote group discussion; Bible within group liturgy & discussion.
Christ as the centre of God's plan for our salvation through the life of the church and its guidance.	God speaks through the events of our lives as well as via Scripture; the church as a 'pilgrim people.'	God continues to speak to His pilgrim people through the events of our lives: Encounter with others leads to encounter with Christ.

3

THE CRITERIA OF THE ANALYSIS AND THE SUMMARY DIAGRAM[3]

The format of the diagram and the selection of material for inclusion have resulted from certain assumptions which, taken together, outline details which show relationships between catechesis in the school situation and educational and theological thinking, without blurring the important distinctions which separate these separate disciplines. This means in practice that the lateral or left to right movement of the diagram is a consideration of catechetical classroom procedures at five stages of gradual development during the time spanned, while the vertical items considered at each of these periods range over the 'constants' of education at the classroom level viz. the teacher-pupil relationships, parental expectations, basic models of teaching employed, the starting points for courses and lessons, the motivation offered to pupils and the criteria used to evaluate success. These educational criteria are followed by five items based specifically on the special character of religion teaching as such viz. the dimensions of religion emphasised (following Ninian Smart's work in distinguishing the doctrinal, mythological and ethical dimensions as basic, but realising that the context in which these are understood provides us with three further dimensions—the ritual, the experiential and the social[4]), the role of a basic text (including the catechism and the position of the Bible in such teaching), the view of Revelation which seems implied, and the explicit or implicit view of the Church.

One final word of introduction. It cannot be stressed too much that the modern catechetical movement has corresponded with a world-wide movement extending the opportunity for some form of secondary education to an increasing number of people, so that those catechized in the school have stayed longer at school, have had better opportunities for formal education than many of their parents, and have probably left school at an older age than their parents did. The five stages selected in the following analysis are to be considered roughly chronological but it would obviously be a distortion of reality to suggest that each stage was consequent on the previous one except by that natural process of dialectic in which a new movement is in some ways an attempt to redress the imbalances of its predecessor.

3. The basis of the preceding diagram is an article in **Catéchèse** No. 35, Avril, 1969, pp. 153-156 by Jacques Audinet. Brother Michael Donnelly FMS adapted Audinet's ideas in an introductory lecture at a catechetical seminar in January 1971 at St. Joseph's, Hunter's Hill, Sydney. I have made use of the insights of both in expanding the criteria used and in developing my personal interpretation.

4. Ninian Smart, **Secular Education and the Logic of Religion**, Faber & Faber, London, 1966, pp. 16-18.

1. The Traditional Approach.

The keynote of this approach is described as 'magisterial' because it was based mainly on the authoritative position of the catechist both as teacher in a school context and also as a person entrusted with a task in the instruction of others in the faith of the church. The major aspects of this position are treated in the following chapter.

A traditional view of authority strongly influenced all aspects of this 'magisterial' approach. The relationship of teacher and taught was in the context of master and pupils, parental expectations presumed that certain verifiable information was taught in a didactic fashion (the parish priest or visiting inspector would examine this), and the principal model of teaching was that best described as "teaching *that*". There was deference to authority also in that the starting point was usually the prescribed catechism at the appropriate lesson, and frequently the method followed was that of an explanation of the text i.e. the question and answer of the catechism. There was attention also to the memorization of both questions and answers with frequent tests of the ability of the pupils to recall exactly. All of this was often part of a concentric plan, ever-expanding the "truths of the faith" according to a syllabus pattern which, contrary to the order of the basic Catechism of the Council of Trent, was based on the sequence of Creed, Commandments, Sacraments and Prayers.[5]

The theoretical motivation for both teacher and taught was substantially the same: he was to teach, and his pupils to learn, the truths of the faith of the Roman Catholic Church of which they were all members. But, as already suggested, the evaluation of this content was often reduced in practice to testing the knowledge of the pupils with regard to the understanding and memorization of the catechism answers. This was undoubtedly of some importance but in itself was hardly likely to ensure growth in knowledge and understanding of the faith of the Church unless there were other factors which helped the pupils to personalize what he had learned and so develop his personal faith. Of course, it was presumed that there were other factors operating so that his personal knowledge and understanding of Catholic doctrine and morality were a complement to his life in a family which gave the example of Christian living and to his personal life as a Catholic in his parish. The duty of the individual pupil to the faith of the Church was emphasised in various ways; he was reminded of his personal responsibility for knowing and understanding it, for showing loyalty and obedience to it at all times, and of living a life which presumed that he was faithful to the regular practices of Catholic

---

5. As Gerard Sloyan has pointed out in **Modern Catechetics**, Macmillan, London, 2nd. printing, 1964, p. 84.

life, attendance at Sunday Mass and the Sacraments. That such an approach was always successful was never presumed as numerous articles and writings about the "leakage from the faith" testified, but at the same time there did seem to be a too easy equation made between instruction in the faith of the Church and the development of personal faith.

It was quite natural that such an approach tended to emphasise the doctrinal and moral aspects of religion much more than the other dimensions, and in certain instances it seemed that the teaching of morality was little more than the inculcation of obedience to a basically natural law based on the Decalogue. The value of a text such as the catechism was apparently in its precision and terseness in indicating what was to be learned, understood and put into practice, but it was all too easy to produce a group of "knowers" who might or might not be "believers." There was practically no direct contact with the Bible except in the citation and learning of Biblical texts, frequently as proof points in polemical comments on heretical opinions expressed by other Christian sects.

To appreciate the viewpoints taken on Revelation and the Church in this kind of approach, the following sequence of questions and answers from the "Catechism of Christian Doctrine" (still in use in Britain) is given:

Question: What is faith?

Answer: Faith is a supernatural gift of God, which enables us to believe without doubting whatever God has revealed.

Question: Why must you believe whatever God has revealed?

Answer: I must believe whatever God has revealed because God is the very truth and can neither deceive nor be deceived.

Question: How are you to know what God has revealed?

Answer: I am to know what God has revealed by the testimony, teaching and authority of the Catholic Church.[6]

This exchange is the prelude to the introduction of the Apostles' Creed, the source of "the chief things which God has revealed."[7] The question here is not one of disputing in any way the answers given, but rather one of highlighting the importance of authority in this magisterial model. Moreover, it is one thing to express these truths in this final form and quite another to try to help a young child or even an adolescent to come to a fuller realisation of the importance of personal faith and of the kind of adherence it demands.

In terms of the position of Catholics in Britain before the 1944 Education Act (and the same thing applies in similar ways in other English-speaking countries) there were strong sociological reasons why a com-

---

6. **Catechism of Christian Doctrine**, Catholic Truth Society, London, 1966, p. 3.
7. ibid. p. 4.

munity which saw itself as a minority against which some form of discrimination was felt to be practised in certain areas of public and private life, found security in just this kind of magisterial approach. This was especially true because of the schools which, generally under the influence of the various teaching congregations of men and women, had provided secondary education especially for the more academically gifted children and, in so doing, had provided the means for a marked social mobility. The success of such schools was often equated with examination results and the avowed intention was to form an elite of Catholics who would represent the Church adequately in public life.[8]

The social mobility of Roman Catholics in the United States and Australia indicates that the same causes operated there also, so that the magisterial model was not simply an English one. With local variations, it is possible to find similar indications in most countries. But besides its educational limitations (to be examined more fully in Chapter 2), the magisterial model was seriously deficient both in its limited view of religion and of what was involved in passing on the truths of the faith to another believer. As already noted, it failed to distinguish sufficiently between this faith of the Church and the development of the personal faith of the believer and sometimes tended to confuse conformity and acceptance of a prevalent pattern of church attendance with personal faith and free response.

This is not to say that it was altogether unsatisfactory. Where the children came from a Christian home which upheld religious values through the example of the parents, it undoubtedly offered a security—perhaps a form of religious certainty at least initially—under the sociological circumstances described in the preceding paragraph. But however consistent the relationship between the teaching model and the community it served, it could only be unrealistic in relation to a rapidly changing secularised world.

2. The Pedagogical Approach.

It would be less than fair to the many gifted catechists of recent centuries to appear to associate them with the worst aspects of the magisterial approach, for there are many instances of catechists who were dissatisfied with a narrow text explanation and memorisation as the chief criteria for the value of their work.[9] Increasingly, however, in the spirit of

---

8. It was from the undoubted success of such policies that much of the social mobility derived. It is an aspect still highlighted by the kind of details given prominence at Speech Days.

9. For example, among the celebrated pioneers of the Method of Saint Sulpice, Père Faillon who remarked that "A child who knows his catechism by heart but is unable to understand the things he has learned if they are proposed to him in other terms, should not be viewed as one who knows his religion." From an article *The Catechetical Method of Saint Sulpice* by Joseph Colomb in Gerard Sloyan (ed.), **Shaping the Christian Message**, Paulist Press, Glen Rock, New Jersey, 1958 (abridged edition) p. 110.

7

the Munich Method, there were applications to the teaching of religion of the main advances in educational thinking, especially in the field of educational psychology and its application to learning. All of this is to be understood under the title of this section. Chronologically speaking, the pedagogical approach followed the magisterial approach; perhaps at times it developed in reaction to it, as was the case with much of the work of F. H. Drinkwater through his magazine "The Sower."[10] Pierre Ranwez of the International Centre for Religious Education, *Lumen Vitae,* noted four sources of improvement of catechetical methods which he cites as:

1 — by starting with concrete facts;
2 — by stimulating an active participation;
3 — by individualizing the teaching;
4 — by encouraging a spirit of work in groups.[11]

The point was that "the application to teaching of increased knowledge and study of psychological factors of teaching and learning" brought about other changes. It is not more semantics to suggest that one teaching in this spirit saw his relationships to his pupils as a teacher, not as a master; as a guide rather than an authority. The psychological emphasis swung more towards pupils learning rather than teachers teaching, even though the extent of the change was often no more than helping the pupil in a situation described as "learning *that.*" It is difficult to specify any marked change in parental expectations as the usual criteria of achievement were still the catechism answers, but from the pupil's viewpoint (and of course, the teacher's) there was quite a marked difference when catechism answers were seen as the end point of an investigation and its summary, not as a beginning. To aid this, teachers tended, as noted by Ranwez above, to look towards reality and the life situation of their pupils as a starting point for any inquiry. While this may have appeared to make no change in the traditional content (being simply a variation in the method of approach), this beginning from the life situation inevitably led to the questioning of the relevance of the catechism answers or of the kind of teaching which began with the life situation only to work towards the catechism synthesis as a kind of pre-packaged set of answers. There was a very real sense in which the more the nature of the inquiry became open and broadly educational in the sense of not looking to aims extrinsic to its own process, the less satisfactory the traditional catechism and magisterial method became. That is why from a traditionalist viewpoint, the application of educational principles regarding the nature and processes of childrens' learning seemed, when all was said and done, to weaken rather than encourage faith! Here again there was the

10. This has been the chief catechetical magazine in England over the period surveyed.

11. From an essay in **Shaping the Christian Message**, p. 3.

false equation between personal faith and the faith of the Church (viewed narrowly sometimes simply as a corpus of doctrine), or only too often, a simple equation was made between knowledge of such a corpus of doctrine and the convinced practice of a Christian life. What we are in a better position to see with the advantage of hindsight was that the lessening of the authoritarian stress in approach and teaching method inevitably led to other changes, and these, far from being final, simply helped to point directions for the future.

In this pedagogical approach, at least in its pre-kerygmatic stage, the dimensions of religion which received most emphasis were still the doctrinal and the moral, especially where the Creed- Commandments- Sacraments sequence remained unchallenged. But as teachers 'experimented' with approaches different from beginning with the catechism questions and answers, the attention to projects and exercises which looked for a more intelligible and life-situated expression of the traditional truths of the faith brought about attention to all kinds of teaching aids which "worked" in other subjects. Thus, in much experimentation in French Catechetics at this time, there were research projects which made use of puzzles, missing answers, crosswords and so on, often leading by various imaginative ways to the vocabulary and precise wording of the catechism answers.

There was also increased attention to Biblical material although this was at first very much centred on Bible History rather than on use of the Bible itself. This was especially true of the Old Testament which was often taught along the lines of that *narratio* commended by St Augustine in *De Catechizandis Rudibus*[12] but which was seen to have value in the school situation principally as an illustration of types and prophecies of the New Testament. A special word needs to be said about this approach to the Bible in the English speaking countries where Roman Catholic opposition to use of the Bible in schools at the time of the various 19th Century Public Instruction Acts e.g. the controversies on the "Bible without note or comment" had led to a curious legacy. One can see the historical problem in the following question and answer as set out in the Dogmatic Catechism commended in its English translation in 1871 by Cardinal Manning:

"Q. Would it not be well to make translations of the Bible into the vulgar tongue so that it might be put into the hands of all, even of the laity?

A. The Church forbids that the Bible, literally translated into the vulgar tongue should be given to be read by all persons indifferently. She even forbids absolution of sins to be given to those who choose to read it, or retain possession of it without permission. The proof that

12. A basic text which has been used and cited at various times in the history of the catechetical movement; for example, Fleury's catechism was based on its principles.

9

it cannot be a good thing to put the Bible into the hands of all persons is, that being full of mysteries it would injure rather than profit the ignorant; and this is manifest from the zeal with which Protestants scatter abroad, everywhere and at great expense, an incredible number of vernacular translations of the Bible."[13]

It should be said, of course, that there was a good tradition of school use of the Gospels and the Acts of the Apostles, and some limited use (at least indicated in some syllabuses) of the Epistles, but the full flowering of the kerygmatic approach was required before the Bible began to take its proper and traditional place in the catechesis of the faithful.

Through all this, there is little indication of any marked change as regards the theology of Revelation or the theology of the Church. But both of these were to be radically influenced by the kerygmatic movement.

3. The Kerygmatic Approach.

The so-called kerygmatic movement (from *keryx* in Greek signifying a herald) owed much of its force to the work of the Austrian Jesuit, Josef Jungmann, whose writings received some notice before the Second World War but whose general thesis was lost sight of in the ensuing controversy as to whether or not there was question of a different kind of kerygmatic theology. The work of Jungmann[14] was popularised after the war through the work of such catechetical leaders as Joseph Colomb[15] and Johannes Hofinger.[16] Jungmann's work looked at the problems of the transmission of the word of God by preaching and catechesis and ascribed the failure of both to an inadequate grasp and understanding of what was the nature of God's revelation to man. As he saw it, doctrinal and moral teaching were carefully organised and carried out, but both seemed to be treated as ends in themselves. There was very little of the "Good News" about most Christian preaching and teaching. He therefore advocated a return to the sources of Christian preaching viz. the Bible and the tradition of the teaching Church, but the Bible was to be seen in its relationship to God's saving plan for mankind brought to fullness through the Incarnation of Christ. His plea was not simply for more scholarly study of texts, but for greater emphasis on that history of salvation in the Old and New Testaments, highlighted and recalled to mind through the liturgical life of the Church. Jungmann's study of catechesis at different stages of

---

13. Quoted by Michael Donnellan in **What to Believe** Logos Books, Gill & Son, Dublin, 1968, p. 21.
14. Translated and published in English as **Handing on the Faith: A Manual of Catechetics**, Burns & Oates, London, 1959.
15. Head of the catechetical institute at Strasbourg and the author of many influential works in catechesis.
16. Author of **The Art of Teaching Christian Doctrine**; co-author of **The ABC of Modern Catechetics; Imparting the Christian Message**; founder of the review **Glad Tidings**. Associated with the spread of the kerygmatic movement in English-speaking countries by his writings and lectures.

Christianity showed how there had been a marked move away from the Biblically oriented teaching of the Apostolic and Patristic ages but showed also by what means the kerygmatic spirit could be regained in modern times. The biggest practical challenge thrown out by him was to the continuing use of the traditional catechism as a manual of theology, particularly where this was the only means used. There were deeper questions relating to the nature of theology and catechesis within the pastoral mission of the Church, the nature of faith and religious commitment—indeed, ultimate questions which involved a radical re-evaluation by all those concerned with the pastoral mission in the Church.

A superficial comparison between the kerygmatic approach and the pedagogical might suggest that the former was more concerned with content, the latter (as the name seems to imply), with method. For comparison purposes this was broadly true, but the kind of separation of content and method implied by the distinction indicates a failure to grasp what was implied by the kerygmatic approach. Obviously, one could hardly proclaim the "Glad Tidings" without the very terminology implying something about the content as well as the method. That is why the diagram indicates a marked change in the relationship of the teacher to his pupils. Emphasis on the kerygma of salvation in Christ was the basis for a less formal relationship, less authoritarian also if only because it stressed *our* salvation in Christ, and gave an evangelical fervour to the role of the catechist who could not restrict himself simply to a teaching role in an exchange in which he was as involved as his students. It is difficult to notice any change in parental expectations although the more widespread use of the Bible and the liturgical emphasis probably did have an effect on those parents who were aware and involved in the catechesis of their own children.

Where the kerygmatic produced its most noticeable change according to the criteria used in the diagram was in the model of teaching it implied. First of all, it undoubtedly produced a "proclamation" model, which, distinct from the "teaching *that*" and "learning *that*" already noted, did concentrate on a more profound understanding of the history of salvation with Christ at its centre. Moreover, with its broader approach and wider attention to the Christian ideal, it looked beyond a school-oriented view of catechesis. It is very difficult to state this concisely but perhaps the phrase "Proclaiming *what*" (i.e. in the sense of 'sharing' with others the Good News of what God has done for us in Christ) indicates both the style and content, especially when associated with the four sources of the kerygma viz. the Bible, the Liturgy, the teaching of Doctrine and the personal and community witness to the reality of what was being proclaimed.

But the major change and indeed the main thrust of the kerygmatic movement was what might be called the "re-discovery" of the Bible. As

11

the quotation cited earlier indicates'[17] generations of Roman Catholics had been brought up with only a second-hand contact with the Bible, especially the Old Testament, except through the medium of Bible History. Even many members of religious congregations engaged in teaching had received little formal training in Scripture studies except under very special conditions. The post-war impact therefore, of the vernacular translations (in England that of Monsignor Ronald Knox and in the United States, the Confraternity Edition) was both a sign of, and a necessary accompaniment to, the kerygmatic movement.

The initial effect of this was on the teachers themselves, whose personal lives were enriched by their "discovery" of the complete Scriptures. Much of the 'witness' value of the early kerygmatic teachers was an overflow from their own new-found enthusiasm. But inevitably, there was besides such benefits, a situation of many ill-prepared teachers who were limited not only in their Scriptural background but also in their understanding of key concepts.

This was especially true of the key concept of kerygmatic teaching viz. the role of Christ in the history of Redemption. But Salvation History,[18] as the shorthand term was called, was essentially an adult concept which required a certain adult ability to view things in historical sequence. As with any other form of knowledge, it needed more than adult commendation to be acceptable to students who failed to see its relevance to their own lives, especially those first generations of students who were introduced to the Bible by enthusiastic teachers in junior classes and continued to hear the same historical sequence from Abraham to Christ so often in their school years that they maintained the "we've heard it all before" attitude which had been their usual attitude to the catechism.[19]

An important bridge between the traditional catechetical method and the kerygmatic approach was the publication of a number of national catechisms written in the spirit of the kerygma. Of these, two were especially influential in English, the so-called German Catechism[20] trans-

17. cf. note 13.

18. For Hofinger and many catechetical writers, this expression is very close to Bible History, i.e. the story of God's saving plan as seen in the Bible. But there are some indications among other Catholic authors of a broader appraisal of 'Heilgeschichte' in Piper's words as "the organising centre of all history. The latter is destined eventually to take part in it, and Heilgeschichte is the power by which purely human history is gradually transformed into a history with God." — **A Handbook of Christian Theology**, p. 163, Fontana Books (ed.), Halverson & Cohen, Meridian Press, London & Glasgow. 1966.

19. For example, cf. Didier Piveteau in **Towards a Future for Religious Education**, edited by Lee — Rooney, Pflaum Press, Dayton, Ohio, 1970, in an article entitled *Biblical Pedagogics*, p. 102.

20. **A Catholic Catechism**, Burns & Oates, London, 1957.

lated into English in 1957 and the Australian Catechisms of the early 1960's.[21]

The main importance of these new catechisms was their redressing of the previous imbalance of the Creed-Commandments-Sacraments sequence by paying closer attention to the Sacraments and liturgical celebration as aids to, or as means of, expressing that form of response which showed understanding and appreciation of what it was to be involved in God's saving plan. But there were still many different viewpoints competing for the attention of the makers of catechisms so that many traditional ideas were retained even in a substantially changed order of content and style of presentation because so much of the work of preparation was done by committees. For example, the German Catechism, which was in the process of preparation before the war, was delayed because the committee which issued the pilot editions between 1952 and 1955 had to consider over twelve thousand suggested amendments.[22]

But the publication of the German Catechism highlighted some very important questions which were basically educational questions and ones which were more likely to arise in regions where the more pedagogical emphasis of the Munich Method had continued to develop:

1 — For whom was the catechism intended? If for school children in a school context, then an attractive text book which bore comparison with other texts used in schools seemed to be required. But this was hardly the kind of book which could be placed beside the Bible as a book to be treasured for one's adult life.

2 — Was the catechism intended to be a manual of theology? If it was, then it could use the terms of traditional theology and could require exact definitions with close attention to exact learning by heart as a safeguard against heretical statements.

3 — Should there not be uniform wording of such texts so that children were not confused by having to learn, at successive stages, different wording in response to what were basically the same questions? If so, why not retain the traditional 'answers' which the parents of the children had learned during their own school years?

It is not surprising that the German Catechism, radical innovation though it was, could hardly satisfy such diverse criteria in one and the same book. In actual fact, it became a child's text book, quite the best of its kind up to that time admittedly, but still very much a text, and to that extent not the kind of book which could be carried through to adult life, especially as one of the appealing features—the very fine pen and ink

---

21. **Catholic Catechism**, E. J. Dwyer, Sydney, 1963.

22. F. H. Drinkwater in *Revolution in Catechism Making*, p. 65 in **Telling the Good News**, Burns & Oates, London, 1960.

drawings—were in a style not appreciated by many adults. Curiously enough also, although the text was written in the spirit of the kerygma, its use of Scripture tended to be mainly as a supporting role for doctrine. Each chapter of its 136 chapters was either prefaced by a Scriptural quotation or else accompanied by a section entitled "From Scripture." It was true that there was a very important link evident between doctrine as such and its foundation in Scripture but the point being made here is that in a number of cases the selective use of Scripture in this way as argument or proof seemed to highlight a functional use of Scripture which was contrary, in spirit at least, to the kerygmatic vision, and easily communicated to children a very limited idea of what the Scriptures were all about.

The sequence of the German Catechism was undoubtedly kerygmatic, for its four main sections were:

1 — Of God and our Redemption;
2 — Of the Church and the Sacraments;
3 — Of life in accordance with God's commandments;
4 — The four last things.

In its terminology and attention to memorization, it remained a traditional catechism but the publication by Josef Goldbrunner of three detailed manuals for the use of teachers helped to guard against the likelihood of the text being used simply in a text-explanatory manner.[23] More important than the catechism and its contents was the degree of understanding of those making use of it, and, one must add, their personal appreciation of the kerygma itself. It is not without importance that to the more obvious signs of the kerygma—the Bible, doctrine and liturgical celebration—there should have been added the important role of personal witness.

The Australian Catechism of 1962 undoubtedly owed much of its success to the pioneering work of those who worked on the German Catechism, but it is for its better appreciation of the central role of the Bible that it is especially important, because as the Teacher's Handbook makes clear:

"The Bible will be used by the teacher in catechetics; it is irreplaceable. It is possible for a teacher to look upon the Bible as a thoroughly reliable source from which he can quarry texts to prove points of doctrine... The Bible is more than that, immeasurably more than that."[24]

---

23. **Teaching the Catholic Catechism**, 3 Vols. Burns & Oates, London, 1959.
24. **Catholic Catechism Book One, Teacher's Handbook**, E. J. Dwyer, Sydney, 1963, p. 26.

14

To appreciate the impact of these new catechisms, it should be remembered that there was substantial re-education of teachers both by means of the specially prepared manuals for teachers as well as the series of conferences and workshops which were organised at the same time.

To attempt to draw together the diverse matters already treated under the ten criteria being used to evaluate each stage being studied, it may be of interest to try to see where the kerygmatic movement was successful and in which matters it was still deficient. However joyful and transforming the message of what God had done might have been to the informed believer, it was not simply a question of repeating this message and simply hoping that it was assimilated by the hearers. Such a transfer of training, however desirable, was unrealistic for the young people for whom the content of the message and perhaps the whole historical vision it implied were outside the real world they knew. The life-style and witness of dedicated teachers undoubtedly helped to bridge this gap, but in many cases, such enthusiasms were viewed with suspicion by pupils whose family and parochial background were more powerful and lasting influences. The point can be well-illustrated by the development in the wake of the kerygmatic approach of what were called "paraliturgical services or ceremonies."[25] This attention to class ceremony and ritual as part of the whole approach in education had all the theoretical strengths of the traditional religious assembly in British schools, especially as it was possible to assume that all the members were of the same religious faith. Paradoxically, the very freedom and spontaneity of worship in such paraliturgies often served as a contrast to the formality and remoteness of the usual parish liturgy, even to the extent of some teachers questioning whether it was a good thing for pupils to take part in something so different from what they would find in the ordinary parish situation. This debate is still going on with regard to the present day experiments with the celebration of Mass for small groups. In terms of its association with the kerygmatic approach, the question was whether such paraliturgies were really part of the life the students regarded as the real world.

Certainly, as regards the dimensions of religion emphasised, the kerygmatic projected a much fuller vision. Even allowing for the tendency towards a kind of 'fundamentalism' in the use of the Scriptures just at a time when Christological studies were becoming increasingly critical,[26] the kerygmatic movement in general emphasised the importance

---

25. ibid., p. 75. "Paraliturgy—a corporate service of prayer and Scripture planned along the lines of the liturgy, and leading those who take part in it to a better understanding of the Liturgy and a wish to participate in the Liturgy."

26. For example, the popularization of the work of Bultmann and the continuing expansion of Roman Catholic scholarship following Divino Afflante Spiritu in 1943.

15

of God's saving plan in Christ and saw the historical evolution of doctrine within this history of salvation. More importantly, such an approach saw morality as the function of the Christian's deeper consciousness of his position as one created and redeemed in God's great saving plan, and looked more and more towards the celebration of these events through the liturgy. Moreover, as already treated, these factors taken together helped to place the catechism in an important place, admittedly, but as one means only in the whole pattern.

From a theological viewpoint, the Christo-centric emphasis of the kerygmatic approach also led to a wider Trinitarian emphasis because it was impossible to treat of the history of salvation without recognising the different functions of each of the Divine Persons. Perhaps, in the long run, it was the attention to Incarnational theology and to the theology of the Holy Spirit which were the most important 'developments'. But no sooner has this been said when it becomes evident that any serious treatment of the history of salvation must lead to questions about God's manner of revealing Himself to us, especially if this history has a present and a future as well as a past. And depending on the viewpoint developed in such studies, the role of the Church could hardly be maintained without many accommodations to such new insights. With hindsight, it is possible to see that the changes brought about by Vatican II, were possible mainly because of the deepening begun by the kerygmatic movement and the questions to which it led.

Finally, with regard to the limitations imposed by the methodology of the comparison table itself, there are four general observations which need to be made with regard to the long-term aspects of the kerygmatic 're-discovery.' The first, and potentially the most important, was the significance of the change of attitude to the widespread use of the vernacular Bible. It is likely that nothing has been more more conducive to a genuine ecumenism than the *de facto* ecumenism which has seen five major English translations in the past twenty years, including the "Revised Standard Version" widely accepted by Catholics, the "New English Bible," and the "Jerusalem Bible" in its various translations, used as a common text by scholars. Secondly, there has been the obvious broadening that has extended the sense of catechesis from the limited idea of instruction prior to the reception of first Sacraments and an expansion and memorisation of basic doctrine over the years of schooling, to a wider appreciation of the relevance of religious belief and practice in life and of the importance of the support of a believing community in liturgical celebration and social action. Thirdly, there has been the contribution of the kerygmatic approach to an enlargement of what constitutes the 'historical.' The point may be illustrated in a practical manner by comparing the inward looking nature of much traditional apologetics in the upper forms of secondary schools where the concentration was on post-Reformation polemics, and the wider vision which resulted when the concept of salva-

16

tion history was seen to have a present and future context as well as a past. Fourthly, we should note again the importance of the German and Australian and other national catechisms as attempting to make a transition from the post-Trent model to one more suited to our time.

In the light of all this, it may appear strange that by the mid-sixties Alfonso Nebrada was writing of "Kerygma in Crisis"[27] and a certain taking stock of the situation had succeeded the initial euphoria. Researchers and commentators on the working of the Religious Instruction Act in Britain since 1944 could have offered some valuable advice because of their experience of the thoroughly boring activity to which Scripture study could be reduced in the school situation. And indeed, so it was proved before long in many Catholic schools which had taken up the kerygmatic approach with such enthusiasm. There were undoubtedly many different reasons for this, but to suggest some of the more likely ones has an important bearing on the nature of this investigation.

Firstly, we have already indicated the dangers inherent in a situation where enthusiastic teachers had little background in Scripture study just at a time when the impact of modern biblical research was beginning to descend from the scholarly to the popular level.

Secondly, as Goldman[28] and Loukes[29] showed in their various ways as regards the situation in the county schools of England, the Bible was not an easy book to teach even where it was accepted as the "word of God." Whether viewed in terms of form or content, the Bible was not something from which to teach apologetics by selected quotations, nor was it to be worked through chronologically like a text-book or novel, not again was it something simply to be proclaimed as always "good news" for pupils! But unfortunately, for various reasons, it sometimes became for some teachers their only text, and for some pupils, their whole staple of religious instruction around the general theme of salvation history.

Thirdly, and this was a particular danger in Roman Catholic schools, the failure of many teachers and parents to understand exactly what their colleagues in catechesis were attempting to do was based on the long standing traditional model based on the catechism. Knowledge and understanding of the Bible was frequently deficient in those very senior teachers without whose support any new venture was unlikely to succeed.

---

27. Alfonso Nebrada, S.J. **Kerygma in Crisis**, Loyola University Press, Chicago, 1965.

28. Ronald Goldman, **Religious Thinking from Childhood to Adolescence**, Routledge and Kegan Paul, London, 1964.

29. Harold Loukes, **Teenage Religion**, S.C.M. Press, London, 1961, and **New Ground in Christian Education**, S.C.M. Press, London, 1965.

4. The Anthropological Approach.

As a general introduction to the nature of the change of direction which is more marked in the next two stages to be discussed, it could be said that both the magisterial and the pedagogical approaches were characterised by what could be called a "pedagogy of *object*"[30] i.e. the models they relied on were more concerned with the handing on of "the Faith" which was taken as an unchanging and universally understood aim. As is discussed more fully in the next chapter, there were some underlying assumptions which saw such knowledge leading naturally to personal acceptance and a Christian way of life. The kerygmatic approach too could be reduced to this kind of approach if the teachers never realised for themselves the inner essential link between content and method in the approach. But where the kerygmatic approach succeeded, it was precisely in being more of a "pedagogy of *subject*"[31] i.e. it looked towards the recipient of catechesis. This important change is even more marked in the life centred and group approaches.

It has been already suggested that the sequence of the accompanying diagram is to be read more as a roughly chronological sequence of development rather than anything else; it is certainly not meant to be consequential or reactionary with regard to the preceding ideas except, as already indicated, through the normal dialectic which accompanies the exchange of ideas. Thus, it is possible to see now that the high point of the kerygmatic approach was its endorsement at the Eichstaett congress in catechetics of 1960, a meeting devoted to consideration of the theoretical and practical consequences resulting from this view of the relationships between catechesis and kerygma. But, as a later examination of other catechetical congresses indicates, the ideal of a universally acceptable model was much more difficult to achieve.[32]

The keynote of this life-centred approach was basically anthropological i.e. it was concerned with the subject or recipient of catechesis in his life situation. In French catechetical writing, the key word which characterised this approach was *réalité* — the here and now situation of the students. This is the spirit of the quotation "human development precedes and accompanies catechesis",[33] the keynote of this approach. This succinct statement which indicates the conditions under which catechesis may be permanently beneficial, should be balanced by the

---

30. That is, as determined by classical theological considerations, cf. Erdozain in *The Evolution of Catechetics,* **Lumen Vitae,** Vol. XXI, No. 1, 1970, pp. 7-31. Also Gabriel Moran in **God Still Speaks,** Burns & Oates, London, 1968, pp. 149-151.

31. ibid.

32. cf. Chapter 4.

33. Adapted from the 1966 General Chapter Statement of the Brothers of the Christian Schools entitled: **A Declaration: The Brother of the Christian Schools in the World Today,** p. 68.

description of the model which evolved under the description of "the education of (the) faith," a concept to be examined in a later chapter.[34]

This life-centred approach involved a profound change of viewpoint, especially when compared with more traditional models. For example, it was customary to speak of the traditional separation of the values of religion and those of "the world" in the sense in which that expression was used by St John in his epistles. The ideal was here presented as the Christian life lived in the world but sanctified by the attention to Christian values, liturgical seasons and festivals. Here there was close resemblance between the implied ideal and the attempt to attain it by the individual which was the basis for so much natural law morality. By contrast, this life-centred approach turned towards the situation of the believer in this real world, and asked him to reflect on his situation and see how he could bear Christian witness in this situation. In European catechetics the approach was at root level, an attempt to cope with the postwar de-Christianisation, an insight into which was provided by the worker-priest controversy. Hence the diagram indicates the relationship of the members to one another as that of a "faith community" in which the catechist is a leader or initiator, or in a more biblical sense, a prophet or witness to the message he brings. This non-hierarchical role of the catechist was an important change which is very much in line with the less authoritarian positions assumed by teachers in many educational matters around the same time. But such changes cannot be viewed in isolation. Even if the catechist had significantly altered his position, it did not follow that parental expectations had accepted this change of position. Indeed, where parents looked to the catechist to supply doctrinal instruction (and the same thing might apply to the expectations of parish priests), they may have failed to understand the kind of activities in which catechist and pupils shared. Furthermore, in attempting to restrict the catechist to this doctrinal teaching, they may have encountered a certain division of loyalty where pupils supported the catechist and this informal situation against what the parents themselves wished. Of course, this kind of difference of opinion was not simply confined to the area of catechetics.

The most obvious change brought in by this life-centred approach was in the prominence given to discussion methods as a form of learning. The model of teaching called in the diagram "learning *how*" might equally well have been called "learning *why*", because the emphasis was less on the idea that there was a standard content for all, and more and more on the importance of the differences in the life situation of each in his personal response to the Christian message. That is why

---

34. cf. Chapter 4.

the statement of "Real life situations" and "Thematic approaches" is to be understood as a conjunction rather than as a separation. Thematic approaches, indeed, were developed originally as much for pedagogical reasons as for anything else, particularly as an alternative to a strictly chronological study of the Bible. The very concreteness of the themes e.g. bread, light, community etc. were the starting points for individual and group research into many allied fields, as for example, the importance of symbols in Scripture. Thematic teaching was originally associated with the junior school although it had its own importance also with older pupils. Discussion methods were also used at all levels but were of particular value with adolescents.

The field of content caused the most difficulty between the defenders of the traditional methods and the advocates of the experience-centred school, as well as between those whose ideas of experience were limited to the "common experience of mankind", as contrasted with those who looked more towards the importance of the unique experience of the individual. Gabriel Moran characterises the elements of the controversy as follows:

> "The understanding or misunderstanding of the category of experience gives rise to two different educational anthropologies. These two are conflicting anthropologies even though they may use the same words. The first will try to locate thinking elements within experience that would modify behaviour in a way not entirely predictable. The second will seek to get a person to think (or feel) in a way that will make his behaviour conform to some standard. The first is social and practical even when it uses an abstract language... The second anthropology is individualistic and abstract even when it talks about the social and aims at feelings. It works too hard at giving the person the right experience, right ideas and right action."[35]

Jacques Audinet, in his conclusion to "Forming the Faith of Adolescents" underlines the difficulty from the viewpoint of the catechist who is attempting, in Colomb's memorable phrase, "to be faithful to both God and man!"

> "There is one fundamental point that must be stressed. We must learn to express the Christian message in terms that are the terms of experience, without being false either to the experience of the young people or to the richness and clarity of experience in the Church or the Bible."[36]

---

35. **Design for Religion**, Herder & Herder, New York, 1970, p. 65.
36. **Forming the Faith of Adolescents**, Deacon Books, Geoffrey Chapman, London, 1968, p. 81.

20

If these are the elements of a controversy which ranges over the fields of anthropology and education no less than of theology, (one taken up again in the discussion of religious education and catechesis in Chapter 5), it is significant that in terms of content, the description of Curriculum Development is to be preferred to that of Syllabus, the basis of the distinction being that the content is seen to be part of the life situation of the group which can be shown to be related to the living of the Gospel, whereas the idea of Syllabus suggests a pre-determined set of learning experiences to be communicated no matter the life circumstances of the pupils concerned. Theologically, this distinction is based on the important distinction between what a following chapter discusses as a propositional view of Revelation contrasted with an emphasis which sees Revelation as on-going. From another viewpoint, that of the importance of changes of terminology discussed in the appendix, the distinction between Curriculum Development and Syllabus can be related to the distinction that can be made between "pre-evangelization" and "pre-catechesis."

Of the remaining criteria to be noted, the most important is the greater measure of freedom extended in various ways to those catechised. This must not be thought of as having reached an ideal form; the point is rather that, in contrast with the earlier stages, there is the marked growth of the idea of the participants themselves, teachers and taught, being engaged in a common task with such respect for one another's freedom that it is not possible to categorise a uniform or standard product of such interaction.

As regards the specifically religious dimensions, the most obvious is that this kind of approach provides more opportunity for some of the elements of religion which had little opportunity to be appreciated in the more magisterial system. Thus the doctrinal, moral and liturgical dimensions highlighted by other approaches in a more didactic fashion, are all here present but very much influenced by the emphasis on the experiential and the social dimensions. In an open society containing a plurality of religions and none at all, this kind of encounter would tend to raise the questions of ecumenism, the normative role of Christianity in Western society, humanism and natural morality, for these are questions likely to arise from the situations of the participants themselves.

Even a very good catechism text book or manual could have only a limited role in an approach such as this. It may serve as a guide line or reference point, but hardly as a starting point without appearing to continue an image of the Church and its concerns as something apart from life. Emphasis therefore tends to be much more on a diversity of sources — audio-visual materials, newspapers and magazines, indeed all the sources of information encountered in ordinary living. There is a fundamental sense in which it is important not to be specific about particular means, because what is being described arises from the life-

21

situations of those concerned. From a theological viewpoint, this is the emphasis of those modern studies in Incarnational theology which have emphasised the importance of the believer's seeking Christ in human experience generally and not simply in those experiences labelled "religious." This is linked, as a later chapter discusses, with development of the theology of Revelation. Hence Gabriel Moran writes:

> "The whole of man's world is expressive of God's revelation in Christ. Nothing of itself is guaranteed to be a revelatory instrument, but everything by the grace of God has become capable of being revelatory of the Christian God. This fact opens unlimited possibilities for the teaching of the Christian revelation."[37]

Such a viewpoint has led Moran naturally to a different emphasis in the idea of the Christian Church of which he says:

> "For the students to appreciate their Church, to accept a teaching authority within that Church, and to desire to participate in the Church's official worship, all depends upon their eventual realization that Jesus Christ is a living person, that God spoke to him, and that in the glorifying act of raising him, God continues to speak the Word of his love. If that never emerges in the students' understanding all other 'explanations' of the Church's life and doctrine will never be intelligible."[38]

5. The Group-Centered Approach.

In considering this fifth 'stage' of development, it needs to be said again that each of these stages is not necessarily to be regarded as succeeding to the one before it. In this case, indeed, the whole approach may well be regarded as a natural extension of the fourth stage by the attention to group work, a feature of modern educational thinking in reaction to the traditional formality of the school situation. Perhaps the main emphasis here has been an attempt to delimit the position of the teacher as primarily one in authority. This is not to deny, however, that there may be specifically religious elements about this kind of group approach, but they tend to result from the composition of the group rather than from the fundamental nature of the process itself.

The keynote of this approach as expressed in the diagram speaks of "the dynamics of non-directed groups in extra class or non-formal religious teaching." To amplify this in theological terms, the approach looks to the value of the group experience, the presence and witness of fellow-believers in a less formal learning situation as the basis for deepening the questions posed by such encounters. The main emphasis, therefore, as with the preceding approach, is experiential rather than instruc-

---

37. Gabriel Moran, op. cit. p. 140.
38. ibid. p. 98.

tional in any formal sense. In accordance with this, the group may meet most frequently apart from conventional school or formal learning situations.

The characteristics of such group experiences are well-expressed by one of the notable pioneers of this approach, Pierre Babin, when he says:

"Our aim in religious education will not be conducted on the individual so much as on the group and interpersonal relations. This group education supposes less of the presence of the teacher as the sole authority but more of his presence as guide in a fraternal relation."[39]

This role of the teacher means that often the work of the group remains "open-ended", that is, it is not pushed through to a pre-determined conclusion for the sake of a conclusion. It should be added, however, that some kind of attempt by the group to trace their own progress is an important task after a series of such meetings. As an approach it seems best suited for the less-formal situations of out of school activities, and indeed it is not accidental that the catechetical writing of the past decade or so indicates that much of this activity takes place in the "week-end" or "camp" situation.

It is important to recognise in addition to the explicitly educational benefits of such groups, the particular way in which they can serve catechesis. As distinct from the "catechism class" or "class group" to whom religious instruction is given because of the convenience of factors such as time tables or organisational convenience, these extra-curricular groups are the result of free choice and association. Secondly, the stress on "non-directive" in the diagram is intended to confirm a direction rather than state an unchanging attitude. Put another way, it could be said that the aim of the group is less didactic while at the same time the very group process itself makes it likely that the whole aspect of religion is approached with the multi-dimensional approach already noted in the previous stage. Finally, in the liturgical developments of recent years, the possibility of close sharing in liturgical celebration often in an informal situation, seems to afford unique opportunities for the experience of close association with fellow believers and so, to a less formal view of the notion of Church. It should be said, of course, that such benefits are to be seen in the context of the view implied previously in this summary account viz. that they are valuable in themselves in the growth and development of young Christians and a valuable learning experience for a "pilgrim people."

---

39. **Options**, Burns & Oates, London, 1967, p. 130.

CONCLUSION

Now it is obvious that the changes indicated in the lateral movement of this diagram have been strongly influenced by considerations which have been sociological, educational and psychological, no less than theological. The latter aspects form the subject for the third chapter of this work, and the general kind of educational model resulting from this perspective is to be discussed in the fourth chapter. Of more immediate concern is the necessity to establish the main lines of the historical evolution of the traditional catechetical model and then proceed to its evaluation in terms of its explicit and implicit assumptions.

A further point should be noted. It is possible to trace from the diagram, which has been the framework of this chapter, some of the changes of direction in which teachers and pupils have been involved over this period. The group, which seems to have been the least influenced, are often the parents or perhaps, more accurately, the adult groups whose school years most resembled the first or second stages of the table. Is this, perhaps, the origin of the polarization which has taken place with regard to the catechetical movement? Has the general lack of adult programmes in catechesis been responsible for the broadening of the natural gap between generations? This issue will occupy us again in the final chapter of this book.

Chapter Two

AN ANALYSIS AND EVALUATION OF THE TRADITIONAL CATECHETICAL MODEL

The analysis in the preceding chapter, besides indicating what is understood by the traditional model, has already evaluated it at least comparatively according to the criteria there used. In this chapter, the analysis will be deepened and extended by close attention to two different ways of looking at catechesis viz. its historical origin and development within the Christian church, and the assumptions, explicit and implicit, on which it has been based as a form of education.

With regard to this last point, it should be clear that there is no intention of denying the special status of religious belief nor its expression in religious language. At the same time, the activity which is being investigated is taking place in an educational context, and to that extent, must be meaningful to the external observer who seeks to clarify the deeper meaning of what is involved on educational grounds alone. It is at least as unfair to allow the traditional catechetical model to go unexamined qua education as it is to allow any other school activity or method the same exempt status. But, on the other hand, as any judgement of catechesis itself which fails to consider its special character is also defective, some consideration needs to be given to the distinctive requirements for adequately expressing and teaching religious truths and practices.

With these considerations in mind, the sequence of matters considered is as follows:

1. The origin and development of the concept of catechesis.
2. The "traditional pedagogy of the Church."
3. Explicit and implicit assumptions of the catechetical model.
4. Catechism — and the traditional catechetical model.
5. The catechetical model evaluated according to educational principles.
6. The ideal of catechesis in relation to education.

1. The origin and development of the concept of catechesis

'Catechesis' has always been associated with the Christian Church's proclamation of its message. What may be learned from an inspection of catechesis at a given period is how the church attempted to proclaim its message of salvation through Jesus Christ in the circumstances then prevailing. But it is important not to confuse a particular cultural or sociological adaptation with the concept of catechesis itself. Rather, the study of such adaptations helps to show how certain accommodations to circumstances were attempts to preserve the basis of the concept itself in a different set of circumstances. Outstanding examples of this were the rise and gradual disappearance of the catechumenate beween the second and sixth centuries and the particular provisions made for the mass conversions which followed the acceptance of Christianity by the chiefs of formerly pagan tribes e.g. the conversion of Clovis and the Franks. The same point can be made by comparing the root meaning of catechesis with some more recent definitions.

Following the thought of J. P. Christopher in his introduction to his translation of *De Catechizandis Rudibus* by Saint Augustine, the origin of the term 'catechesis' is as follows:

"The compound verb κατηχεῖν which is composed of κατά intensive and ἠχεῖν retained its root meaning 'to sound down' but was applied to the act of informing and instructing by oral repetition, the idea being that children in school were instructed by making them 'sing out' in chorus the answers to the questions asked by the teacher. In this meaning of 'to instruct', 'to inform by word of mouth' occurs first in *Philo Leg. ad Gaium 198*. In the New Testament it is found in this meaning for example in Luke 1:4, Acts 18:25, Gal. 6:6. In the sense of giving instructions to catechumens it apparently occurs first in the oldest homily, the Ps.-Clementine so called Second Epistle to the Corinthians (17:1) written probably before the year 150. The first Latin writer to use "catechizare" in the meaning of "to instruct orally" in the Christian faith was Tertullian e.g. *De Cor. Mil. 9 quem Petrus catechizat*. The word 'catechismus' is first found in Augustine's *De Fide et Operibus*.[1]

Jungmann's account is substantially the same, being a little more explicit in showing how the root meaning of 'sounding down' is the foundation of its special usage in Christianity for "the message of God resounds downwards in the direction of men." His account also stresses that in its transitive usage, it was applied to instruction especially as "an introduction for beginners."[2]

Attention to this literal sense as well as to the object of catechesis is evident in the definition of Marcel Van Caster of the *Lumen Vitae* Centre for religious education for whom catechesis is "all activity which resounds the word of God: all activity which makes divine revelation known and which aims at awakening and developing faith."[3] More tersely, and with less attention to literalness, he describes catechesis

---

1. J. P. Christopher, **The First Catechetical Instruction** in *Library of Ancient Christian Writers*, Longmans, Green & Co., London, 1963.

2. J. A. Jungmann, **Handing on the Faith: A Manual for Catechetics**, Burns & Oates, London, 1959, pp. xiii-xiv.

3. Marcel Van Caster, **The Structure of Catechetics**, Herder & Herder, New York, 1965, p. 12.

elsewhere as "the encounter of God and man in Jesus Christ."[4] The origin, content and aim of catechesis is expressed in another contemporary statement by the staff of the Higher Catechetical Institute of Nijmegen, the authors of the "Catechism for Adults" or "Dutch Catechism" for whom catechesis is:

"Throwing light on the whole of human existence as God's salvific action by witnessing to the mystery of Christ through the word, for the purpose of awakening and fostering the faith and prompting man to live truly in accord with that faith."[5]

Combining both the literal and the developed ideas of these definitions, it is possible to note three ideas as essential to catechesis:

1 — The one responsible for the catechesis speaks of things of which he is personally convinced, with the intention of sharing his belief with his hearers. As distinct from other pastoral activities such as evangelization and preaching (cf. appendix), catechesis already supposes a common faith (at least in terms of all having been initiated into Christian life by Baptism).

2 — The content of catechesis is the life, death and resurrection of Jesus Christ or the teachings derived from these events in the history of man's salvation. This point evidently depends on the point already made viz. that the recipient of catechesis has already made some first act of faith or received some initiation into Christian living, so that the catechesis is a second stage, a deepening of the first response to the message of the Gospel.

3 — The expectations of catechesis, under the diverse forms it may take, are mainly greater knowledge and appreciation of the Christian message leading to an increased fervour in the living of the Christian life.

Historically, then, catechesis has been approached from three different viewpoints depending on whether the emphasis has been on

a — the instruction preparatory to admission to the sacrament of Baptism and the reception of the sacrament itself. This may be most conveniently summarised around the concept of *initiation*.

b — the instruction subsequent to this initiation, especially in the case of the majority of Christians who have been baptized as infants. The key word here is *instruction*.

c — the continuing instruction and aid to deeper understanding of the Christian life which is associated with the official public

---

4. **Lumen Vitae** Vol. XX, No. 2, 1966, p. 134.

5. **Making All Things New**, Divine Word Publications, Techny, Illinois, 1966, p. 88.

worship of the church i.e. the cycle of the liturgy with its reminders of the great truths of salvation etc., plus the homilies or sermons given within the context of such worship. To distinguish this from the second category of instruction in (ii), the word *worship* will be used to signify the two aspects which such worship ideally includes.

In order to appreciate the point of these distinctions in the historical evolution of catechesis, it could be instanced that the traditional catechumenate placed most of its emphasis on 'initiation.' After the widespread acceptance of Christianity, however, and the consequent acceptance of infant baptism as the norm, the early mediaeval church was able to place much more emphasis on the second and third phases of instruction and worship which were, in the unity of Christendom, little separated by our later distinctions of sacred and secular. The growth and extension of opportunities for education in late mediaeval and post-Reformation times, has resulted in a greater emphasis on the second stage while presuming that the third stage was a natural accompaniment to the living of the Christian life.

But these three concepts of Initiation, Instruction and Worship, in the senses in which they have been generally indicated, have not necessarily remained exactly the same at all stages of the history of the Christian church.

Initiation has meant in practice the tradition from the earliest times of administering baptism to infants, thereby implying certain consequences for catechesis which are not always taken notice of, especially when,

1 — the sense of 'initiation' has generally been figurative when compared with the sense of the word in a phrase such as "initiation rites" because in practice it has meant introduction into the church by proxy, without any obvious connection with that free, personal response by which an adult catechumen indicated his faith. Besides the already noted distinction between the faith of the church and that of the individual, there is another theological point. For the initial years of the growth of the child it is impossible to speak of the growth of either kind of faith except in terms of the theological aspect of grace designated *ex opere operato,* i.e. working by the nature of the process itself irrespective of the contribution of the agent since the child by definition has no *opus operantis* to contribute.[6]

2 — because of this, it is quite possible for the child catechized in "the faith" to withold his personal consent or simply to go through a process of learning about something which has no effect on his personal faith. The point may be noted in just this sense when Newman says on the opening page of *Apologia pro Vita Sua.*

---

6. Bishop B. C. Butler in **The Tablet,** 6th October 1972.

"I was brought up from a child to take great delight in reading the Bible; but I had no formed religious convictions till I was fifteen. Of course, I had a perfect knowledge of my Catechism."[7]

3 — Instruction may take place under many different forms, direct and indirect, but the post-Reformation model has been particularly associated with the overriding importance of the printed word in the catechism. In its increasing association with schooling, catechesis has gradually been extended in duration without any great change in its reliance on the catechism—often the same text being used at all levels of schooling—and in its general image of a task to be completed during the period of formal schooling. Such a fixed model has become increasingly unsatisfactory during a period of ever increasing change in the duration and content of education.

4 — Following from the deficiencies of too great an association of catechesis with formal schooling and the implication of its having a verifiable end point, there has been an undervaluing of the importance of the continuing catechesis which the liturgy of the church should be, both in itself and in the continuing instruction associated with it. This is not to undervalue the importance of the didactic sermons on doctrinal and moral subjects, the sequence of which was specified in the Catechism of the Council of Trent, but simply to underline the point already made in the analysis of the opening chapter with regard to the narrowing of the dimensions of religion which this sometimes represented.

The historical analyses of writers such as Jungmann, Colomb, Sloyan and Carter support the thesis of an evolving catechesis in response to the different needs of the Church at different historical periods. For this reason, it seems important to analyse the term found in a number of official documents on catechesis viz. "the traditional pedagogy of the Church."

2. The "traditional pedagogy of the Church"

Although there are many references in Papal statements to "the traditional pedagogy of the Church" it is difficult to be precise about what this description means, except in a post-Reformation context of catechisms. In issuing the Catechism of the Council of Trent in 1567, Pope Pius V included the following in his introduction:

"The fathers, therefore, of the Council of Trent...deemed it further necessary to issue for the instruction of the faithful in the very rudiments of faith, a *form* and *method* (my emphasis) to be followed in all churches by those to whom are lawfully entrusted the duties

7. Op. cit. The Catholic Book Club Edition, 121 Charing Cross Rd., London, 1946, p. 1.

of pastor and teacher...so that there may also be one standard and prescribed form of propounding the dogmas of faith, and instructing Christians in all the duties of piety."[8]

Elsewhere in the same introduction, the ends of religious instruction were stated by the Pope as knowledge of Christ, observance of the Commandments and love of God. The means required to achieve these ends were instruction which was accommodated to the capacity of the hearer, given at all time in a zealous manner; the pastor himself was to deepen his own knowledge by studying the word of God "in Scripture and tradition."[9] The division of matters in the Roman Catechism was set out in a sequence which proceeded from the Apostles' Creed to the Sacraments and from thence to the commandments and the Lord's Prayer. As already noted, however, the majority of diocesan catechisms reversed the order of Sacraments and Commandments with a resulting emphasis on authority and on morality as a form of obedience.

In terms of method, it should be kept in mind in all references to this Roman Catechism as it was also called, that it was not set out in a question and answer format, for the aim of this Catechism was the better instruction of the pastors themselves as the first step to ensure the better instruction of the faithful. For this purpose, it included a Sermon Programme for the whole liturgical year, based on the liturgical readings, and as there was scope for two sermons—one at Mass and one at Vespers —on Sundays and feasts, there was a dogmatic subject and a moral subject suggested for each week. Two important aspects of this should be noted. First of all, it was assumed that there would be continuing instruction for the faithful all their lives, and secondly, this instruction was given in the context of a liturgical ceremony. All were included, adults, adolescents and young children and there was an unexpressed assumption about the educational value of being a member of this believing community and about the gradual deepening of faith which would accompany regular attendance at the ceremonies where this instruction was given. Small wonder then, that it was this catechism which was so highly commended by various Popes, especially as the development of public education during the nineteenth century raised the whole question of religious instruction. Pope Pius IX advocated its use in 1849:

"We are certain that these same parish priests will devote themselves with ever greater zeal to the teaching of the basic points of Christian

---

8. **Original introduction to the Catechism of the Council of Trent**. Translated and annotated by McHugh and Callan, B. Herder, London, 1958, 15th Impression, p. 4.

9. ibid., pp. 6-9.

doctrine to children, since they are fully aware that this is one of their principal duties. They must be warned to keep before their eyes, in their instruction both of children and of the laity, *the Roman Catechism...*"[10]

Pope Leo XIII in 1878 spoke of the same work in these terms: "In order to educate the hearts of the young to virtue, why not avail oneself of the *Catholic Catechism,* in which we find the most perfect method and the most fertile seeds of a healthy education."[11]

Commending the work of an institute devoted to the work of Christian education, Pope Pius X wrote:

> "In spite of the obstacles raised by official programmes, the "Association of the Institutes of Christian Education" has the magnificent record of constant attempts to preserve the methods approved by the *traditional pedagogy of the Church"* (my emphasis added)[12]

We may learn something about this elusive "traditional pedagogy" at least by implication in the following statement opposed to "Pedagogic Naturalism" by Pope Pius XI in the celebrated *Divini Illius Magistri* of December 31st 1929:

> "Every method of education founded, wholly or in part, on the denial or forgetfulness of original sin and of grace, and which relies on the powers of human nature, is unsound. Such generally speaking, are those modern systems bearing various names which appeal to a claim of self-government and to unrestrained freedom on the part of the child and which diminish or even suppress the teacher's authority and action, attributing to the child an exclusive primacy of initiative, and an activity independent of any higher law, natural or divine, in regard to this education."[13]

But if all this is negative, there are some positive claims made in the following paragraph from the same writings:

> "If any of these terms are used less properly, to denote the necessity of a gradually more active co-operation on the part of the pupil in his own education; if it is intended to banish despotism and violence from education, which, by the way, are not to be confused with just punishment, this would be correct, but in no way new. It would mean only what has been taught and reduced to practice by the Church in traditional Christian education, in imitation of the

---

10. **Papal Teachings on Education**, St. Paul Books, Boston, 1960, par. 13, p. 39.
11. passim par. 70, p. 76.
12. cf. note 1 above.
13. **Papal Teachings on Education**, par. 279, p. 229.

method employed by God Himself towards His creatures, of whom, he demands active co-operation according to the nature of each."[14]

There seem to be two main aspects of this "traditional pedagogy" referred to or assumed in the preceding quotation. The first is the central position occupied by the catechism, and the second is the simple conjunction of the necessary content supplied by the catechism with a method which ensures certain verifiable criteria of success viz. memorised catechism answers, didactic teaching by masters and so on. Each of these aspects is to be inspected more closely in later sections of this chapter. But before examining the explicit and implied assumptions of the traditional model, it should be said firmly that the existence of a model known as "traditional" should not confer on it a kind of exempt status. To do this is to run the danger of confusing some fundamental idea of tradition with what a tradition attempts to preserve.

3. Explicit and implicit assumptions of the catechetical model.

The title of this section is important because some of the assumptions inspected are discernible from the historical perspective on catechesis set out earlier, whereas others are true only of the catechetical model in the educational context in which it has just been studied. Some assumptions therefore have a kind of universal application to catechesis as a concept — even though they are more explicitly made in some circumstances rather than others — whereas others are more relative to the kinds of variations in the catechetical model we have just established.

There are three sets of assumptions to be considered. The first are those concerned with catechesis as a duty of the teaching Church, the second with the duty of the catechist to his mission within the Church, and the third with the explicit and implicit educational assumptions of the catechetical model in an educational context. These latter are examined separately in the final section of the chapter.

But prior to a consideration of these matters in more detail, there is one basic assumption which is intrinsic to the nature of catechesis itself as it is distinguished in the appendix from other forms of the ministry of the Word. Catechesis is not evangelization nor is it preaching in the strict sense of both these terms. It is the instruction in the faith of those who are implicitly believers, or more precisely, those who have been accepted by Baptism into membership of the Church and have, if not personal faith, at least that *habitus fidei* or potential for faith, which has always been seen by the Christian Church as the particular grace of Baptism. The practical point which results from this may be stated simply: in catechesis, a believer is assumed to speak to a fellow believer. This is the foundation assumption of all catechesis no matter the circumstances in which it is carried out.

---

14. ibid.

There is a second assumption which, at root, is a practical result of the first: all catechesis is related to the Bible. This may seem a strange point to be taken as a fundamental assumption when, practically speaking as the discussion on the Bible in the opening chapter indicated, a long period of catechetical activity made very little explicit use of the Bible as a whole, however much it did use the New Testament. But in commenting on the catecheses of St. Cyril of Alexandria, Sloyan remarks:

"In a sense doctrine is not so much taught as assumed. The credal explanation of the catechumenate days just before Easter is totally available to them, and the writer does no more than re-word its elements with the illustrative aid of both Testaments. He goes from Pentateuch to prophets, epistles to gospels indiscriminately. Here in classic form is the oldest catechetical assumption: that the Bible or the oral teaching based upon it is the source place of all doctrine for Christians."[15]

For Liége, in his seminal article "From Kerygma to Catechesis" the same is true, for his thought may be summarized:

Catechesis flows from the Gospels. As a result, all catechesis should be Christo-centric and should bring man back to the initial act of his first conversion. In the measure that conversion has not been chronologically distinct from catechesis as for baptized infants, catechesis will always have a *dialectic* period of evangelization, without which it would be mere religious instruction.[16]

(a) *Assumptions underlying catechesis as part of the teaching mission of the Church.*

To examine the assumptions which underlie catechesis as a part of the teaching mission of the Church, two key statements from *Gravissimum Educationis* the statement on Christian education from Vatican II provide us with a focus:

1 — "In discharging her educative function, the Church is pre-occupied with all means appropriate to that end. But she is particularly concerned with the means proper to herself, of which catechetical training is foremost. Such instruction gives clarity and vigor to faith, nourishes a life lived according to the spirit of Christ, leads to a knowing and active participation in the liturgical mystery, and inspires apostolic action."[17]

Three points are to be noted:

a — The Church claims an educative mission proper to itself.

15. **Shaping the Christian Message**, p. 16.
16. André Liége, *Readings in European Catechetics,* Lumen Vitae Press, 1962, pp. 33-34 (paraphrased).
17. W. M. Abbott (ed.), **The Documents of Vatican II**, Geoffrey Chapman, London, 1966, par. 4, pp. 642-643.

b — The Church claims means "proper to herself" because of the distinctive activity being carried out.

c — The claims made for "such instruction" obviously rely on the already noted fundamental assumption of catechesis viz. believer speaks with believer. As noted earlier on the discussion on the role of faith, Coudreau's distinction is here understood:

"To catechize is neither to instruct *or* form, nor instruct *and* form but instruct while forming or better, it is transmitting a doctrine *for* living. The catechist should teach in such a way — and this is the definition of his pedagogy — that doctrine is received in the one catechized at the level of faith, awakens in him a living faith, provokes in him an act of faith, arouses in him a living faith, provokes in him an act of faith, arouses in him the life of faith . . . The final goal, the ultimate objective is to establish "a believer."[18]

The aims of a Christian education are expressed in the second key statement from Vatican II:

2 — "That as the baptized person is gradually introduced into a knowledge of the mystery of salvation, he may daily grow more conscious of the gift of faith which he has received; that he may learn to adore God the Father in spirit and truth (c.f. Jn. 4:23), especially through liturgical worship; that he may be trained to conduct his personal life in righteousness and in the sanctity of truth, according to this new standard of manhood. (Eph. 4:22-24)

Thus, indeed, he may grow into manhood according to the mature measure of Christ (cf. Eph. 4:13), and devote himself to the upbuilding of the Mystical Body. Moreover, aware of his calling, he should grow accustomed to giving witness to the hope that is in him (1 Pet. 3:15), and to promoting that Christian transformation of the world by which natural values, reviewed in the full perspective of humanity as redeemed by Christ, may contribute to the good of society as a whole."[19]

If we sharpen these general aims of Christian education and apply them specifically to catechesis in the context of Christian education, three assumptions are being made:

1 — There is to be a gradual handing on of the Christian message resulting in a growth of knowledge and understanding of Christian truths, as well as an acceptance of Christian moral principles and a life lived according to these norms.

2 — The aims presume a response on the part of those who receive the message.

18. Francois Coudreau, *Introduction to a Pedagogy of Faith* in **Shaping the Christian Message**, op. cit., pp. 138-139.

19. Abbott (ed.), op. cit., par. 2, p. 640.

3 — The Christian's life is aimed not simply at passive acceptance of these norms for his own life: he is positively concerned with being a witness to a Christian way of life which will help to transform society.

It seems important to emphasise in the light of such clearly stated aims that there is an internal contradiction if the means adopted to achieve such ends effectively negate the principles of the Christian message. It is obviously possible to achieve certain knowledge aims by indoctrination, understood in a pejorative sense; it is possible to uphold at least certain external aspects of objective morality if one controls government or law-enforcement; the externals of religious observance may be carried out simply as a form of obedience, and so on. But in all these cases, the basic assumption of believer encouraging free response from his fellow believer is denied.

The point needs to be emphasised in a more practical manner. The *de facto* situation in which most school catechesis takes place is one in which those baptised as infants receive continuing instruction in the Christian faith. But the right balance must be maintained between the faith of the individual i.e. his growth in knowledge and understanding of what it is to be a Christian, and the faith of the Church i.e. the doctrine, morality and obligations of being a member of the Church. As emphasised earlier, failure to distinguish these two related senses is a likely source of confusion in the catechetical situation.

So, the assumptions of the Church with regard to her mission, her fidelity to the message and to forms of activity proper to that message and mission are subject to the spirit of the Gospel message itself, which invites rather than commands. Freedom is to be the balancing point. But as a later discussion will treat more fully, it is not a question of assuming a neutral position and maintaining a kind of fundamentalist attitude that truth will necessarily be discovered. The assumptions of the Church with regard to mission and her activity in carrying out that mission through various means, including catechesis, require her to make use of all legitimate means in carrying out this task. This balance, Joseph Colomb expresses in terms of a double fidelity: "Fidelity to God and fidelity to man."[20]

On the practical level, this double fidelity is the responsibility of the catechist entrusted with his particular mission by the Church.

(b) *Assumptions underlying the mission of the catechist.*

The assumptions made with regard to the duty of the catechist in regard to his task, may be concentrated on the four following statements:

---

20. The basic division of Colomb's first section of **Le service de l'évangile.**

1 — The catechist has a mission in the Church.

2 — His role in this mission is not simply that of an intermediary for he is expected to be a witness to the truth of the message he brings.

3 — He must therefore be faithful to the nature and content of the message.

4 — His task is to help produce "believers" as contrasted with "knowers."

The importance of the work of the catechist as teacher and initiator of others into a deeper knowledge and experience of the Christian life has been well illustrated in the opening chapter. In addition, it should be recalled that included in the prime mission entrusted to the Catholic priest at his ordination is that of "preaching the word of God." In the thought of the Second Vatican Council "it is to be hoped that, where it seems opportune, catechists who are duly trained will receive a 'canonical mission' in a publicly celebrated liturgical ceremony."[21] But as the second and fourth assumptions indicate, the catechist has a task which is not to be fulfilled simply by increasing the knowledge of his hearers: he is to attempt to produce 'believers', and, for this, must be prepared to offer the witness of his own Christian life and that of the community. In addition, as the third assumption indicates, he must be faithful to the message he brings. This notion of 'message' deserves some attention. It is not the same thing as doctrine. A message is addressed to someone and by its nature, invites a response. Because of the nature of the message itself, the believer's reflection on it and its continuing re-formulation in language appropriate to the age, there are necessarily diverse manifestations of the truths represented (how different this is from the uniformity of the catechism!), truths about God and truths about man—the recipient, the celebration of these mysteries in the litur-gical event and the moral response which flows from man's awareness of the dignity to which he has been raised. But the action essential to the catechist (as distinct from either apostle or evangelizer) is precisely the handing on of a message, of engaging in dialogue with another, of offering instruction and example and awaiting a reply. The value and importance of the message is that this is the announcement of God's salvation addressed to human beings through Christ.

In short, everything he does in this regard rests on the fundamental point already noted of believer speaking with believer. This enlargement of vision is evident in the Eichstaett conference's concentration on the four main sources of Doctrine, Liturgy, Bible and Witness as discussed in Chapter 4.

---

21. Abbott (ed.), op. cit., par. 17, p. 606.

36

But to state and elaborate these assumptions even in this summary fashion underlines an important distinction between the role of the catechist in the school situation and the role expected of the teacher in other subjects or activities. This important question will arise again in Chapter 6, but the following remarks are called for here.

1 — Assuming as normal, the continuing tradition of infant baptism and the attempts at progressive development of the faith of the one catechized as already outlined in summary fashion, does the teacher/catechist always assume as an unchanging "given" the faith of those whom he addresses in the ordinary school situation? Are they pupils? or believers? or pupils who *are* or *might be* believers? Put another way, is his role basically an instructional one viz. that of handing on the "deposit of faith" or the teaching of a Christian apologetic to members of his classes who are all assumed to be practising members of the Church?

2 — The catechist's mission to arouse and develop faith must be exercised in such a way as to respect the faith and freedom of those whom he addresses. As Cardinal Heenan remarks with regard to this question: "...religious instruction is essentially different from any other kind of teaching. There are two main differences. In the first place the religious teacher (i.e. in context, the teacher of religion) does not merely give instruction but actually provides the means of grace... The second difference is that the value of a lesson in arithmetic or geography is in no way dependent on the moral character or virtue of the teacher."[22]

Accepting the distinction made without necessarily accepting the second difference uncritically, it could be said that on such a view part of the teacher's work is showing his personal faith in action and attitude. This is quite opposed to an authoritarian "teaching what the Church teaches" attitude which in practice assumes either that his listeners are outside of the Church or that they need prescriptions to be followed without examination. As Coudreau remarks in this regard:

> "In catechesis...one proceeds to faith from knowledge of the revealed data. The person catechised is not primarily in search of a better knowledge of revelation, but in search of an object for his faith, truth from God in which to believe. In this regard one might say that catechesis is *Intellectus quaerens fidem*."[23]

(3) As has been indicated earlier, those teacher/catechists who proceed in an authoritarian manner towards certain ends without regard to the internal contradictions brought about by the means they employ, really fail to regard their hearers as 'fellow believers'. Their reduction

22. **Teaching the Faith**, Catholic Truth Society, London, 1972, p. 8.

23. **Basic Catechetical Perspectives**, Paulist Press, Deus books, New York, 1969, p. 136.

of the Christian message to doctrinal or moral statements, satisfies the claims of an apparent orthodoxy but in so doing, runs the risk of reducing the interior development of faith and progressive commitment in that faith, to the position of being simply consequent upon factual knowledge. The question here is whether the teacher wishes the pupil to have his i.e. the teacher's faith, or whether he is ready to appreciate that the pupil's faith must be his own, attained to by personal choice (anguish? decision?) rather than accepted in a passive fashion. This is an important aspect of the present catechetical controversy in the Roman Catholic Church.

(4) The very reluctance of some teachers to take religious instruction lessons seems to arise from an implicit recognition of the special kind of relationship required of them as catechists. They are often reluctant to assume a position which they see as requiring and witnessing to a Christian commitment.

A special difficulty of another kind may arise where teachers or catechists called upon to fill this position, may appear to do so because of their special religious calling i.e. their status appears to give them the right to special pleading. This is an important consideration when so many members of religious orders are engaged in the teaching of religion, especially in circumstances where they are assigned this work in preference to the laity.

4. Catechism — and the traditional catechetical model.

"The use of the catechism is perhaps the most controversial topic of discussion among teachers of Religion in Junior Schools. Its use as a text-book has presented formidable difficulties, not least because of its vocabulary. This is inevitable, since it is a book of concise, accurate definitions originally intended for adults, and, of course, takes no cognizance of a child's mental development. But more difficult in fact than the vocabulary are the abstract concepts of Grace, Hope, and some of the Sacraments.

Yet when due note is taken of all these, the world-wide trend of opinion "in the Church must have its weight. Nothing better has yet been found, and it is in use everywhere."[24]

This quotation from "The Teaching of Religion in Catholic Schools" published for the Catholic Teachers' Federation of England and Wales in 1954 illustrates the curious inconsistencies which seem to persist in present controversies on catechetics. Even after all kinds of reasons have been outlined as to the educational deficiencies of the catechism whether it be concerned with its terminology, its content or the likelihood

---

24. **The teaching of Religion in Catholic Schools** edited by J. J. Branigan, for Catholic Teachers' Federation, Macmillan & Co., London, 1954, p. 88.

of its being used simply in a text-explanatory method, there still seems to be some kind of justification based on vaguely specified criteria such as tradition, parental wishes, or even a kind of "better than nothing" approach which effectively prevents any new initiatives finding favour. The point is well illustrated in 1972 by Cardinal Heenan who can write at one point of his pamphlet "Teaching the Faith":

> "No modern teacher would defend the old mechanical use of the catechism. It is doubtful if the catechism by itself ever led people to love their religion. Its language was clear but it was dry and dispassionate precisely because its purpose was simply to define concepts. It would be difficult to imagine a manner of teaching more remote from that of the Sermon on the Mount."[25]

But at a later point, in attempting to place the use of the catechism in its historical context, he writes:

> "The old definitions learned at school have been a source of strength and consolation to many a Catholic. Certain definitions of doctrine are put so neatly and rhythmically in the catechism that only those who discard their religion will entirely forget them. It must however be stressed that the catechism is not a primary source but only a reserve."[26]

If the argument here is simply that not everything done in the past was wrong then it can be accepted. If there is an assumption that teaching religion is different from other forms of teaching, this too is acceptable but the criteria of such successful teaching of religion would need to be broader than those here implied. Some key statements from the Catholic Catechism Teachers' Book already cited afford a close view of theoretical and practical points for emphasis. It is suggested that the inconsistencies which appear between some of the statements are not due to a haphazard selection but reflect an underlying confusion of aims. The following statements are made with regard to the role of the catechism in religion teaching. Note the assumptions.

1 — The Catechism is our most important tool...in the hands of a skilful and willing teacher it will ensure that a child will live his faith and remain steadfast to the end of his life."[27]

2 — "...the Catechism is still the best, the most remarkably clear and logical treatment of the truths of our religion... Its answers are categorical statements of fundamental truths, and in its frequent

---

25. **Teaching the Faith**, Catholic Truth Society Pamphlet, London, 1972, p. 8.
26. ibid., p. 16. Cf. also *Suggestions for Teachers for those using the Westminster Syllabus of Religious Instruction*, 1951, p. 14: "Well-taught, the Catechism supplies the Catholic with clear-cut summaries of his religious beliefs and practices, with simple slogans to remind him of his duties, with ready made answers to sincere inquiries or carping critics of his religion."
27. op. cit., p. 15.

appeal to proofs from Scripture it is very definitely Christocentric. It formulates completely the Christian life."[28]

3 — "Yet it (i.e. the catechism) cannot be replaced by oral teaching *tout seul,* it must never be omitted. Any attempt on the part of teachers to teach without it throughout the school life of a child will inevitably lead to an incomplete, and possibly heretical version of our Faith."[29]

4 — "It is essential, therefore, that the Junior School Course contains in an elementary fashion all that a Catholic needs to live a full and active spiritual life."[30]

The general picture presented by these quotations belongs to the model described as "Magisterial" in the analysis of the last chapter and it is obvious that there are different kinds of assumptions being made at different levels. But it is now possible to outline the chief features of the "catechism approach," where the catechism occupied the main position in the teaching of religion:

a — in practice it was often used as a text to be explained and subsequently learned by heart;

b — knowing and understanding the catechism was considered to be the best way to ensure the development of personal faith i.e. personal faith and the 'Faith of the Church' were complementary processes and acceptance on 'faith' when young was a likely step towards adult understanding;[31]

c — exact knowledge of the doctrines of the faith was a safeguard against heresy and an assurance of orthodoxy;

d — it was from the security of the catechism answers that one could apply the faith to one's conduct and to public questions of adult life.

It should be stressed that this discussion is not meant to be principally an historical evaluation of something which characterised religion teaching in the past. In the Downside Symposium of 1968 on Religious Education, Derek Lance, in an article called "Catholic Children and What they are being taught" wrote as follows:

---

28. op. cit., p. 13.

29. op. cit., p. 14.

30. op. cit., p. 16.

31. This issue, already opened up in the commentary on Chapter 1, is treated by Barbara Hosegood in *The Faith and Indoctrination* in **Catholic Education in a Secular Society**, Sheed & Ward, London, 1968. "A more profound sense of confusion still seems to me to be in the other aspect, that of 'the faith'" (p. 169) and "(The faith) is not just a set of facts but a way of life which must permeate the whole place (i.e. the school) and the conduct of all its inmates," (p. 193)

"In many schools to-day the content and methods of religious education are still those of 1900. In practice this means essentially the use of what we know as the "Penny Catechism" and the text-explanatory method. This is, to take a catechism answer as the starting point and to explain it perhaps with the aid of supporting scriptural proof texts and then to make sure that the pupils learn the question and answer by rote. . ."[32]

In evaluating this system for himself, Lance continues:

"The belief of the advocates of such a system is that the children will have memorised a handy collection of brief, theologically approved statements; orthodoxy will have been safeguarded. . . As to understanding. . . the many abstract religious concepts. . . they will come to understand them later. This, alas, is just not true."[33]

Lance justifies this viewpoint by a reference to Goldman whose conclusion on this point was as follows:

"We are forced to the conclusion that religious concepts introduced too soon may lead to regressive thinking in religion and not only retard later insights, but may prevent them developing at all."[34]

One should add, as indeed Lance does later, that the very safeguarding of orthodoxy is a specious activity when it anticipates real understanding and remains a merely verbal orthodoxy because the imbalance produced by precise theological statements memorised without real understanding can often lead to misunderstandings which make it unlikely that important concepts will ever be grasped properly.[35]
A just appraisal of the important role of the catechism in the past and a clear indication as to its basic unsuitability for school use today is the following statement of the Newman Association:
"For those involved in educating Catholic children of a deprived and despised community of the 1870's, the catechism must have been a godsend—simple precious truths, learned by heart in the short time available, if any, that there was for children to gain the rudiments of education and religious instruction. The approach, like the age, was uncomplicated and authoritarian and "commanded obedience to all lawful superiors" (answer to question 198 of the catechism). It may well be that the stress on learning by heart was because many could not read and little Christian literature was available. The catechism was revised in 1870 and again

32. Jebb (ed.), **Religious Education: Drift or Decision**, Darton, Longman and Todd, London, 1968, p. 41.

33. ibid., p. 42.

34. **Religious Thinking from Childhood to Adolescence**, Routledge and Kegan Paul, London, 1964, p. 227.

35. Lance Derek, op. cit., p. 46.

revised but little changed in 1871. Many people still express a great loyalty to the penny catechism but the situation for Catholic children today is unrecognisably changed even by the standard of our own parents. As we have said, the dedication of previous generations has provided schools where sophisticated education is achieved in the humanities and the sciences. Catholic children, like their peers in non-denominational schools, are encouraged to think deeply, they read widely and are familiar with a plurality of ideas. In this context, the catechism denies them the wealth of Christian understanding that will enlighten all the other ideas they have found. Definitions can so easily be taken as final and put limitations on the full truth of the statements."[36]

CONTENT OR METHOD?

It is significant that the phrase "teaching the catechism" has been one of the synonyms for catechesis. As indicated in the appendix, the verb "to catechize" owes part of its meaning to its context, as its particular meaning is affected by both its subject and its object. But the model suggested by the term "teaching the catechism" is quite restricted in that, grammatically and logically, it indicates that the object of the teaching done is the transferring of a determined content. As has been amply illustrated in the quotations already given, this kind of thinking separates content and method in a way which restricts the teaching to an infusing, filling-up kind of activity. Such an activity, it is being suggested, is educationally defective on the following grounds:

1 — In an extreme form, it easily becomes anti-educational in that the reliance on infusing a certain content condones or ignores the means used to achieve this end, thereby disregarding the freedom of the individual or his personal understanding or ability to understand. The criterion of success achieved is wrongly taken as the ability of the recipient to recapitulate in some form or another, the exact catechism answer. Such a result achieved by such means may well be a form of indoctrination in every pejorative sense.

2 — To talk, in Hofinger's phrase, of method as the "handmaid of the message" is only to indicate its position relative to the content. But while appreciating the force of the distinction, there is a sense in which the very way in which the message is conveyed helps to determine its acceptance or rejection. To adapt McLuhan's phrase, there is a sense in which the method is the message and the message determines the method. The very freedom proclaimed by the Gospel must always respect the listener's freedom to respond; the invitation of Christ and the Gospel leaves the hearer to reject as well as to receive. The point is well illustrated if we focus on the role of the one who catechizes. In a fundamental sense, it

36. **The Newman** No. 2, May, 1972, 15 Carlisle St. London, p. 54.

has been asserted that catechesis only takes place where believer speaks to believer. Even to talk of 'catechesis of witness', personal or communitarian, is to underline the essential unity of the message proclaimed and the Christian life-style and values of the one who proclaims. Ideally, at least, this is a necessary rather than a contingent relationship, for then there is an inner logic of content which has its own dynamic and which to a certain extent dictates what is taught and how it is taught.

3 — Too easy a separation of content and method can be either an under-estimation or an over-simplification of the Christian message. The first tends to limit the content to what we may describe as the 'factual', and it tends towards the 'teaching about' situation. This is a model to be examined more closely later but it may simply be pointed out here that it lacks the fundamental point of catechesis viz. believer talking with believer.

An over-simplification results from either excess or defect. In the first case, like the sacred/secular dichotomy or the dualism which has found certain classical manifestations in history such as Manicheanism, Albigen-sianism and Puritanism, it may present the Gospel in terms of law rather than love. At the other extreme it is so man centred that God is invoked only from outside and the whole significance of God's gracious intervention via the Incarnation is lost sight of. The restored position of the kerygma in our own day was a necessary redressing of an imbalance brought about by this defect. It has been truly stressed that the essential of the Christian message is some*one* rather than some*thing,* a point well understood by St. Paul. But besides this kind of excessive emphasis on the objective 'law' outside of man, there is a different kind of over-simplifica-tion which results from defect in that it presents only one aspect of the Christian message as being the whole. Besides the impersonal doctrinal approach of which the catechism has been the main type, one would have to recognise also the defective view implicit in a kerygmatic approach which never progressed past the simply historical.

Part of the difficulty about the content/method separation arises from the failure to appreciate the various senses of content between which it is possible to move. Broadly used, it is a rough equivalent for *curriculum* in the general sense of those factors which constitute learning experiences. Used thus, it includes things done and things experienced as well as things said by a teacher; it is a discovery of God and Revelation in everything around us. If the word is given an apparently more restricted sense, it is synonymous with knowledge to be acquired, but this is capable of extension into all the senses in which we use the term 'knowledge', so that we are into the vast realm of theories of knowledge. Gabriel Moran is thinking of this when he writes:

"It is assumed that there is a body of materials that is the content of Christian faith, and that the teachers's role is to convince people to

43

accept this content as true... I mean not only that the religion curriculums of elementary and secondary schools are impossibly and absurdly large. I mean much more basically that at no level of education is there a specific and definable content that is the religion course."[37]

Earlier in the same essay, Moran points up the defects of concentration on this content/method discussion which has tended to be the history of catechetics in this century, by showing that the question does not do justice to the really important matters which this kind of discussion overlooks:

"Those who speak about the 'biblical-liturgical approach' almost invariably have a well-defined content in mind... much of the recent catechetical effort has been misdirected to 'content' rather than to persons and personal understanding."[38]

The very nature of the content and the way in which it is presented to the potential believer are inter-dependent and must always be considered so. The teacher who, in an authoritarian way, speaks of the love of God and of his mercy, may through such a method effectively negate the content by his own mis-representation of what it is to be a Christian believer. The teacher who intellectualises his approach may well leave the hearer confused, puzzled or simply apathetic with regard to the great Christian truths because they appear to have no meaning or relevance to the here and now.

4 — There is another important observation which requires to be made with regard to a rigid distinction between content and method, in the catechetical situation. It is the view taken of the theological concept of Revelation, and in relation to this, the assumed view of the Church.[39] If the notion of Revelation is accepted which sees it as given once for all, contained in the Bible, interpreted by tradition and the practice of the historical Church claiming to be historically descended from the Apostles, then the separation of content and method has a certain neat finality. For, given such assumptions, to be a faithful member of the Church one must first of all know what the Church teaches. To ensure this, one requires to be instructed formally in the teaching of the Church, to be able to prove one's orthodoxy by recitation from memory of certain hallowed and traditional formulae taken as the criteria of Church membership. In all of these senses it is obvious that the traditional catechism is a method of ensuring such content. The only question then is that of variation or

37. **Vision and Tactics**, Burns and Oates, Herder and Herder, London, 1968, p. 63.

38. ibid., p. 59.

39. cf. schema of Chapter 1 and the discussion of Revelation in Chapter 3.

development of method to be sure that such content is easily understood and verified. In practical terms, the separation of content and method is precisely what the traditional catechism method lends itself to because of its firm subjection of method to content and its easily verifiable proofs of successful teaching. But from a theological viewpoint one should ask:

a — What happens if the view taken of Revelation follows the direction of more recent thinking where the emphasis is on the notion of "on-going" Revelation and the response of the individual to his personal situation?

b — Is there not some danger in this "content" approach, of over-stressing the uniformity of response to the Gospel and indeed of confusing Christian response with the fulfilment only of certain external norms of conduct?

If this content/method separation model is not tenable, what of the general aspect which underlies the model viz. that there is a message to be handed on? This "transmission" model now needs to be examined.

A 'TRANSMISSION' MODEL?

James Michael Lee, in an article called "The Teaching of Religion," has noted the widespread use of what he calls a 'transmission' model.[40] If we consider simply some authors cited in the discussion of the kerygmatic approach in Chapter 1, the following titles emerge:
"Imparting the Christian Message";[41] "The Art of Teaching Christian Doctrine or The Good News and its Proclamation";[42] "Catechetics, a Theology of Proclamation"; [43] "Handing on the Faith";[44]

Lee's comment on this continues by noting how Domenico Grasso places catechesis within the more encompassing term 'preaching' in the following terms:
"What the term 'catechesis' fails to express is that religious instruction is not simply a communication of ideas, but rather the transmission of facts and actions that are intended to become principles of thought and moral conduct. But this deficiency resides in the nature of preaching itself, of which catechesis is merely one form. For this, too, the term 'preaching' is preferable to any other for describing the phenomenon of the transmission of the message."[45]

40. **Towards a Future for Religious Education**, edited by Lee-Rooney, Pflaum Press Dayton, Ohio, 1970, p. 56.
41. Johannes Hofinger, **Imparting the Christian Message**, Univ. of Notre Dame Press, Indiana, 1961.
42. Johannes Hofinger, **The Art of Teaching Christian Doctrine or The Good News and its Proclamation**, Univ. of Notre Dame Press, 2nd edition, 1962.
43. Alfred McBride, **Catechetics, A Theology of Proclamation**, Bruce Publishing Co., Milwaukee, 1966.
44. Jungmann op. cit.
45. Domenico Grasso, **Proclaiming God's Message**, Univ. Notre Dame Press, 1965, p. 247.

In his detailed criticisms of such an approach, Lee emphasizes that "the teaching model does not center itself in the teacher or the content (as does the transmission theory and the preaching model) but rather in the learner"[46] whereas the transmission model is the reverse of this:

"Speculatively, this conception of teaching is based on the "transmission theory" which postulates that teaching consists in the transmission of a given message from the teacher to the student. The more intact this message is received by the student, the better the teaching is. The passionate devotion of specialists in religious instruction to the transmission theory can be illustrated in a recent attempt by one such specialist to transmute transmission from the methodological sphere into the realm of theology."[47]

The author referred to in the above statement, Alfonso Nebrada, does indeed entitle his article "The Theological Problem of Transmission" but in context seems to be arguing for nothing more than others who advocated the kerygmatic approach:

"It is, then, necessary to point out where and how the main road of Catechesis went astray, and to realise that the type of catechesis which most of us learned when we were children is an unfortunate recent deviation from the true tradition of catechetics in the history of the Church."[48]

In a footnote citing the important work of P.A. Liégé for the recognition of the importance of the kerygmatic approach, the argument continues:

"It is a fact that in the Catholic Church, little by little, primacy has been given to 'doctrinal teaching' and that the stage of kerygma has practically disappeared from the catechesis. Doubtless it was believed safeguarded when the children were baptised in Christian countries and received their Christian education in the faith as from a mother."[49]

But the question which concerns us in the evaluation of the "transmission" model is the attitude which stresses all learning simply from the viewpoint of those entrusted with the "passing on" and the short-sighted move to equate all learning as the result only of formal didactic teaching. Of all recent commentators on this question, Sebastian Moore, writing in the 1968 Downside Symposium comes closest to appreciating what the real question involves when he writes ironically:

". . . when the Church teaches, man is purely the receiver, grateful and docile. She brings to him a revelation, truth that he could never

---

46. **Towards a Future for Religious Education**, pp. 58-59.
47. ibid., pp. 56-57.
48. **Lumen Vitae** Vol. XX, No. 2, p. 311.
49. ibid., footnote 2.

have found for himself... It will not be a venture into the unknown on the part of teacher and taught alike. It will be the purveying of the supernaturally known, on the part of her who is possessed of this precious knowledge with the mandate to pass it on."[50]

Taking exception to this kind of model, however, Moore continues:

"If it (i.e. in context, the question of content) was raised, this would involve a new look at the major premise of our educational policy, the Church's authority to teach—I mean, more precisely, a fresh attempt to understand the event of the Church teaching, to answer our question "What exactly is happening when the Church is teaching?"[51]

In his detailed answer, Moore stresses that something happens to both teacher and taught. For each, "it is that the experience of being a man has become more meaningful."[52] Moore, in his highly arresting and original way, is obviously opposed to a simplistic 'content/method' model but he also raises an important question mark about the transmission model in itself, no matter whether it has a doctrinal or a kerygmatic orientation.

Although he does not use this same term to describe the model he opposes, Jacques Audinet, in "Forming the Faith of Adolescents" is evidently opposed to this 'transmission model':

"The expression 'to get over the Christian message' carries its own condemnation. The jockey has to get his horse over the obstacle. But tricks will never help people to reach a knowledge of the faith. If we must speak of 'getting across' the message of faith, let us do so with misgivings. For our part we prefer to speak of an 'approach' when we describe that movement of encounter between the young person and God's plan, for this is what our teaching must bring about."[53]

5. The catechetical model evaluated according to educational principles

It is now important to proceed to an evaluation of each of these manifestations of the catechetical model. Whether we call it "the traditional pedagogy", "the catechetical method with the catechism content" or "the transmission model" there are certain common features which need to be appraised from an educational viewpoint. There are three main areas to be treated. viz. the catechetical model and authority, the role of the teacher, and that of the pupil.

---

50. **The Teaching Role of the Church**, Chapter 10, pp. 246-247.
51. ibid., p. 249.
52. ibid.
53. Jacques Audinet, **Forming the Faith of Adolescents**, Burns & Oates, London, 1968, p. 21.

1 — The catechetical model and authority.

We have already noted the consistency of terminology which speaks of "handing on", "transmission", "imparting" with respect to the teacher's role. It is worth underlining just how easy it can be for an 'authority' role to become 'authoritarian' in the traditional sense of one entrusted with a specific mission in the Church, the teacher/catechist is both *in* authority and regarded as *an* authority. In the first sense, what he imparts is the message of salvation carried by the Church; to his pupils he represents the teaching Church. If he is identified closely with the Church as an ordained person or as a member of a religious order, his very distinctness endows him (in the eyes of pupils and parents) with a position which makes him also *an* authority.

Both of these senses of authority were heightened by the tendency in the past, especially evident in the use of the catechism or an appeal to it as the final arbiter in any discussion, to concentrate on the teaching of doctrinal truths. In schools for many years this emphasis was indicated by the title of 'Christian Doctrine'. Indeed, the very wide range of terminology even at the present probably reflects the under-lying confusion surrounding the teaching of religion in many places. Thus, besides Christian Doctrine, there are also to be encountered at present in English Catholic schools, Catechism, Religious Instruction, Religious Education, Theology, Religion and Doctrinal Knowledge. As the preceding chapter indicated, the description of the keynote as 'magisterial' was justified by the widespread usage of the model characterised by "teaching *that*". Even the movement described in the sequence of the preceding chapter which has lead to the more widespread use of models of "teaching *how*" and "teaching *why*" has not necessarily influenced all teachers. To the extent, therefore, that much teaching in the generally accepted traditional catechetical manner relied so heavily on doctrinal statements in an authoritative form expected to be learned off by heart, it easily ran the risk of being authoritarian or of appearing so to pupils. This was especially the case where the emphasis was on the final form of the orthodox statement in its exact wording rather than on discussion, explanation and understanding. Even in traditional topics such as apologetics with senior pupils, the very appearance of open inquiry and discussion failed to mask the fact that there were certain definite conclusions to be drawn and certain statements to be made in the end.

2 — A Teacher-centred Model?

A closer inspection of the "teaching that" model emphasises other ways in which it was at variance with educational theory. Most obviously, it postulated *teachers teaching* as its norm rather than pupils learning. Even where the pupil's role was made explicit, it only emphasised this situation, requiring as it did that he learn and memorize prepared statements. While there were certainly good teachers who arrived at this final position with pupils only after genuine inquiry, the model hardly encouraged the idea of pupils and teacher in a co-operative enterprise of learning together. Pupil learning was always seen as the result of teachers teaching. This is all perfectly natural in the "catechism" situation, in the content/method division and equally of course, in the transmission model also, for in all of these cases what was emphasised above all was the language and thought of adult theologians, rather than the natural expression of pupils. This was the case even where some kind of concession appeared to have been made by requiring younger pupils to learn only selected answers from a national catechism. Whatever quantitative restrictions this implied, the strictures of Sloyan on the practice are worth noting:

> "The device of asterisks to indicate questions proper to the very young is especially harmful because it puts on young minds the burden of seeing the same panorama of faith the adult sees but aided by fewer landmarks of the same type. To employ the same or similarly phrased answers for ages six and sixteen is to fly in the face of all we know about the development of the human mind and personality. Here it is not a question of simplified phrasing (important though this might be) but of a whole way of thinking foreign to him."[54]

With regard to the teacher-centred situations implied in the three aspects of the catechetical model, Lee comments:

> "Lecturing, telling, reciting, teacher-directed questions, and other teacher-centred pedagogical devices constitute the ultimate in the deprivation of student freedom, for in these situations the students are encased in an extremely narrow range of free-acting. In other words, in the traditional teacher-centred, transmission approach, the students are free solely to react in a certain way clearly delineated by the teacher, or not to react, to listen or not to listen, the teacher is the sole source of control."[55]

Moran is also critical of the transmission approach:

> "The oft-repeated principle that the role of the religion teacher is to "deliver the message" must be challenged... The teaching material must largely be discovered in the common search by teacher and student though the teacher should obviously contribute more because of his background of competence and experience."[56]

Of the many sources of dissatisfaction with the traditional catechisms, nothing seems to have aroused more opposition (and often for the wrong reasons!) than the question of memorisation. Sloyan rightly notes:

---

54. Gerard Sloyan (ed.), **Modern Catechetics. Message and Method in Religious Formation,** Collier-Macmillan, London, 1963, p. 92, note 56.
55. Lee-Rooney, op. cit., p. 61.
56. **God Still Speaks,** Burns and Oates, London, 1967, p. 46.

"This raises the root ambiguity of catechisms, which must be terminated if they are to have any efficacy whatever. The lists for memorization were devised for the adult penitent; handbooks like Bellarmine's for unlettered adults; Canisius' basic book for the relatively small student population that was getting basic training in letters during late adolescence; and the manual prescribed by Trent for the guidance of the clergy."[57]

But in the "teaching-centred passive pupils" discussion, one has only to consider such things as the use of the formal question and its precisely worded answer to be memorized, so different from the question which arises from the pupil himself; the assumption by means of the official answer that all inquiry must eventually lead to this knowledge and no other; the arbitrary end-point of the catechism answer itself (even worse when as Sloyan noted, it was the beginning, middle and end!); the inevitable restriction of inquiry—and in consequence of opportunity for personal growth—when precise attention to formulae was required to avoid statements which were materially heretical, and the final position of formal orthodoxy was attained possibly at the expense of personal understanding!

3 — Passive pupils?

The natural corollary is that there will be passive pupils where there are dominant teachers. Any conserving or transmitting model implies certain expectations with regard to pupils' learning, so that the degree of passivity of the pupils may well bear some relationship to the attitude of the teacher. But the very nature of the subject (and often its sociological background in a more sectarian age) plus the obligation felt by many teachers to produce a certain kind of 'product', often resulted in the activity of pupils being restricted to acquiring facts and memorising answers. That this was due as much as anything else to the inadequate preparation (or lack of theological background) of teacher/catechists who made literal use of the catechism because they were not really capable of teaching without it is highly likely, although it is only fair to consider that the ideal put forward in *Divini Illius Magistri* by Pope Pius XI remained "active co-operation on the part of the pupil in his own education."[58] The passivity of pupils or at least a less active co-operation on their part is a natural result from any kind of "transmitting" model, because if the process is viewed as instruction rather than education, it is difficult to avoid a situation where the process seems to be mainly a handing on of facts.

57. Gerard Sloyan (ed.), **Modern Catechetics**, p. 92, note 56.
58. cf. note 14 of the present chapter.

Coupled with this notion of passive pupils should be noted the lack of recognition of the value of the pupil's experience. This reached quite ridiculous lengths in certain aspects of what was called "teaching the liturgy" when the whole notion of worship and sacrificial offering, was taught in the classroom without any attempt to relate it to the life and experience of the pupil. The point being made here is not that explanation of worship was something unsuitable for the classroom but rather that the descriptions, history of rites and so on, had little relationship to the actual worship which the pupil attended in his local church.

Perhaps a subtle variation of this is still to be found in what some teachers refer to as "experience centred" teaching when what they are referring to is the manipulation of pupils' ideas or emotions to arrive at a position held by the teacher himself, or thought desirable for pupils to hold. This is not meant to be a condemnation of everything but the most objective teaching. What is being affirmed positively is that a broad view of education which should have its place no less in the teaching of religion, sees value in the very process of teaching and not simply in the end-product; it recognises the value of 'knowledge' gained via the emotions through personal and vicarious experiences as of equal importance with those cognitive skills gained through intellectual application; it regards the activity of pupils and teachers as a joint activity which leaves everyone changed through the very interaction, without, however, requiring arbitrary criteria of success.

6. **The ideal of catechesis in relation to education.**

After the detailed analysis of this last section in which the "actual" traditional model of catechesis has been inspected, it remains now to consider some explicit and implicit assumptions which result from the nature of catechesis as a special form of educational activity. In other words, this last section considers the ideal rather than the actual. There are four areas to be considered:

1 — Catechesis must include positive instruction in the truths of the faith and of the traditional moral discipline of the church.
2 — Successful catechesis transcends the acquisition of factual knowledge and looks to changes in attitude i.e. to the development and deepening of personal faith as the basis for conduct.
3 — Catechesis in the school situation is a continuation of that work of initiation and instruction already begun by the intervention and example of parents, so that the catechist's mission is ideally an extension of that of the parents.
4 — Catechesis proceeds as already noted on the assumption of catechist and pupil sharing the same beliefs and it looks towards ensuring positive and lasting commitment to this by the pupil.

The first of these expresses an important right of the Church: the truths of faith as well as moral principles may be learned in various ways, but the Church here insists that the learner has the opportunity to hear these truths presented by formal teaching under favourable circumstances. Two extremes have to be avoided. The first is that emphasis on truths of faith and morality are not meant to be a complete summary of all that religion entails, nor is it something which can be reduced completely to credal formulas and catechism answers. Coudreau rightly insists however:

> "It goes without saying that the importance of actual instruction in catechesis needs to be frequently repeated. Certain present-day methods of religious education, though oriented towards bearing witness to the faith and toward dedicated Christian living, sometimes tend to minimize the indispensable role of this positive presentation of doctrine. It seems that insistence on this necessity is not out of place at this very hour, and that those responsible for the pedagogy of the faith should honor, defend and clarify the role of informative teaching in religious educaton."[59]

The second extreme to be avoided, however, is the use of un-educational or even anti-educational means, such as indoctrination, to ensure a result which effectively disregards the freedom of the individual. For some writers, there seems to be a particular suspicion of formal didactic religious teaching as inevitably leading to indoctrination. For example, J. P. White, takes as paradigm cases of indoctrination "communist systems of political education or, perhaps, the teaching of religion in Roman Catholic schools".[60] The term is used in this regard often enough to justify a more detailed comment on the concept, which will be looked at again in Chapter 5 on religious education.

Indoctrination is one of those words which have taken on mainly a pejorative connotation since the publicising of methods of "brain-washing" in totalitarian regimes since the second World War, but the word has a neutral sense as referring to the teaching of doctrine. In a pejorative sense, the term is applied to teaching facts without giving reasons, teaching as factually true what is an aspect of the private beliefs or opinions of the teacher, teaching without open discussion of the matter taught, or neglecting to employ or to accept rational criticism of a factual presentation. Indoctrination may result from content, intention or method, separately or all in conjunction. J. P. White would add a fourth kind viz. the view

---

59. Coudreau, op. cit., p. 136.

60. **The Concept of Education**, edited by R. S. Peters, Routledge & Kegan Paul, 4th impression 1969. *Indoctrination*, p. 181.

of those child-centred theorists who oppose the introduction of any matter not arising from the spontaneous needs and interests of the child.[61]

In his discussion of "Indoctrination as a Normative Concept", Willis Moore offers a simple model:

"It would seem to be more in accord with reality to consider the 'indoctrination' and the 'education' of the earlier liberal educators to be the polar extremes of a continuum of teaching method along which actual teaching may move in keeping with the requirements of the situation. With infants in nearly everything and with mature reasoning adults in very little, the teacher will use indoctrinating procedures. Between the two extremes the proper mixture of the one method with the other is appropriately determined by the degree of rational capability of the learner with regard to the subject matter before him and the degree of urgency of the situation."[62]

On this basis, and with the support of assumptions already noted, the catechist fulfils his mission to the children, their parents and the Church, precisely by providing those whom he catechises with the content of truths called the faith of the Church. This does not justify indoctrination either of method or intention but if the word is used for the very literal sense of teaching the doctrine of the Church, it must be seen to have no pejorative overtones.[63] This matter will be referred to again in relation to the notion of "teaching about" in Chapter 5.

THE DEEPENING OF FAITH

With regard to the second assumption viz. transcending the acquisition of factual knowledge and looking to changes in attitude and the development and deepening of personal faith, there is first of all a certain amount of resemblance to R. S. Peters' general notion of education as essentially an 'improving' process. In this view, the person is rightly the object of education and the acquisition of factual knowledge is regarded not as an end in itself, but as an intermediate stage of a complete process. What is implied, however, in the catechetical situation seems to be a cause and effect relationship between the acquisition of new knowledge and a change in attitude on the part of the learner. But such a relationship is at the most, contingent rather than necessary. The already noted confusion over the terms "teaching the *faith*" i.e. teaching the official doctrines of

---

61. op. cit., p. 180.

62. **Studies in the Philosophy of Education**, Vol. IV, No. 4, p. 401.

63. cf. the model proposed by Barbara Hosegood op. cit. where she considers all except the first as constituting indoctrination: "(1) the presentation of truth truthfully; (2) the presentation of truth dogmatically; (3) the presentation of dogma truthfully; (4) the presentation of dogma dogmatically." **Catholic Education in a Secular Society**, edited by Tucker, Sheed and Ward, London, 1968, p. 185.

the Church and the development of personal faith would come under the same strictures. There is no doubt that the development and deepening of personal faith may often take place because of the greater knowledge and understanding acquired by the learner, but there is nothing logically necessary about this sequence and the desired result. But from an organisational viewpoint—and from the viewpoint of the Church looking for the development of personal faith—the acquisition of such factual knowledge is an important means. The outcome of successful catechesis, however, depends on factors apart from this preparation because it is concerned with a process which, as a special form of knowledge and experience, depends also on the theological concept of God's grace and on the co-operation of the individual person with that grace. We are back again to the fundamental idea of catechesis as believer speaking to believer in a faith context, explicit or assumed. The verification for success in such an enterprise cannot be reduced to proof of the acquisition of factual knowledge; perhaps there is no one way of making any final verification. Indeed, is this the catechist's task? But the assumption does point towards certain guidelines, even though they may remain as vague as those of the "educated man" of R. S. Peters.

CATECHESIS WITHIN CHRISTIAN EDUCATION

The relationships between catechesis and education in general and the particular responsibilities of teachers to parents are both implied by the next assumption. The traditional Catholic viewpoint in the century since Catholic schools were established separately from those of the state in various countries, has been that the teacher receives his mandate by delegation of the parents. This principle laid down by Pope Leo XIII in *Rerum Novarum* and adopted by Pius XI in *Divini Illius Magistri* in 1929, is stated in *Gravissimum Educationis* as follows:

> "Parents... have the first and inalienable duty and right to educate their children... But let teachers realise that to the greatest possible extent they determine whether the Catholic school can bring its goals and undertakings to fruition... Above all, let them perform their services as partners of the parents."[64]

These statements out of many similar ones indicate the juridical position of the teacher in the catechetical situation in school. He is entrusted often with young children and is concerned with their initiation to the Sacraments of Penance and Eucharist. As part of his work with all age groups, the catechist has the duty to help form the consciences of those whom he teaches and to act as a witness to the truths he teaches. Does this necessarily assume that the catechist's task is always bordering on

64. Abbott (ed.), op. cit., par. 6, p. 644; par. 8, p. 646.

54

indoctrination? On the lines of the analysis already given, this is not so, although there may be special difficulties where the school is private and the financing of the school and the payment of teachers' salaries is the responsibility of the parents. Is the catechist/teacher bound under natural justice to do just what the parents require? The question is a little finer than this. The rights of the parents in education are fundamental but this does not mean that they are the only people with rights. The situation encountered in boarding schools and in forms of institutional care of young offenders, cannot be resolved entirely on a transferred parental mandate in a way which supposes that parents have the right to indoctrinate their children and a simple transfer of responsibility throws the same onus onto teachers. Certainly, accepting the Willis Moore continuum description has as much application to parents as to teachers. Both share a common enterprise but the precise differences between their roles must always be appreciated and the role of the catechist qua catechist may necessitate his taking view-points different from those of parents. Parental rights are not absolute and must be balanced against the growing ability of the young people to make their own choices. Encouragement and help towards personal autonomy is directly threatened by an approach which is narrowly prescriptive and which presses for completeness of knowledge and understanding and fullness of commitment before the young person is ready for it. This is not to underestimate the dilemna of the catechist who at times has to balance the dual fidelities quoted previously. It is possible to envisage a situation where the catechist feels obliged to support his pupil's attitudes against those of the parents, just as it is to imagine a situation where his mission in the Church requires him to oppose attitudes which may alienate him from his pupil. Finally, there is the important factor that there can be ethical relationships between teachers and pupils which may not be shared with parents.

THE END RESULT

The fourth assumption is that which seems to be made when the expectations of catechesis in the school context are being considered. It is difficult at times to distinguish the expectations resulting from a Christian education from those of the more limited term, catechesis, but from this set of assumptions being treated, the following amalgam should result ideally:

The catechised person is an instructed believer who knows and understands his faith and Christian duties and has committed himself to live according to them. In practice such a person would act according to the set of norms which are taken as norms of Christian life and conduct.

Such outward criteria are assumed to be the outward manifestation of his interior dispositions towards these religious/devotional practices.

55

Where people who have received the opportunity for such instruction do not follow it, terms such as "falling away from the faith" or "leakage from the faith" are used.[65] This description is important because its norms are sociological rather than particularly religious. The very supposition of a completeness at some arbitrary terminal stage is something to be wished for, hoped for and indeed prayed for by the catechist, but if the product is obtained by uneducational means, the result is illusory.

From an educational viewpoint it is particularly defective, subscribing implicitly as it does to a functional view of education and of catechesis by looking to ends outside of the process itself. This kind of thinking is evident in the following statement of Branigan:

> "Since the aim in the secondary sections of school life is to prepare pupils for the time when they leave school, a much more informed knowledge of Christian Doctrine will be necessary, along with such a course of elementary apologetics as will fit them not only to defend their Faith but to satisfy their own possible misgivings and doubts at a very critical age."[66]

Such statements often deny implicitly the educational aims to which teachers subscribe in other activities. Pupils trained to be critical of evidence, to detect prejudice in the emotional tone of some writing and in the empirical sciences in particular, to be aware of the value of demonstration as proof, will necessarily examine their religious teaching in the same way. This easily leads to shallowness and rejection of religion unless religion has been taught in terms of its own special character. The commitment which one might hope for would be a commitment to truth and to its pursuit in all circumstances. Such a view of commitment is something progressive, always in a state of development. It is to believe in the value of the educational process as a whole thing, rather than look only towards a finished product.

CONCLUSION

The examination in this chapter of the catechetical model and of the assumptions upon which school catechesis appears to be based, is intended to help clarify the principal relationships between education and catechesis. It does not pretend that catechesis will necessarily be the better because it is undistinguishable from education or the educational process. To proceed thus would be to fail to respect the separate concepts involved, something discussed in Chapters 5 and 6.

---

65. Hosegood, op. cit., p. 192.
66. Branigan, op. cit., p. 165.

56

What may be clearer from the foregoing analysis may be concentrated around the following ideas.

1 — To the extent that school catechesis is part of the educational process, it needs to harmonise with the educational methods, procedures and attitudes in which it has its place. In practical terms, catechesis carried out in an authoritarian teacher-centred, didactic manner with pupils who in other aspects of their formal schooling rarely encounter such attitudes and methods, runs the risk of being considered distasteful and irrelevant.

2 — The true catechetical situation cannot be simply a matter of time slots on a time-table. If the fundamental catechetical assumption i.e. believer talking with fellow believers is true, then pupils brought together for instructional aims where there is compulsory schooling and minimum school leaving ages, are not necessarily a community of believers, let alone a voluntary association. The catechist may not proceed as though these conditions may be assumed. This is possibly the most important point to be considered about catechesis in the school situation.

3 — The evolution of the school and the interaction of such changes on catechetics and on pupil-teacher relationships, indeed all the factors looked at in the general view of the preceding chapter, are of the greatest importance. The deschooling movement, and theoretical and practical changes in the structure and organisation of education all have important implications for the traditional catechetical situation, especially if these movements threaten the traditional grounds upon which catechesis in the school has been based.

Chapter Three

THEOLOGICAL INFLUENCES ON THE MODERN CATECHETICAL MOVEMENT

INTRODUCTION

The concern of this chapter is to trace in more detail some of the important theological influences already pointed to in the analysis of the opening chapter or in the evaluation of the traditional model. The first way of doing this in summary fashion is by a treatment of the influence of the Second Vatican Council. But it is very important to specify that the consideration which follows takes Vatican II both as an event and also as expressing a movement i.e. while the Council itself was undoubtedly a landmark in twentieth century theological thought, it was preceded and followed by an important theological ferment. The second part of the chapter considers in particular the influence of the post war studies in what has been called Incarnational theology and concludes with an assessment of the contribution made to the catechetical movement in English speaking countries by Gabriel Moran's important "Theology of Revelation."

The fundamental relationship between the Council and catechesis may be expressed as follows:

If it is to be consistent with its particular role of the instruction of believers as part of the pastoral mission of the Church, what catechesis must *do* results from what the Church *is*. Since therefore, the Church made as thoroughgoing a self-appraisal in relation to the contemporary world as the Vatican Council proved itself to be, the catechist has been confronted with the task of interpreting this event to his fellow-believers. But this cannot simply be an historic survey of what happened as *event*. As already stated, the Council needs to be interpreted also as *movement* because of its general acceptance in its thinking as expressed in the Vatican II documents, of the principle of a dynamic view of life and of social change. In the survey of the opening chapters, it has been shown that catechesis, has tended to be interpreted with a post-Tridentine bias, and in a narrow but widely-accepted sense, has been understood only as the handing on of the traditional faith of the Church in time-hallowed formulae. But it was just this aspect which Pope John XXIII laid open to question in his opening address:

"...the authentic doctrine...should be studied and expounded through the methods of research and through the literary forms of modern thought. The substance of the ancient deposit of faith is one thing and the way in which it is presented is another. And it is the latter that must be taken into great consideration with patience if necessary, everything being measured in the forms and proportions of a magisterium which is predominantly pastoral in character."[1]

To speak, then, of a catechesis in the spirit of Vatican II is not simply to ask for a final re-statement in different terminology of the traditional doctrinal and moral statements, the 'unchanging deposit of the faith.' The concepts of Church, Divine Revelation, Liturgy, Ecumenism, Missions as expressed through the sixteen documents are of varying quality, and far from ending discussion, some of them have provided the starting point for important advances. But it is not with the history of Vatican II nor with a theologian's examination of the documents that we are concerned. It is rather with the new vision of the Church and its mission face to face with the contemporary world, because this is what the catechist is concerned with when he confronts his fellow believers in the catechetical situation.

To do this, we shall consider those documents which relate specifically or by implication, to the four sources of catechesis: the Bible, Liturgy, Doctrine and Christian Witness. But as the catechist's task is to assist in the pastoral work of the Church, it is the Dogmatic Constitution on the Church in the Modern World which reflects the Council's vision of the Church. Therefore, the sequence of this first part of the chapter is a consideration of the following matters:

1—The Bible, with special consideration of the Constitution on Divine Revelation, and the principle of "development of doctrine."

2—The Liturgy, especially through the Liturgical Constitution itself but also through the movement which has followed this document.

3—Doctrine, especially in the light of important concepts regarding the Church and the concept of the "People of God."

4—Christian Witness, the role of the laity and the universal call to holiness.

5—In the last section, there are some special aspects of the notion of catechesis which seem to be implied by the broadening in thinking which has accompanied the growth of the modern ecumenical movement. In particular, there are certain questions which relate to the fundamental inquiry of this work as regards the concepts of catechesis and religious education which are proposed by the direction of certain documents, notably those on Ecumenism and the Non-Christian Religions.

---

1. W. M. Abbott (ed.), **The Documents of Vatican II**, Geoffrey Chapman, London, 1966, p. 715.

Part One

1. The Bible and the Constitution on Divine Revelation[2]

The document *Dei Verbum* is generally regarded by theologians as one of the major achievements of the Council both in itself and in its implications.   In the long term it may well prove to have been the foundation for a dialogue involving all Christians, for not only did it recognize the kind of *de facto* ecumenism which had been achieved by those scholars engaged in Biblical research and criticism since the broadening of Roman Catholic attention to Biblical studies following the letter of Pope Pius XII, *Divino Afflante Spiritu,* in 1943, but in its re-emphasis on the importance of the Scriptures, it made possible an ecumenical dialogue which has been hailed as the end of the Catholic Counter-Reformation. In its attention to modern methods of criticism and exegesis as well as in its reliance on the work of scientific investigations it effectively recognised the autonomy of certain human sciences and methods of investigation.

Attention has already been drawn both to the importance of the Biblical renewal which inspired the kerygmatic movement and the widespread attention to the concept of salvation history, which was, as we have seen a growing focus of attention for over a decade before the Council. The special contribution of *Dei Verbum* may be considered from the following points:

1 — The uniqueness of the Christian religion has always been in its explicit acceptance as a ground point, that it is based upon God's revelation of Himself to mankind.   Such a claim has been rejected by various groups throughout history, but the Roman Catholic Church has always maintained its belief in God's revelation to man and in the power and duty of the Church to interpret this revelation, as for example in the statement on Revelation from the First Vatican Council. This latter statement, however, seemed to favour what was called a *propositional* view of the matter, that is, one which seemed to regard the uniqueness of Christian revelation precisely in its making known truths about God which were otherwise incapable of being discovered by man for himself.   Whether this was a correct interpretation of the Vatican I statement is less important than the observation that too much stress on this aspect tended to neglect the importance of the recipient of the revelation, man, who receives this revelation of God in a certain historical context and who, in this reception, enters into some kind of relationship with God whose revelation is primarily, at least, a revelation of Himself.   In other words, discussion of whether or not a propositional view of revelation is acceptable or not, is not the main issue,

---

2. Abbott (ed.), op. cit., pp. 111-128.

however much man's account of this encounter with God's self-revelation can be expressed subsequently in terms of propositions.

2 — It was the re-emphasis on the personal aspects of revelation — the God who reveals Himself through the saving event of Jesus Christ in a certain historical situation to man — which put into its correct perspective the long-standing discussion of theologians as to whether or not revelation was contained in scripture alone, in scripture and partly in tradition, or in scripture and tradition without any separation of the two sources, by emphasising

a — the unity of revelation both as historical event and as personal communication in the life of the believer;
b — the unity of deeds and words necessary for the full understanding of revelation, within the context of God's saving history. This meant that tradition must be looked to not simply in the recorded traditions but also in the subject of the tradition, man himself.

The statement which resolves this historical questions concludes:

"It is clear, therefore, that sacred tradition, sacred Scripture, and the teaching authority of the Church, in accord with God's most wise design, are so linked and joined together that one cannot stand without the others, and that all together and each in its own way under the action of the one Holy Spirit contributes effectively to the salvation of souls."[3]

3 — Another aspect of *Dei Verbum* which has opened out new and important directions for theologians, was its bold formulations of the principle of the 'development of doctrine',[4] which, while explicitly referred to in the First Vatican Council's Dogmatic Constitution on the Catholic Faith,[5] had not been viewed favourably by those who sometimes made the mistake of identifying a theological truth with a particular method or mode of expressing it. In context, the reference seems to be made especially with regard to establishing the inter-dependence of scripture and tradition, but, as the following quotation shows, there is a wider connotation:

---

3. ibid., p. 118.

4. This idea, the subject of Newman's essay on the Development of Christian Doctrine in 1845 was greatly helped by the Catholic theologians of Tubingen, but the idea as a whole suffered from the conflict between traditional Catholic theology and Modernism. cf. **Concilium**, Vol. 1, No. 3, January 1967, p. 53. *Recent Catholic Views on the Development of Dogma,* by Herbert Hammans.

5. Footnote 18, Abbott (ed.), op. cit., p. 116 acknowledging Chapter 4 *On Faith and Reason of Vatican I* (Denziger 1800).

"This tradition which comes from the apostles develops in the Church with the help of the Holy Spirit. For there is a growth in the understanding of the realities and the words which have been handed down. This happens through the contemplation and study made by believers, who treasure these things in their hearts through the intimate understanding of spiritual things they experience, and through the preaching of those who have received through episcopal succession the sure gift of truth."[6]

In his discussion of the development of doctrines, Bernard Lonergan points out "that there is not some one manner or even more limited set of manners in which doctrines develop. In other words the intelligibility proper to developing doctrines is the intelligibility imminent in historical process. One knows it, not by *a priori* theorizing, but by *a posteriori* research, interpretation, history, dialectic and the decision of foundations."[7]

Having related one mode of development of doctrine to the ongoing discovery of mind and shown how the movement to a systematic position is itself sometimes challenged either from a more developed idea of consciousness or by a reversion to first sources, Lonergan observes:

"Often enough development is dialectical. The truth is discovered because a contrary error has been asserted."[8]

The acceptance or not of this principle lies behind the sharp division between those who perceive catechesis in a limited role of handing on exact formulae e.g. those who would support the continuing use at all stages of schooling of a traditional catechism, and those who prefer to begin from an existential or at least experiential position.

4 — The attention to the Scriptures and "the ministry of the word" was a marked contribution to the recognition of the major emphasis of the Protestant churches, so that, along with other developments such as the extension of the chalice to the laity, at least in principle, and the emphasis on the priesthood as a role of service rather than of hierarchy and privilege, so much impetus was given indirectly to the ecumenical movement. As already indicated briefly in earlier chapters, the 're-discovery' of the Scriptures was central to the kerygmatic renewal, but the further designation of "pastoral preaching, catechetics, and all other Christian instruction, among which the liturgical homily should have an exceptional place"[9] as various forms

---

6. Abbott (ed.), op. cit., par. 8, p. 116.

7. Bernard Lonergan, **Method in Theology**, Darton, Longman & Todd, London, 1971, p. 319.

8. ibid.

9. Abbott (ed.), op. cit., par. 24, p. 127.

of the ministry of the word, was an important change in emphasis especially for traditional catechetics. In this view, the criterion of the Christian's living and of the catechist's instruction is not the theological statement nor the exact catechism answer, but Scripture. This attention to the Bible flowed over into the lives of many members of religious orders, both as teachers and as groups responsible for the training of catechists, from the application of the norms for the Appropriate Renewal of Religious Life in *Perfectae Caritatis* in which the previous imbalance on the notion of Rule was redressed by attention to the scriptural basis and justification of all religious orders.

5 — The very history of the 'growth' of *Dei Verbum* from its first rejection by the Council to its final acceptance three years later in a greatly changed form is not without importance, for the kind of discussions and re-formulations which were the background to this development had their own importance as one commentator has observed:

"Far from ending discussion on the nature of revelation, the Council has provided a framework within which more fruitful discussion may now proceed . . .   One thing above all is certain: it is the nature of revelation itself that is now in question."[10]

In this connection, it is not surprising to find that one of the major resolutions formulated during the International Congress on Catechetics in Rome in 1971, was a call for further work by theologians on the nature of revelation and in the application of these new insights to the tasks of catechesis.

2.   The Constitution on the Liturgy[11]

Despite the greater theological importance of other documents of Vatican II, notably in addition to *Dei Verbum,* the Dogmatic Constitution on the Church and the Declaration on Religious Freedom, it was the Constitution on the Liturgy which first brought the influence of the Council on the Church as a whole, and as one of the sources of catechesis, contributed directly to the advancement of new and much broader ideas in the past decade.

Perhaps the most remarkable of these advances, the emphasis on the use of the vernacular, was almost an indirect result, at least in the minds of those responsible for the document.   The renewed emphasis on the 'theology of the word' necessitated widespread changes in the or-

10. Gabriel Moran, **Theology of Revelation**, Burns and Oates, London, 1967, p. 18.

11. Promulgated 4th December 1963, see Abbott (ed.), op. cit., pp. 137-178.

ganisation and selection of scriptural readings, so that it was only natural that these be done in the vernacular. Moreover, the central position and organisation of the readings gave new point to the development and use of the homily, which, unlike the formal sermon as organised by subjects for the whole year in the Catechism of the Council of Trent, was based on the scriptural readings which were increased in number and more carefully planned around central themes of the history of salvation. In a remarkably short time, a vernacular liturgy for the Mass and the administration of the sacraments was a reality, and even though this was a logical result of the efforts of the pioneers of liturgical reform from the time of Jungmann in 1936, it was no less startling for that. Just to mention one important aspect which would otherwise have been delayed on purely practical grounds, it would not have been possible to see much practical implementation of the Decree on Ecumenism without this rapid change over to the vernacular. Indeed, the very search for suitable translations of prayers and rituals and, even more so, for suitable musical settings of hymns and Masses, provided an ideal starting point for the kind of *de facto* ecumenism which, as already mentioned, had come about with the Scripture scholars. There were even stronger factors working for ecumenism, for as the celebrant at Mass now needed to be audible, to face his congregation and to be prepared to present a homily on the scriptural readings, his particular role of service to the community was better appreciated in terms of function rather than of hierarchy. The provision for occasional extension of the chalice to the laity[12] and the encouragement of concelebration[13] rather than separate 'private Masses' without congregation, were important advances in themselves but even more so because of the better appreciation of the role of the faithful themselves. It was not long before an expression which had for centuries hardly been used except as a reference to the "errors of Luther" was heard by Roman Catholics: the priesthood of all believers. This expression, used in a number of the later Council documents, was certainly implied by the following passage from the Constitution on the Liturgy:

> "Mother Church earnestly desires that all the faithful be led to that full, conscious, and active participation in liturgical celebrations which is demanded by the very nature of the liturgy. Such participation by the Christian people as "a chosen race, a royal priesthood, a holy nation, a purchased people" (1 Pet. 2:9; 42:4-5) is their right and duty by reason of their baptism."[14]

12. ibid., par. 55, p. 156.
13. ibid., par. 57, pp. 157-158.
14. ibid., par. 14, p. 144.

65

What has been said to this point confirms the opinion of Schille-beeckx who lists the main achievement of this document as follows:

"The fundamental gain of this constitution is that it broke the clergy's monopoly of the liturgy. Whereas it was formerly the priest's affair, with the faithful no more than his clientele, the council regards not only the priest but the entire Christian community, God's people, as the subject of the liturgical celebration, in which each in his proper place is given his own particular, hierarchically ordered function—a theological view with all kinds of practical repercussions."[15]

Another matter with very far-reaching results was the practical acceptance of a plurality of forms of religious worship according to the different peoples and regions of the world, a change of great importance for the Church in traditional missionary areas. This kind of adaptation to native cultures which the first Jesuits in China and the East had tried to effect in the sixteenth century from their very experience was at last accepted and indeed recommended. The change, significant in itself and in its recognition of the importance of the native culture, was even greater when considered against the accumulated rubrics of centuries which had regulated even the slightest movements and gestures of the celebrant in the uniformity of the Roman rite. The return to a more biblical notion of sacrifice and to the affirmation of the centrality of the Paschal mystery, the "demythologization" which accompanied the demise of Latin and the increased understanding available to all by the use of the vernacular, were responsible also for the delegation of certain roles to the laity e.g. that of reader and even in some cases the distribution of Communion, and to degrees of experimentation which continue to have great importance for catechesis. For example, the removal of much of the mystique which accompanied vestments, incense, ritual, rigid uniformity of movement and gesture etc. led towards experiments in liturgy which included group Mass in informal settings, folk music, dialogue homilies, reception of Communion in the hand and similar kinds of developments, all of which laid stress on the experiential element of worship.[16] It is generally true that these developments often took place in the informal situations of camps, week-ends, or private houses rather than in the formal settings of traditional churches, although much pioneer work in this regard came from the old mediaeval church of St. Severin in Paris. It hardly needs to be added that these settings were generally characterized by a strong sense of community and there was great stress on dialogue as a form of mediation of the word of God.

15. E. Schillebeeckx, **Vatican II: The Real Achievement**, Sheed & Ward, London, 1966, pp. 27-28.

16. cf. Chapter 1 (diagram) and discussion in Chapter 4 of modern developments in catechesis.

From the viewpoint of catechesis, the very involvement of people in the preparation for such activities seemed to lead many to a more profound sense of understanding of the aims, intentions and even satisfactions of religious celebration, factors not always discovered in the formal ecclesial setting. Perhaps one of the strongest examples of this has been the adaptation of the principles of the group Mass to classroom settings in schools as a means of achieving that community of worship which can be such a formative influence in a religious education.

In his introduction to the Constitution on the Liturgy in the Abbott Documents of Vatican II, McNaspy points out that the spade work for the document had been carefully prepared, so that it was able to channel the kind of thinking which had ebbed and flowed since the beginning of modern liturgical reform with Pius X in the early years of the century.[17] In this sense, the document simply made available to the whole Church, the kind of thinking which had developed in some places e.g. the re- cognition of the priesthood of the faithful which was to find expression in the term 'People of God', used in the Dogmatic Constitution on the Church. We may therefore summarize the contribution of this liturgical Constitution to catechesis in the Church around the following points:

1 — The revised attention to the liturgy of the Word—and were not the already noted 'paraliturgies'[18] referred to in an earlier chapter an indication of this—makes the scriptural education of the faithful at least more likely, especially as the revised series of readings attempt to combine readings from the Old Testament and from the New around a central theme in such a way, that over a three year cycle, the greater part of the Bible is read. If this is beyond the likely experience of most Christians, at least the readings in the vernacular help to provide the background for the liturgical homily.

2 — As noted in the preceding chapter, the possibility of instruction within the liturgical context—the continuing catechesis of the liturgy—was made more likely when the language used was immediately intelligible both by being heard and easily understood. This is not to deny the mystical aspects of the traditional liturgy with its emphasis on posture and silence and the centuries of traditional Latin settings in music, but it seems realistic to believe that children who have been brought up with the Bible in a way not previously experienced by many generations of Catholic parents, may be more than compensated by the more easily understood and recognised attention to the Scrip- tures in the vernacular.

3 — That view of catechesis which was particularly linked with "initiation" has been made more intelligible by the use of the vernacular for the

17. Abbott (ed.), op. cit., pp. 133-134.
18. Chapter 1.

sacramental life of the Church. There are indications that the traditional symbols associated with some of the sacraments may be given different forms in mission countries to be better appreciated as symbols in the particular culture in which they are used.

4 — Perhaps it needs to be said that the value of liturgy should not depend on extraneous considerations. As a form of worship it is an integral dimension of religion, both in the primary sense of offering homage to God but also in the form of communal activity in which such homage is given. As Jacques Bournique says:

"It is the profound intention of the Constitution to make clear the role of the community—a community which is called and gathered together by the Word of God, which hears, listens to and assimilates this Word, and is thus able to respond to it... Liturgy exists at one and the same time for God and for man. It is the homage of God, but it must also involve and transform man, and implies a catechetical dimension."[19]

It is in this catechetical dimension that it may involve both pupils and teachers in a common activity involving different forms of learning —the explicitly doctrinal, the experiential dimension of social worship, the social presence and involvement which necessarily accompany it, as has already been indicated in the schematic treatment in Chapter One.

3. Doctrine—and the Church of Vatican II

Under this general heading we are particularly concerned with the Church's self-understanding and her mission, for it is in the light of this understanding that the perhaps traditionally overemphasised role of Doctrine may best be understood. In this sense, no document of the Council was of greater importance than the Dogmatic Constitution on the Church, known as *Lumen Gentium*[20] in which the Church set out her own understanding of her own nature. From every point of view, such an understanding was of the greatest importance for those engaged in catechesis in any form, for it was necessary both for their understanding of their own mission within the Church as well as for their attitude towards those whom they were instructing in the doctrines of the Church, that they appreciate the nature and force of the Church's view of herself.

For the purposes of this chapter, then, it is necessary to consider the structure and content of this longest document of Vatican II and to point out changes in attitude and self-understanding which had the greatest

---

19. *Catechetics after the Council,* in **Presenting the Christian Message to Africa,** Deacon Books, Geoffrey Chapman, London, 1965, p. 118.

20. Promulgated on 21st November, 1964. See Abbott (ed.), op. cit., pp. 14-96.

import for catechesis. This means that a general sequence of the document is followed, giving special attention to statements or attitudes which are either new, or different in emphasis from that previously understood by the teachers/catechists who were brought up on ideas resulting from Trent and Vatican I. This last point is important for, unlike these other Councils, Vatican II did not promulgate any new doctrine, but it did pay a great deal of attention to reformulation of its traditional beliefs face to face with the contemporary world. One last point needs to be made. Although this is called a 'dogmatic constitution' there is no *a priori* determination of what the Church *should be*. Instead, the language is essentially biblical rather than legalistic as for example in the former Code of Canon Law, so that this very attempt to confine its vision to that of the history of salvation is strongly in accord with *Dei Verbum* and the general open attitude of looking at the 'real' rather than 'ideal' situation. Such a view is hardly consistent with a literal 'transmission' model of catechesis.

1 — *The Mystery of the Church*[21]

The very title of this opening chapter, stressing as it does, the central view of the Church as the presence of God amongst men, is the very opposite of the kind of triumphalist attitudes with which traditional Roman Catholicism has claimed a monopoly of the truth; this new vision is of "a church always in need of reform". It is centred in that sense of the word 'mystery' which stresses the intervention of God rather than the organisation of men and the fidelity of God rather than the permanence of a human fabrication. The Church, moreover, is presented in the doctrinal setting of the Trinity as the foundation doctrine of Christianity, and it is only from within this doctrine that God's gracious plan of salvation can be known and understood. Here we find that broad sweep of salvation history discussed earlier in Chapter One in connection with the kerygmatic movement, with its stress on God's preparation for the sending of the Son, not simply for the Chosen People of the promise, but for all men. The document here makes use of the expression first used by Schillebeeckx of the Church as Sacrament i.e. as sign and source of grace for mankind. It is by the incorporation of those who receive the gift of redemption through Christ and the Spirit that the union (and communion) and fellowship of the Church comes into being. In this sense, the union of people in worship i.e. their acknowledging of their dependence on the work of Father, Son and Spirit, is the form of the Church, both in the local sense and in the wider communion that this represents. This last point is quite important

---

21. ibid., p. 14.

69

for the different perspective it casts on the notion of Church as Mystical Body, the classic affirmation of Pius XII made in *Mystici Corporis* in 1943. Where this latter document stressed the idea of "Church as society", the present document follows more closely the thought of St. Paul i.e. the church is the communion of those redeemed in Christ, and it is the concrete acknowledgement of this in worship which forms the Church in a given situation. From the individual Church, it is possible to envisage the communion of many such bodies, a position expressed in the idea that "the Church is a fellowship of men with Jesus. Church is Christ's presence through the Spirit in the midst of his People."[22] Where *Mystici Corporis* equated the mystical body of Christ with the Catholic Church, this Constitution much more carefully states: that "This Church, constituted and organised in the world as a society, *subsists in* the Catholic Church, which is governed by the successors of Peter and by the bishops in union with that successor, although many elements of sanctification and of truth can be found outside of her visible structure." (my emphasis)[23]

This is a very important change of the traditional attitude particularly the narrow interpretation often made by the traditional "Outside the Church, no salvation." Later chapters are consistent with this broadening, particularly in rejecting any tendency to identifying the "Kingdom of God on earth" with the Roman Catholic Church. The implications for catechesis of this carefully stated modification of viewpoint are particularly with regard to other Christian churches, as well as to the wider ecumenism with regard to non-Christian religions. Both matters are to be considered in relation to these specific decrees later in the chapter.

2 — *"The People of God"* [24]

Perhaps nothing has seized the imagination of Christians more generally than the second chapter's description of the 'faithful', "the People of God," as a pilgrim community.[25] Viewed however in the broader perspective of the history of salvation, this pilgrim people, like Isreal of old, is always in a stage of seeking, still seeking a final fulfilment. In this position, she is still able to acknowledge an ideal of holiness to be attained, but she is also quite realistically aware of her historical shortcomings, her many and continuing failures to live up this ideal of holiness to which all are individually and corporately called. In

22. Gregory Baum, **Commentary on the Constitution of the Church of Vatican Council II**, Deus Books, Paulist Press, New York, 1964, p. 23.

23. Abbott (ed.), par. 8, p. 23.

24. ibid., par. 9, p. 24. This is the title of Chapter 2.

25. ibid., p. 24.

other words, the Church "always in need of being purified continually follows the way of penance and renewal."[26]   Such an attitude of being pilgrims is an aid to that necessary detachment from wealth and ambition as well as identifying the Church with the various needs of people all over the world in their common quest for justice.   Furthermore, a stress which recalls many of the 19th century tensions between Church and State, reminds the members that the Church must transcend particular cultures and national boundaries in its pilgrimage towards the end-time, for if the Christ is the "source of unity and peace",[27] this is not to be confused with uniformity.   Nor is there to be a hierarchy of privilege but only one of service, for by baptism "the common priesthood of the faithful and the ministerial or hierarchical priesthood are nonetheless interrelated."[28]   This theme of common priesthood, already referred to, is developed subsequently in the chapter on the Laity, but for the nature of this present chapter, it is worth noting the emphasis on the faithful confessing before men "the faith which they have received from God through the Church."[29]

Developing the point already noted in the first chapter on membership of the Church, paragraph 13 begins with the statement that "all men are called to belong to the new People of God."[30]   If the Catholic faithful are regarded as "fully incorporated into the society of the Church", the Church recognizes the many links shared with those Christians not in union with her, and while regretting this absence of complete unity, praises the qualities of these Christian churches, not in a condescending way, but with clear recognition of the common heritage shared with them, and of the scandal of disunity.   This unprecedented commendation after four hundred years of anathemas and condemnation, has been the basis for Catholic response to the growth of ecumenism in recent years.   As regards the content of catechesis—especially from the negative view of much of the historical apologetics of the past as well as the study of world religions at present—this has major implications to be considered briefly later.

Further than this, the solicitude of this document extends to those so far outside the Christian faith.   Anticipating the later public revocations of traditional attitudes towards the Jewish people, "this people remains most dear to God,"[31] there is mention too of those who acknowledge the Creator, notably the Moslems "professing to hold the faith of

---

26.   passim, p. 24.
27.   ibid., p. 26.
28.   ibid., p. 27.
29.   ibid., p. 28.
30.   ibid., p. 30.
31.   ibid., p. 34.

Abraham."[32] It goes on to speak of those who through no fault of their own, do not yet know the Gospel but who strive to follow what they believe is right and who can thereby attain salvation. From this there is a natural progression to a consideration of the missionary work of the Church, of the duty of everyone to respond to the plea to "preach the gospel to every creature," not, as in a former emphasis to save the unbelievers from a perdition for which they were otherwise destined, but to try to share the benefits of the Gospel with all. Such a viewpoint is of central concern for the catechist, both as regards his own task, and also for having his pupils understand their concern for all men.

3 — *"The Hierarchical Structure of the Church and in particular the Episcopate."*

From this interesting and carefully argued chapter, two aspects are selected because of their implications for catechesis.

a — The discussions on the principle of collegiality redresses the historical lack of balance, the legacy of Vatican I, which, shortened by the outbreak of the Franco-Prussian War, proceeded to define Papal Infallibility without indicating fully its relation to the episcopate generally. The affirmation indicates the two aspects of collegiality viz. the responsibility of the individual bishop to teach, sanctify and govern his own church on the one hand, and the union of individual churches to form the "communion of Churches" with the resulting collegial action of bishops on behalf of the universal church. This last point, affirmed by the post-conciliar creation of the Synod of Rome for regular meetings with the Pope on behalf of the whole church is important for more than its administrative aspects. Perhaps more important in the long run is the establishment of a principle of dialogue between the bishops themselves and between the Pope. Gregory Baum has suggested that perhaps the true measure and importance of this development will be an important modification of the exercise of authority on all levels.[33]

b — The discussion of the priesthood and the re-introduction of a permanent diaconate where it was requested by the bishops, has led to the return to a practice well known in the early church. Perhaps equally important with the 'service' aspect implied by the origin of the word itself and the implications for a better understanding of the function of the ministerial priesthood, has been the ordination to this office of married men. Inevitably, this has led to study and discussion of the question of celibacy as intrinsic or relative to the

---

32. ibid., p. 34.

33. Baum, op. cit., p. 38.

priesthood, and though at present there has been a tendency to re-affirm the traditional practice of the western church, the very raising of the question indicates an attempt to understand the essence of the priestly ministry, separated from other considerations.

4. Christian Witness—the Laity

In these sections of the Constitution, we are particularly concerned with the fourth source of catechesis viz. that of Christian witness. The continuing discussion of the Constitution will concentrate on the role of the Laity, the Universal Call to Holiness, the role of Religious and the Eschatological Nature of the Pilgrim Church, devotion to the Blessed Virgin, these being the principal remaining sections of the document on the Church.

1 — *The Laity*

The designation of a special chapter for the laity is meant simply to specify their special duties as the "People of God", those, who by baptism have been "made one body with Christ," but who not in holy orders or members of a religious order," seek the kingdom of God by engaging in temporal affairs and by ordering them according to the plan of God."[34] It is important to note the positive importance with which the laity are designated "in terms of their baptism and their active role in the People of God," and as a common vision is extended through this chapter directly through the Decree on the Apostolate of the Laity and implicitly in other documents on Ecumenism, Christian Education, Communications, Missions and so on, it is only with the more general perspectives with implications for catechesis that we are concerned.

First of all should be signalized the fact that there was a chapter in this document and a further separate decree on the laity, both in themselves marking innovations of great importance and markedly different from such things as statements on Catholic Action made by previous Popes, where the presumption always seemed to be that any apostolate which the layman shared was by association with that of the official ministers of the Church. Theoretically, neither this chapter nor the later decree adds anything fundamental which was not implied by the description of "People of God" and "pilgrim people" of Chapter Two, but such expressions are themselves their own indication of a different cast of mind from that implied by the more traditional description in which the 'faithful' (*sic*) were the undifferentiated mass supporting the apex of a hierarchical priesthood.

Secondly, no less than the other sections of the Constitution and indeed the Decree on the Apostolate of the Laity itself, the foundation

---

34. Abbott (ed.), op. cit., p. 57.

and justification are expressed in biblical terms. As the majority in the Church, the laity share too in the mystery of the Church and from this viewpoint, other ministries including that of the clergy are designed to aid the laity in their common task of spreading the Kingdom of God on earth. And this is particularly a task of Christian witness. The document is at great pains to stress the inter-dependence of the lay and clerical ministries in terms which are striking:

> "Therefore, by divine condescension, the laity have Christ for their brother, who though He is the Lord of all, came not to be served but to serve... They also have for their brothers those in the sacred ministry who by teaching, by sanctifying, and by ruling with the authority of Christ so feed the family of God that the new commandment of charity may be fulfilled by all." [35]

This is an important distinction because it is not here a question of the laity simply acting as collaborators of the clergy—something they are encouraged to do elsewhere—but rather an affirmation of the apostolic tasks of the laity because of the unique responsibilities and influence they have as laity "called in a special way to make the Church present and operative in those places and circumstances where only through them can she become the salt of the earth." [36]

Thirdly, the particular competence possessed by the laity should be availed of for specific functions in the Church, notably those associated with missionary work (in its literal sense and in its transferred usage in de-Christianized areas), and with liturgical functions. It is suggested that they may serve on parochial and diocesan councils where their special gifts can be of direct service to the ministry of the hierarchy, or even be deputed to some kind of ministry normally reserved to an ordained person. The post-Council perspective makes it possible to see these aspects as major contributions to the parochial life of the Church.

The relevance of all this for catechetics is particularly well-drawn in the Decree on the Apostolate of the Laity where the sixth chapter, Formation for the Apostolate, provides a practical programme for catechesis.[37]

In this, the lay person is seen ideally as one who is active and well-informed in his own society, learns to base his life on his self-realisation as a Christian, dependent on the continuing guidance of the Spirit and witnessing to these values by the quality of his life. Ideally, he has a solid doctrinal formation as well as general cultural and practical training,

---

35. ibid., p. 59.
36. ibid., p. 59.
37. Abbott (ed.), op. cit., pp. 517-519.

and by pursuing a prudent policy of see, judge and act, he helps to further the Kingdom of God.

Such training is recommended from early childhood but "in a special way...adolescents and young adults should be initiated into the apostolate and imbued with its spirit." There is a particular duty incumbent on those responsible for Christian education to ensure that this happens, so that within the family, children are made aware of their wider responsibilities within the community, notably in the parish. Priests and teachers are considered to have special duties of cultivating this kind of response from the young, especially in those circumstances where young people are unable to receive such formation in Christian schools.

Besides the encouragement of Christian knowledge both for its own sake and as a means of social contact and influence, there is emphasis on the importance of opposing materialism by the witness of an evangelical life, and on the practical performance of works of compassion so as to be habituated towards helping those in need.

With all this, there is obviously no quarrel at all although there does seem sometimes an assumption about the general learning and education of the priest which while it is undoubtedly true of individuals and may have been even more true at least comparatively in former years, is strangely out of touch with the generally higher and more diversified education received by the laity as a matter of course in developed societies. Perhaps, it might be stressed that the special competence which the laity require of their priests is more in those things which pertain to their special vocation as preachers of the word of God, offerers of sacrifice in the name of the community and attention to the provision of the opportunities for the laity to participate fully in the liturgical and sacramental life of the Church. This aside is all the more important, it seems, because of the traditional tendency to consider the laity solely in terms of their parochial life, a dichotomy which has always been as unrealistic as it has been unsatisfactory.

2 — *The Universal Vocation to Holiness in the Church*

The title of this section is self-explanatory but there are a number of matters which have particular implications for catechesis.

a — All the people of God are called to a perfection of charity as a result of their baptism in Christ. This does not mean a uniform kind of achievement but one which allows for a diversity of forms and expressions, according to the work of the Spirit in each.

b — Some specific remarks are addressed to members of the community who carry out specific tasks — priests, deacons, married couples, parents, labourers, the sick and so on. It is noticeable that the document in its various modifications from the scheme first presented to the Council, lays great stress on a positive view of what is to be done rather than a negative one. In particular there is a complete absence of any idea that Christian holiness is a kind of automatic result of obedience to a set of Commandments. Rather there is the ideal of a Christian life which develops from the faith begun in baptism and is aided through the sacramental life of the Church. Such a view does not see holiness as a kind of alternative to involvement in life situations, but rather makes no distinctions between the Christian's duty in the world and the growth of holiness.

3 — The Eschatological Nature of the Pilgrim Church and its Union with the Church in Heaven

This highly praised seventh chapter of the Constitution is deserving of treatment of itself. But it has certain emphases which offer important considerations for the content of catechesis especially in those areas where the Roman Catholic belief and practice are most at variance with certain aspects of the Reformed churches and seem to provide important obstacles to ecumenism viz. questions relating "to the role of the saints and the state of the individual after death." [38]

In its first two sections the document argues for a clear understanding of the "final age of the world"[39] not as something which is to be expected in the future, but rather as something already present, "for even now on this earth the Church is marked with a genuine though imperfect holiness." [40] But because of her present pilgrim status, such holiness can only be achieved in a limited way, although what is achieved provides both an achievement and a reminder of the perfection to be realised in the end time.

Those who have already died and "sleep in the peace of Christ" [41] are already more closely united with Christ, but they are not by this dissociated from the Church, "for after they have been received into this heavenly home... they do not cease to intercede with the Father for us." [42] This traditional faith of the Church subscribed to by all Christians who give assent to the Apostles' Creed, extends no less to the veneration of the memories of those predecessors in the faith who have been outstanding for their Christian lives. Such example provides its own inspiration for those still engaged in the struggle, leading as it does, not to an unbalanced veneration of individuals, but rather, to a strengthening of our knowledge and appreciation of the exemplar of all, Christ.

The document also points with ecumenical delicacy to the traditional pre-Tridentine practices of the Church as regards the suffrages offered for those "who are still being purified after death." [43]

---

38. Baum, op. cit., p. 51.
39. Abbott (ed.), op. cit., p. 79.
40. ibid., p. 79.
41. ibid., p. 81.
42. ibid., p. 81.
43. ibid., par. 50, pp. 81-82.

From the viewpoint of 'reform' in catechesis, such a chapter does much to redress an only too well noted legalistic and at times Manichean tendency associated with the Commandments, Creed, Sacraments sequence already discussed in the section on catechisms. It is not too strong to say that many generations have heard much more of hell and punishment than they did of Good News or of Redemption in Christ, because of this kind of imbalance. A chapter such as this reaffirms the traditional faith of the Church in a balanced fashion.

It is within this same context that we should note the attitude of the Council towards the traditional Catholic veneration for the Blessed Virgin Mary. Originally the topic of a separate scheme, the Council (by a small majority) voted to include the treatment of this topic into the final chapter of the Constitution on the Church. In the event, this was done in three sections entitled respectively:

1 — The role of the Blessed Virgin in the economy of salvation.

2 — The Blessed Virgin Mary and the Church.

3 — Devotion to the Blessed Virgin in the Church.

The Commission which produced the document indicated that the intention of the first section was to present the role of Our Lady in the whole history of salvation so as to be consistent with the style of the Constitution and "so that there can be no discrepancy between the mother of Jesus in the Gospel, the Virgin Mary of our theological treatises and the Madonna of popular devotion." [44]

The second section, after beginning with careful attention to the importance of Christ as sole mediator goes on to say:

"The maternal duty of Mary towards men in no way obscures or diminishes this unique mediation of Christ, but rather shows its power."[45]

The remaining sections concentrate on this aspect while showing how particular titles and invocations are eventually related to this principle.

The same spirit runs through the third section but while tracing the history of Marian devotion in the Church from the Council of Ephesus onwards, it does recommend to theologians and preachers "that in treating of the unique dignity of the mother of God, they carefully and equally avoid the falsity of exaggeration on the one hand and the excess of narrow-mindedness on the other." [46]

---

44. Baum, op. cit., p. 55.
45. Abbott (ed.), op. cit., p. 90.
46. ibid., p. 95.

This general treatment is evidently sensitive to the traditions of other Christian churches while at the same time maintaining a traditional Catholic attitude based on scripture and tradition. Perhaps in the catechetical situation, the most practical implications relate to the devotional practices inculcated by the school. It would not be untrue to say that in some instances, traditional practices have lacked the clarity and balance of this treatment.

5. Catechesis in other Documents of Vatican II

If at first sight it is strange to find fewer than a dozen explicit references to catechesis in the documents of Vatican II, it is surely significant to recall that the early activity in the first months of the Council to produce a uniform and definitive catechism for the Church was successfully resisted, and even the appointment of a sub-commission on catechesis itself was unable to come up with a document of its own. Further thought might suggest that, as already indicated in the first section of this chapter, the explicitly catechetical depends on the understanding of doctrinal formulations and their implications which as the last sections have indicated, are very far reaching. This section, then, will consider the nature of the explicit statements before turning to the far more important implications of the documents on Christian Education, Religious Freedom, Ecumenism and the attitude towards the non-Christian religions.

The three longest sections of the documents referring specifically to catechesis — they are paragraphs only — occur in the Decree on the Bishops' Pastoral Office in the Church. The first of these is as follows:

"Catechetical training is intended to make men's faith become living, conscious, and active, through the light of instruction. Bishops should see to it that such training be painstakingly given to children, adolescents, young adults, and even grown-ups. In this instruction a proper sequence should be observed as well as a method appropriate to the matter that is being treated and to the natural disposition, ability, age and circumstances of life of the listener. Finally, they should see to it that this instruction is based on sacred Scripture, tradition, the liturgy, the teaching authority, and life of the Church."[47]

This is an important paragraph which deserves closer inspection. First of all, it is evident that the view of catechesis is not so much one of instruction for its own sake, but rather one which has for its aim at all times, and to diverse groups of people, the development of faith. This is a key point for us to recall when we come to the analysis of the concept of catechesis in the following chapter.

47. Abbott (ed.), op. cit., par. 14, p. 406.

Secondly, there is no supposition that catechesis is something which is only applicable to beginners requiring instruction. Rather, it is pointed out that it is to be given to various age groups at every stage of their lives.

Thirdly, it is surely indicative of the influence of the human sciences in our day and of the inner consistency of much of the Vatican II thought, that there is emphasis not simply on sequence and method— familiar enough in catechesis—but also on the natural dispositions i.e. the psychological readiness, we might say, of those to receive or to be involved in catechesis.

Lastly, it is only at this stage that the actual content of catechesis is specified viz. Scripture, tradition and so on, in other words the explicitly theological follows *after* the human experience of the recipients.

In the second paragraph cited, the implications of the individual and collective roles of the bishop have obviously been considered, for the idea of a uniform set of directives seems set aside, for besides the "individual directories concerning the pastoral care of special groups of the faithful, as the different circumstances of the particular nations or regions require", the passage continues:

> "Another directory should be composed with respect to the cate-
> chetical instruction of the Christian people, and should deal with
> the fundamental principles of such instruction, its arrangement, and
> the composition of books on the subject." [48]

This in itself is a notable development on the ideal referred to above, because of the recognition that catechesis in a particular region must be related to the special character of the region itself. That this principle, however, has not been universally recognised was evident in the attempts made during and subsequent to the 1971 International Congress on Catechetics in Rome, to give a juridical status to the *Directorium Catechisticum Generale* issued by the Sacred Congregation for the Clergy in May 1971. Other local directories have appeared, notably one produced by the Italian hierarchy, which has been the basis for the important adaptation and translation into English carried out for the Australian Catholic Hierarchy in August 1970 and entitled "The Renewal of the Education of the Faith." [49]

The only other major references are those in the Decree on the Missions and on Christian Education. The latter statement maintains the Church's traditional position of being "particularly concerned with the means proper to herself, of which catechetical training is foremost" for "such instruction gives clarity and vigor to faith, nourishes a life lived

---

48. ibid., par. 44, p. 428-429.
49. Published by E. J. Dwyer, Sydney, 1970. cf. Chapter 4.

according to the spirit of Christ, leads to a knowing and active participation in the liturgical mystery and inspires apostolic action." [50] The former passage calls for an increase in the number of schools available for catechists to study Christian doctrine, scripture and liturgy, calls for opportunities for them to attend refresher schools and to have their work signalized by the bestowal of a canonical mission at a public liturgical ceremony in order to give them greater authority in their work.[51]

Of the document on Christian Education itself, the following points should be noted to be taken in conjunction with the discussion on Christian education in later chapters.

1—Although basic principles relating to Christian education are stated, there is no suggestion that this is anything more than just that, recognizing as the Council does, that "these principles will have to be developed at greater length by a special post-conciliar Commission and applied by episcopal conferences to varying local situations." [52] This willingness to accept such diversity is a welcome change as regards education itself, and catechesis also, The principle, it is presumed, should apply with equal validity to differences in age, family background, experiences of the faith etc. when any group is being considered in relation to catechesis also.

2—The Declaration is realistic also in recognizing the diversity of school situations open to pupils, so that it does not proceed simply on the assumption that all Catholic children will necessarily receive their education in Catholic schools, nor that catechesis is necessarily the task of the school, either in the real or the ideal situation.

3—In at least tacitly acknowledging the possibility of Catholic pupils in state secular schools, the document recognizes the necessity of other agencies taking responsibility for the catechesis of such children. It is, nevertheless, difficult to see a clear statement on some possible means of resolving the necessary tensions between the rights of parents as regards the religious instruction of the young, and the implementation of this right by such attention to separate schools that there is little official concern by the Roman Catholic body for the catechesis of those in the state schools.[53]

---

50. Abbott (ed.), par. 4, p. 643. Some of the implications of this document have already been treated in Chapter 4 part 2 viz. the educational assumptions underlying catechesis.

51. ibid., p. 606.

52. ibid., Introduction to Decree, p. 639.

53. cf. **The Future of Catholic Education in England and Wales**, Catholic Renewal Movement, London, 1971, pp. 15-18.

1 — Religious Freedom, Ecumenism, Non-Christian Religions

No treatment of the influence and importance of Vatican II, especially as regards its catechetical implications, would be complete without some indication at least of the profound significance for both content and method of the Declaration on Religious Freedom, the Decrees on Ecumenism and the Missions, and the Declaration on the Relationships of the Church to Non-Christian Religions. The following points are worthy of attention:

a — The open discussion and courageous development of ideas which marked the Declaration on Religious Freedom has appeared to some observers as the major achievement of the Council, for by asserting the right of the human person to religious freedom and an "immunity from coercion" by individuals or societies in religious matters, the Council has underlined the right of the individual to search for the truth about God, about himself and his destiny. In other words, the *freedom from* coercion is complemented by man's own responsible use of his *freedom for* the ascertaining and following out the truth as he discovers it. Such a right to freedom is exercised in a social setting, so that personally, and as one responsible for others as a parent (or teacher), there must be ideally a choice in the religious training of the young and the right to avoid "lessons not in agreement with their religious beliefs, or if a single system of education, from which all religious education is excluded, is imposed upon all."

b — If this appears to be condoning a complete relativism and the unrestricted supremacy of the individual conscience (without, for example, specifying the necessity for the conscience to be informed to act as a true arbiter), it should be noted

  i—that the Declaration affirms most directly the position of the Roman Catholic Church as trusting not in itself but in its fidelity to its belief that it is an integral part of God's saving plan for man. As Bishop Butler observes, "The Catholic Church teaches, and Catholics believe that the Church is not simply a contingent outcome of the divine revelation in and as Christ, but is part of the 'economy of salvation' established by God in Christ." [54]

  ii—that, as Schillebeeckx notes, "compared with the official attitude of the Church, in former times, this declaration reflects an entirely new attitude of mind, based on the unassailable dignity of

---

54. Bishop B. C. Butler in **The Tablet**, 16/9/1972, p. 876.

81

the human person, down to his personal (perhaps objectively erroneous) outlook on life";[55]

iii—that individuals and groups have the right to spread their religion, and indeed the Church claims this as a duty incumbent on herself, but a distinction should be observed between what might be called missionary activity as compared with the basically unfair means used in proselytising. This latter point as described fits the pejorative models of indoctrination described elsewhere.

It is easy to see how this leads naturally towards preparing for the growth of ecumenism in a traditionally Christian society, but the same momentum carries it also to an appraisal of the Church with regard to the non-Christian religions and indeed, to its role in a pluralist society. With regard to the former, the "separated Christians and communities", the text on Ecumenism carefully avoids the former practice of describing such groups as heretical or schismatic and, while speaking of the Church of Christ as one that "subsists in" the Catholic Church, it speaks also of the "positive significance in the mystery of salvation" of these separated Churches and communities.

"Nevertheless, our separated brethren, whether considered as individuals or as Communities and Churches, are not blessed with that unity which Jesus Christ wished to bestow on all those whom He has regenerated and vivified into one body and newness of life— that unity which the holy Scriptures and the revered tradition of the Church proclaim. For it is through Christ's Catholic Church alone which is the all-embracing means of salvation, that the fullness of the means of salvation can be obtained." [56]

With regard to the non-Christian Religions, a similar balance is called for between the tensions imposed by truth and charity, a position well summed up by a noted ecumenist in the following terms:

"How then do we find theological room for the "wider ecumenism?" I think we must say that the other religions may be true to the extent that what they teach is not in contradiction with the Christian faith: and we can surely add that these true elements may in many cases have an aspect of divine revelation about them. We can further add that, when we compare Christianity as it is actually being lived with these other religions as they too are actually lived, we may find that they have much to teach us which, while compatible

---

55. Schillebeeckx, op. cit., pp. 41-42.
56. Butler, op. cit., note 54, p. 877.

with and even at least implicit in the Christian faith, has been over-
looked or underemphasised in our day to day Christian teaching and
practice." [57]

Part Two

THEOLOGY OF INCARNATION AND GABRIEL MORAN'S
THEOLOGY OF REVELATION

Mention has already been made of the growth of ecumenism in the
post-war era through the common attention of Christian scholars to the
study of scripture. In an earlier chapter, discussion of the kerygmatic
movement has made prominent the varying notions of *Heilsgeschichte* or
'salvation history' which in varying ways has been a kind of indicator of
the directions sought by modern theology.[58] Specifically resulting from
this same movement was the development of what has become known as
incarnational religion or theology, one of the most influential factors for
those engaged in the teaching of religion in the past decade, and associated with it and derived from the same sources, has been a much
more flexible notion of the theology of revelation. It hardly needs to be
added that from these three movements there has developed a changed
notion of what is to be understood by the nature and function of the
teaching church, and, by implication at least, the tasks of catechesis in
view of all this. As it is with the importance of these changes for
catechesis that we are mainly concerned, the treatment of incarnation
and revelation will be particularly related to the influence on catechesis.
But as the sources of incarnational theology and theories of revelation
are located in the important scripture studies of our era, and are closely
linked by their common appreciation of Christ as the revelation of God,
many of the practical consequences of these studies for catechesis, have
already been encountered in the commentary on the schematic presentation of the first chapter.

6. Theology of Incarnation

The theology of the incarnation — God becoming man — is as
old as the Christian church, the early history of which is simply a series
of refinements or re-statements as successive Councils tried to express
the already known and accepted Trinitarian mystery. These early periods
of confusion and doubt, the early heresies as they were called, were
attempts to be clear about the two natures of Christ as God and man.

---

57. ibid., p. 876.
58. cf. note 18, Chapter 1.

First there was the problem of late Gnosticism with its implicit denial of Christ's humanity, followed by the variation of Docetism which taught that Christ's humanity was present only in appearance; later, there was the failure of Arianism to accept Christ as truly divine and that of Nestorianism to unify the two natures it so carefully distinguished. In response to these contestations, the Fathers of Chalcedon in 451 made use of a dualist formula by which, "Jesus is the God-Man, He is God *and* man. At the same time, He possesses two natures, the divine nature and the human nature, united in only one divine person." [59] But the modes of thought within which this dualist formula is used, must be seen as limited if only because the terms and concepts are categories of thought derived from Greek philosophy, terms which no longer have the same meaning in modern thought.

Hence, modern Christology is still concerned with the same topic viz. the work of man's redemption accomplished through Jesus Christ, but its approach is different, because to continue to express the traditional faith only in the same terms as Chalcedon with its stress on the doctrine of the two natures i.e. the union of the divine and human in the one person of Jesus, God and man, is to fail to appreciate,

1 — the historical reasons why such expressions were a necessary final form to put an end to the controversies of the 4th and 5th centuries,

and

2 — the necessity of embodying these truths in a language and form which are easily evident to the men of to-day.

What this means in practice is that modern Christology has been concerned to know and understand the historical Christ as well as the glorified Christ. As a second-order reflection such a theology depends on the knowledge of God's saving plan for mankind, both as demonstrated in the past, as it continues at the present and as it will be fulfilled in its eschatological promise. Hence Yves Congar writes,

"We know how unwearyingly the Fathers repeated: 'The Son of God becomes man so that man might become God.' This means that the incarnation is what God willed that it be, and is what He made it, only if we keep in mind the link which it possesses or intends to effect with creation as a whole, and most particularly with man who is creation's summing-up and point (microcosm)." [60]

Later he adds this comment to show how different starting points may be found — "From one standpoint, the incarnation is connected to

---

59. Robrecht Michiels, *Incarnation*, **Lumen Vitae**, vol. XXV, no. 4, 1970, p. 642.

60. **Jesus Christ**, Geoffrey Chapman, London, 1966, pp. 20-21.

the world, whose meaning it restores...From another standpoint, the incarnation is connected to the entire salvific activity of Christ." [61]

If we examine the reply of a modern Roman Catholic author to the question:

'What is incarnational religion?' we learn:

"It is not an abstract idea but the concrete reality of the work of our redemption in its impact on the world through the people Christ won for himself. It is the remoulding of man by grace in Christ. At the creation, man was given the power to multiply and fill the earth. In the new creation, the supernatural order, God's people is given the power, helped by Christ's presence to make children of God. In the world-wide mission of the Church, this involves re-forming peoples and their cultures. In the name of Christ, the Church must pass judgement on the aspirations and achievements of nations... Incarnational religion affirms at the same time the absolute value of the individual human person and the religious value of human solidarity." [62]

If we ask how this is to take place, it is necessary to consider two contemporary trends with important bearings on our understanding of the reality of the incarnation:

1 — The modern scriptural movement with its superior exegesis has shown us that the historical Christ whom we know from the early church, is the result of a certain interpretation made by those early believers of all that Jesus did and said. Moreover, post-Bultmann exegesis is confident, as Michiels states, that it has discovered the Jesus of the early Church and the Christ of faith as the one person.[63]

What this means is that the exegetes are confident that there is a marked continuity between the historical aspects of Christ's life and the traditional interpretation of these events by the faith and tradition of the church. Better appreciation and understanding of the literary forms of the Bible has set a limit to some of the excesses of 'demythologization.'

2 — Man's scientific advances have so advanced his control over nature that it is possible for a modern society to rid itself of that long-standing 'sacred-secular' dichotomy in which man tended to have recourse to the gods to try to exercise some semblance of control

---

61. ibid.

62. Ralph Woodhall S. J., **Theology of the Incarnation**, Mercier Press, Cork, 1968, pp. 55-56.

63. Michiels, op. cit., p. 647.

85

over many areas of life beyond his scope. This 'man come of age' however, in ridding himself of the necessity of having recourse to the god's as a substitute for doing something himself, is more capable of appreciating man's position in the Bible as one made in the image and likeness of God and placed over the whole of creation. In such a view, man and God are truly partners and God's works are especially seen in man. Reality, then, is one and the sacred is simply a deeper dimension of the secular; God, far from being remote and intervening only occasionally, is, in Tillich's phrase, the very 'ground of being.' Such a view eliminates what Bonhoeffer referred to somewhere as using "God as a stop-gap for the incompleteness of our knowledge," but much more than that, it reminds us that Christ was experienced by his contemporaries as *man,* that he valued human things such as love, friendship and kindness, and that his teaching showed intimate acquaintance with all the details of ordinary human life. Hence the modern phenomenon of secularization (to be separated clearly from secularism, of course), far from weakening true religion, should help us to recognize and confess God's presence in the world, both in the history of mankind and in the lives of men made in God's likeness, but especially in the person of Jesus Christ.

This is the clear sense of the Pastoral Constitution on the Church of the Second Vatican Council, *Gaudium et Spes,* which thus balances out the concern of the Christian for earthly progress and the growth of the kingdom of God:

"Earthly progress must be carefully distinguished from the growth of Christ's kingdom. Nevertheless, to the extent that the former can contribute to the better ordering of human society, it is of vital concern to the kingdom of God. For after we have obeyed the Lord, and in his spirit nurtured on earth the value of human dignity, brotherhood and freedom, and indeed all the good fruits of our nature and enterprise, we will find them again but freed from stain, burnished and transfigured... On this earth that kingdom is already present in mystery. When the Lord returns, it will be brought into full flowers." [64]

When we attempt to consider the Man Jesus (rather than the God who became man) some of the implications of an incarnational theology may be perceived.

1 — Jesus as Man belongs to the created order, but he is so in a unique and special way as the high point of the revelation of God. This point will be looked at and developed in the following section.

64. Abbott (ed.), op. cit., Chapter III, par. 39, pp. 237-238.

2 — The incarnation shows us a "visible, audible and tangible" Jesus, completely man, not in any figurative way nor even simply as a bearer of divine oracles as did the prophets, but as someone like us in all things save only sin.

3 — Beyond a vague Deism, or Docetism, Arianism or Nestorianism, the incarnation asserts the humanity of our God. It interprets the traditional *descendit de caelo et homo factus est* of the Nicene creed as a literary expression of the truth rather than as a straightforward description of God intervening from outside of our world; the God Man is part of this world.

4 — Perhaps the whole emphasis of modern Christology may be seen as a redressing of the balance between the breathless *God* became 'incarnate' of the early believers who, knowing Christ as Man came to believe that he was God, and the 'God became *incarnate*' of incarnational theology.[65]

One concluding observation is that if these ideas at a popular level are particularly associated with such names as Bultmann, Bonhoeffer, J. A. T. Robinson and Harvey Cox, it helps to underline the ecumenical convergence of christological thought.

7. Theology of Revelation: The thesis of Gabriel Moran

Our concern in this section is necessarily limited to the relationships and mutual influence of the theology of revelation and catechesis, some practical aspects of which have been indicated in the opening chapter. In particular, the thesis of Gabriel Moran's "Theology of Revelation" is considered.[66]

The special aspect of Christianity which distinguishes it from many others is its claim to possess the revelation of God. This revelation is something which has taken place in man's history, for God's communication has been in "deeds and words having an inner unity: the deeds wrought by God in the history of salvation manifest and confirm the teaching and realities signified by the words, while the words proclaim the deeds and clarify the mystery contained in them. By this revelation, then, the deepest truth about God and the salvation of man is made clear to us in Christ, who is the Mediator and at the same time the fullness of all revelation." [67] Here is the intimate connection between the two matters of this second section, for the high point and focal point of this

---

65. Adapted from Michiels, op. cit., p. 650, note 1.

66. For a better understanding and appreciation of Moran's book, I am indebted to Dom Iltyd Trethowan's analysis in **The Absolute and the Atonement**, Muirhead Library of Philosophy, 1971.

67. Abbott (ed.), op. cit., Chapter I, par. 2, p. 112.

revelation is the historical event which we call the Incarnation. This is the basis of that 'salvation history' discussed earlier as the root of the kerygmatic movement. But it is important to note that the event of the Incarnation occurs at a certain historical time, within the wider historical manifestation of God.

The development of a theology of revelation in modern times is therefore closely linked with the already noted biblical revival, and as such, it is essentially ecumenical in origin. Broadly speaking, the description of a Roman Catholic 'return' to scripture has some validity if it describes a corrective to the post-Tridentine emphasis on the role of tradition and its authority in the life of the church. In the aftermath of Bultmann and those who followed his ideas, the work of many Protestant scholars has tended to lessen the fundamentalist attitude to the scriptures which had been broadly characteristic of certain aspects of the Reformed tradition, and has brought into prominence the role of the bible as history, as well as the importance of the Christian tradition as the incorporation of doctrinal and moral truths. But as the earlier discussion on salvation history has shown, it is possible for all of these developments to have comparatively little influence on one another so long as the historical notions of revelation have remained rooted in the past and are regarded as something outside of the experience of modern man who receives such a revelation only in a propositional form.

It was the merit of Gabriel Moran's "Theology of Revelation" [68] that it reflected accurately the concerns of contemporary theologians but pointed past the peripheral aspects to the question of the nature of revelation itself. It seems worthy of note, too, that the thesis was developed at the Catholic University of America under the direction of the author of some of the most basic studies of catechesis in English, Gerard Sloyan, and that Moran himself as a member of a religious order internationally concerned with catechesis was in the forefront of the catechetical movement in the United States. Lastly, the publication of Moran's book so soon after the final text of *Dei Verbum* (contained as an appendix to the first edition), and the application of the thesis of "Theology of Revelation" to "Catechesis of Revelation" (published in England as "God Still Speaks") [69] and the later "Visions and Tactics" [70] reached and influenced many catechists who may not have been likely to grapple with the implications of a specifically theological text. For the intrinsic merit of Moran's contribution to the catechetical ferment

---

68. Burns & Oates, London, 1967.
69. op. cit., note 36.
70. Burns & Oates, London, 1968.

of the sixties and for the theoretical underpinning which it provided for some of the best pioneer work based on little more than pragmatic assurances that "it worked," "gained the interest of pupils" and so on, the remainder of the chapter provides an outline of the thesis proposed in relation to the incarnational theology already summarized in the first part. The earlier schema shows the practical influence of these studies.

Moran is at pains to stress the unique claims made by Christianity for itself as based on the revelation of God to man. His concern is that the emphasis has traditionally been on the fact of revelation rather than on its nature and, within the Roman Catholic church, at least, the advent of the modernist crisis in the early years of the century had largely stifled fresh investigation. Influenced, however, by modern biblical scholarship, philosophy, ecumenism and the catechetical movement which followed recognition of Jungmann's work, theologians have been increasingly concerned with the question of revelation. Moran's thesis is presented under the following points.

1 — The relationship between revelation and history is explored, especially the root ambiguity of the word 'history' itself, as well as the Jewish attitude to it, and the problem of a revelation apparently restricted to a particular time and place, for "they (i.e. the Jews) accepted the thoroughly temporal character of human life, believing that the human temporal events possessed a depth of meaning." [71] But it was the biblical concept of 'word' which contained so much that was important, because it was in the elucidation of this, that the prophets and biblical authors not only linked past and present time but "could not help but project an image into the future though the conscious realization of what they affirmed for the future was beyond their comprehension." [72]

2 — Stressing God's fidelity in spite of man's failings, Moran stresses that "revelation in its most basic sense is neither a word coming down from heaven to which man asserts nor an historical event manifesting a truth. It would be better to begin by conceiving of revelation as an historical and continuing intersubjective communion in which man's answer is part of the revelation." [73] This leads him to lay great importance on the interpersonal aspect for "unless one considers in all seriousness the human person who is himself within the revelation and not outside it, all attempts to unite 'revealed truths' with 'revelatory events' will be unsuccessful." [74]

---

71. **Theology of Revelation**, p. 41.

72. passim, p. 48.

73. ibid., p. 50.

74. ibid., p. 51.

3 — It is in this connection that Moran reveals his dissatisfaction with much of the emphasis of the then contemporary kerygmatic movement with its catch-cry of 'salvation history' as the two following quotations illustrate:

a — "It is a most remarkable contention in much theological and catechetical writing today that revelation will become relevant to men's lives if only they will study the history of Israel and realize that God revealed himself in the events of Israelite history." [75]

b — "The talk of a personal presentation of revelation as 'salvation history' has not greatly impressed anyone outside of a rather narrow circle, because the rooting of man's life in past events not only does not restore value to human history, but, on the contrary, seems to be the most direct denial of it.[76]

The key point here is whether a past revelation can be thought of in the present unless it is formulated in some kind of propositional form which has a perennial appeal by its fundamental relationship to the nature of man. Moran's observation that "an event in which one participates and a story about an event in someone else's past are quite different things,"[77] leads him to contrast the 'continuing revelation' of some Protestant theologians with the ambiguity of the Catholic situation which talks about the 'closing of revelation' as well as the continuing call of God.[78] The question is eventually refined to the following forms:

"How can revelation be anything other than truths or objects if it is handed down from one generation to another: or, reversing the question, how can a revelation consisting of personal events in the past ever be a present revelation!" [79]

4 — It is the answer to this question which constitutes the central thesis of Moran's work for "the key to a personal revelation in the twentieth century lies in the emergence of a human consciousness that is extremely receptive to God revealing and that remains among men to continue that revelation." [80] This is examined in a chapter called "Christ as Revelatory Communion" where the significant change denoted by the description of Christ as the "revelation of God" is looked at under the following headings:

---

75. ibid., p. 53.
76. ibid., p. 54.
77. ibid., p. 51.
78. ibid., p. 52.
79. ibid., p. 56.
80. ibid., p. 56.

"1) that God's revelation not only reaches a high point in Christ but is recapitulated in him;

2) that the participating subject who first receives the Christ revelatio is not the apostolic community but Christ himself;

3) that the fullness of revelation reached at the resurrection cannot perdure in books or institutions but only in the consciousness of the glorified Lord." [81]

The full working out of this thesis is beyond our scope here but a number of observations need to be made:

1 — The personal relationship aspect of revelation is shown to be compatible with an historical past as well as with a continuing and developing process because it takes place in the mind of Christ.

2 — It is obvious that such an idea of 'growth' of Christ's mind presupposes the already noted incarnational emphasis on Christ as man, and this logically leads to the idea that there was a "fullness of revelation" at the moment of Christ's death.[82]

3 — The importance of the resurrection and the understanding of revelation by the apostles—especially important for the claims of the Christian church—are expressed as follows: "The resurrection was for the apostles not so much a proof of his divinity as the light of understanding which was cast upon all the facts of his life... At the end of the forty days and then the pentecostal experience, the apostles had received the revelational communion of God's love. They did not receive it, however, in the same way and to the same extent as Christ did (and does). If God's revelation is not to fall off from its high point, it must remain in the one consciousness where it is totally accomplished. The risen and glorified Lord is the one place where revelation continues to happen in fullness." [83]

5 — From the thesis as stated, there follow important conclusions to the dilemma proposed earlier:

1 — The apostles witnessed to the whole of revelation for the church through the work of "the indwelling Spirit who made potentially and implicitly to the apostles the whole of revelation. In this sense it is possible to maintain the traditional statement

---

81. ibid., Chapter 3, pp. 57-76.
82. ibid., p. 74.
83. ibid., pp. 74-75.

91

that revelation came to an end with the death of the last apostle.[84]

2 — But to be taken in conjunction with this last statement we must add with Moran that "what had taken place in the consciousness of Christ and had been shared in by the apostolic community was never to be surpassed, but never was it to cease since Christ had come for all men" or as put elsewhere, "God reveals and man believes; there is no revelation unless God is now acting and unless a human consciousness is now responding." [85]

3 — Moran appeals to a key section of *Dei Verbum* for its reconciliation of the scripture and tradition controversy: "This sacred tradition, therefore, and sacred Scripture of both the Old and the New Testament are like a mirror in which the pilgrim Church on earth looks at God, from whom she has received everything, until she is brought finally to see Him as He is, face to face." (cf. 1 Jn. 3:2)[86]

The implications of Moran's thesis are carried through chapters dealing with the questions of continuing revelation in the church, the church's understanding of the revelational process (with an impressive discussion of the notion of the development of this revelation in the church, the participation of the individual in revelation (especially the relationship between revelation and personal freedom), revelation to all the earth (leading to ecumenical relationships and the questions raised by the non-Christian religions), and finally, the discussion of revelation in regard to eschatology.

CONCLUSION

With the insights provided by the general view of theological developments sketched in this chapter, it becomes possible to appreciate from a different viewpoint the inadequacies of the traditional catechetical model. From a positive outlook, however, it indicates the scope of the next chapter. Is there another kind of catechetical model emerging from the pressure of theological, sociological and educational factors? Is it possible to trace from the analyses of the preceding chapters some characteristics of such a model?

---

84. ibid., p. 85.
85. passim, p. 90.
86. Abbott (ed.), op. cit., Chapter II, par. 7, p. 115.

Chapter Four

THE CONCEPT OF CATECHESIS AND A CATECHETICAL MODEL FOR OUR TIMES

INTRODUCTION

The analysis of the preceding chapters leaves no doubt that a uniform catechesis, — if it ever did exist before — has little chance of doing so at present or in the foreseeable future. This is not to deny that there have been attempts to impose such a uniformity, especially by the use of catechisms supposedly based on that of the Catechism of the Council of Trent.[1] Confusion of uniformity with unity was evident in the decision of the International Catechetical Congress at Rome in 1950 to press for a uniform wording in national catechisms "so that the same words will be used to convey the same truths."[2] Church leaders in the last century and in the early years of this discussed the publication of a uniform catechism for all the Church.[3] A preparatory commission on catechetics at Vatican II did aim to produce a uniform and definitive catechism for all the Church but significantly, failed to gain sufficient support;[4] moreover, the production of the General Catechetical Directory in June 1971, just prior to the International Catechetical Congress of the following September, was certainly viewed by some authorities as a prescriptive text rather than a set of guidelines, as the Council itself had requested. But, as the temper of that Congress showed, an imposed uniformity could only hinder the growth of a catechesis suitable for our times.[5]

What is increasingly evident from the preceding chapters is that the concept of catechesis is approached most satisfactorily by looking for reference points rather than precise definitions i.e. it seems to be of more importance to look for the central core of the concept and to re-cognise certain poles within which this core can be specified, than to try to specify a completely uniform model unless the statement of such a model is in terms which have sufficient flexibility to accommodate any number of variations. There is no intention, therefore, of deriving the core of the concept of catechesis from a set of *a priori* assumptions, but rather, of extracting from the analysis conducted in the preceding chap-

---

1. cf. discussion in Chapter 2.
2. Gerard Sloyan (ed.), **Modern Catechetics, Message and Method in Religious Formation**, Collier-Macmillan, London, 1963, p. 63.
3. ibid., pp. 64-66.
4. cf. Chapter 3, section 5.
5. ibid., D. S. Amalorpavadass, an outstanding contributor to the Congress, re-ceived spontaneous applause in a plenary session when he countered a sugges-tion that there should be more uniformity.

ters, the central core of what each historical, theological or sociological modification has tried "to preserve" by its very advocacy of change.

To do this, the chapter proceeds by the following stages:

1 — It is important to note that it is not only the traditional model which has been rejected. Consideration needs to be given to some representative writings by prominent catechetical writers which show the inadequacies of some more recent emphases and point some positive directions for the future. In similar vein, an overall survey of the change in emphasis in the sixties can be traced in the six explicitly catechetical congresses held between 1960 and 1971.

2 — The catechetical model has been increasingly identified in this past decade with the idea expressed in the French expression — *l'éducation de la foi* — the education of (the) faith. The meaning of this expression is examined in establishing (a) the core of the concept of catechesis, and (b) the poles within which the concept may be stated.

Finally, "the education of (the) faith" is further elaborated with regard to the following matters:

a — the importance of the idea of 'education' in this model;

b — the role of the teacher/catechist;

c — the interpretation of the model in certain basic practical situations.

1. Rejection of the traditional model

The analysis in Chapter 2 has attempted to show the inadequacies of the catechism-based model for catechesis in our times. This is not to condemn it out of hand as having been always misleading; in its limited way it provided a valuable means of helping many generations of Christians to know and understand their religious beliefs and practices at a time when there was little else to do the same.[6] The eclipse of such a simple model is a natural evolution which represents progress of an important kind. If the catechumenate, that first and greatest innovation of catechesis was so successful that it eventually became unnecessary in the changed social conditions after the sixth century, this is perhaps an important precedent on which to reflect. Just as the very special circumstances of our time have brought about the restoration of many forms of the ancient catechumenate without making it necessary to reintroduce all the old forms which marked it, especially its mainly oral aspect, so too, the special circumstances of an age in which visual media

---

6. cf. note 36, Chapter 2.

are taking over whole areas formerly served only by the printed word, seem to require fresh attempts to adapt what was best about the use of the catechism—simplicity of statement, a summary of the beliefs of the Church etc.—in ways which will be acceptable and helpful to the men of to-day.

It is important to be clear about this. The rejection is of the catechism model with its exaggerated emphasis on authority and categorical statements in question and answer form as the main form of the instruction of Christian believers; it is *not* of the value of such statements of Christian beliefs and traditions, as for example, in "A New Catechism: Catholic Faith for Adults", better known as "The Dutch Catechism" which stresses in its foreword:

> "But 'new' does not mean that some aspects of the faith have been changed while all the rest remains as before... The whole message, the whole of the faith remains the same, but the approach, the light in which the faith is seen, is new. Everything that lives has both to remain itself and to renew itself. The message of Christ is a living thing, and hence this new type of catechism tries to present the faith of our fathers in a form suitable to the present day."[7]

The former model, as noted in Chapter 2 because it was historically linked with the instruction of children, did, in Moran's phrase, "suppose a priest in a pulpit talking to little children or at least to adults being treated like little children."[8] Moreover, it was easy for a false idea of 'church' to receive an emphasis which stressed the passivity of the believer rather than his activity. In addition to the comment made earlier on this point, it is interesting to note two remarks of Brian Wicker in "Culture and Liturgy." He is concerned about the kind of language used, for example, about adult conversion to Catholicism — "he has been received" or "he has made his submission."[9] On these, Wicker comments that they "betray in fact a concept of the Church as the dominant and unchanging partner in a relationship to which the convert has to adapt himself unilaterally. There is no awareness of the truth that, in every conversion, the Church is changed as well as the individual concerned."[10] Secondly, he instances the traditional emphasis on the motherly care of the Church which "is properly directed to the care and protection, but equally to the adult maturing of the individual Christian...

7. **A New Catechism: Catholic Faith for Adults**, Burns & Oates, London, 1970, Foreword, p. V.

8. **Commonweal**, 18/12/1970, p. 299.

9. **Culture and Liturgy**, Sheed & Ward, London, 1963, p. 51.

10. ibid.

It is a mistake to emphasize the protective function of her motherhood at the expense of its ultimate purpose, which is a certain independence from her protection."[11]

The schema of Chapter 1 showed how the kerygmatic movement was amplified (and in the opinion of some, complemented)[12] by the anthropological phase, centering on man in his life-situations. There were two distinct phases in this, the first (although the point can hardly be 'proved'), tending to arise from the practice of good teachers who were simply looking for motivating points to arouse the interest of their pupils, so that they could find an opportunity to introduce what they really intended all along viz. doctrine, Bible, liturgy, apologetics etc., and a second much more significant one which, in the light of a better understanding of that theology of Revelation and of Incarnation with the kind of emphasis treated in the second part of Chapter 3, eschewed the sacred—secular dichotomy, and pronouncing boldly in favour of the value of the human for its own sake, tended to stress the importance of the true education of the believer as essential in the whole task of catechesis.

It is probably true that there was a mixture of both these ideas in the development of group activities, discussions, the acceptance of the principle of 'non-directivity' and the other practices mentioned in the schema as positive replacements for a kind of 'catechism' no longer found tenable. It is for the important insights which are offered during this important period of change that mention is made of three representative articles which illustrate, not simply the rejection of the traditional model but also of the inadequacies of some recent emphases for which too much has been claimed. Joseph Colomb's "Catechesis Contested"[13] is an overall survey and appraisal of the whole picture, but first of all, let us mention two articles which by their titles no less than their content, had a certain 'shock' value because of the writings and general standing of the authors in the catechetical movement from the mid-sixties: Pierre Babin's *J'abandonne la catéchèse* of 1968 in an issue of *Catéchistes* entitled *Nous faut-il encore catéchiser*[14] and Gabriel Moran's explosive *"Catechetics R.I.P."* of 1970.[15]

As a general comment on these articles, it seems of key importance to note that much of the dispute about catechesis refers to that given in a school context or in circumstances analogous to it e.g. release time in the United States, Sunday schools etc. This raises the very important

---

11. ibid., p. 53.
12. Luis Erdozain, *The Evolution of Catechetics*, **Lumen Vitae**, Vol. XXV, No. 1, 1970, p. 20.
13. Joseph Colomb, *Catechesis Contested*, **Lumen Vitae**, Vol. XXV, No. 3, 1970,
14. **Catéchistes**, No. 76, October, 1968, pp. 415-428.
15. **Commonweal**, 18/12/1970, pp. 299-302.

question as to whether or not the difficulties stem solely from the nature of catechesis, or whether they are related more to questions of formal schooling or similar organisations. In an age which sees in developed countries the periodic advancement of the school leaving age as well as the greater opportunities and necessity for tertiary studies of some kind, it is important to judge whether or not the problems of catechesis are peculiar to itself or whether they form part of the wider discontent which finds expression in the de-schooling movement and the radical re-appraisal of formal education in our time. This is of key importance in noting Babin's article written soon after the events of May 1968 in France, but to the extent that much formal schooling has suffered similar if less violent experiences in recent years, the continuation of the authoritarian aspect of the catechetical model has been untenable in schools for purely practical reasons.

Secondly, the combined impact of secularization in modern society and acceptance of a religious pluralism, has meant that the 'initiation-instruction-worship' sequence which was the constant background of Christianity from the catechumenate to the end of the mediaeval period, and which persisted in many traditional forms in society to the present century, has had a diminishing influence because it is no longer the accepted standard and indeed, is often publicly ignored or flouted in many aspects of national life. In an important study of the effects of such secularization, Pierre Delooz instances the growth of two aspects of what he calls "distancing" i.e. gradual separation from previously held uniform norms, which he characterizes as 'doctrinal selectivity' and 'compartmentalization', the former referring to those who appear to make a choice among the official truths, and those who "confine their beliefs in a compartment of their lives where they have scarcely any influence on the rest, which proceed quite independently."[16]

Besides this loss of any generally accepted set of norms to judge the religious believer—and is not this in itself a practical repudiation of the traditional model? — there has been an important set of changes in the role of the teacher, both as viewed by teachers themselves as well as by their pupils. As this has already been presented schematically in Chapter 1, one comment will suffice. French catechesis, in particular, seems to have been greatly influenced by the vogue of 'non-directivity' mainly from the works of Carl Rogers, but as so much traditional French education has tended to be magisterial, the relaxation of rigid discipline is the more noticeable, particularly with middle and upper school pupils. But since the use of discussion, group activities and such like have become the main educational models, it is difficult from a traditionalist viewpoint to see what functions as the authority in such a

---

16. Pierre Delooz, *Catechesis and Secularization*, **Lumen Vitae**, Vol. XXIV, No. 2, 1969, pp. 200-201.

situation. And as the older catechetical models were nothing if not models of authority, there can appear to be an important gap in the whole catechetical practice, a fact instanced by articles in more recent years in catechetical journals, questioning the extent of such non-directivity in catechesis.[17] This is certainly a significant gap, particularly where the question of the magisterium of the Church is raised or invoked.

(a) *Pierre Babin — "J'abandonne la catéchèse?"*

All of this is an important background to the article of Pierre Babin already referred to, because the catechesis which he maintains he is abandoning in October 1968 is neither the traditional, magisterial model nor its pedagogical development, not even the 'faulty' kerygmatic, but that life-centred approach of which Babin himself had been the main exponent by his writings over nearly twenty years. After stating the main lines of his argument, Babin continues:

> "Are we going to abandon catechesis? It is with the faith and the uncertainty of a man of to-day that I would reply, mindful of the risks and uncertainties of the vast revolution taking place... To give up the catechesis of these past twenty years, I will reply, yes! It corresponds to a period between Christianity and modern pluralist societies. But to give up any form of offering the Gospel to the young people at this particular stage of their lives, definitely not!"[18]

The remainder of the article concentrates on what Babin regards as three very valuable directions for catechesis at the present time and for the future.

1 — Following the thought of Gabriel Moran, which he acknowledges, Babin considers that if catechesis is to address itself principally to the conscience and freedom of the recipient, it must be addressed more than previously to adults. The catechesis formerly addressed to children and adolescents was inextricably mixed with sociological and philosophical systems which are no longer accepted. There is no point, he continues, in ridiculing such systems nor the kind of adolescent catechesis we tried to give over these past twenty years: they were both "the Incarnation of Christ of a certain age"[19] but they have now disappeared.

---

17. Catechesis Contested cit. supra cites two articles on this point, one asking "Is non-directivity a good course to follow?" note 2, p. 372.

18. op. cit., in **Catéchistes**, No. 76, October, 1968, p. 415 (my translation throughout).

19. ibid., p. 419.

2 — Babin's second direction is in favour of what he calls *l'animation culturelle*[20] — perhaps best translated as a 'cultural development'. In accepting with some reservations the necessity for a 'fallow period' following catechesis from infancy, he is of the opinion that "what the young person rejects is not so much catechesis but the world of childhood to which it is so closely tied."[21]

His description of what this cultural development should be is of central importance for us. He is radically opposed to any "pseudo-course of religious instruction" which explores all kinds of ingenious ways of finding an excuse to speak of God or to "discover" the Gospel. Rather he is concerned to propose a "cultural development through study, meetings and reflection (group and personal), having for its object to develop young people in their knowledge and personal abilities, so that, in union which others, they can revolve the problems of life and growing up which present themselves to everyone, problems which always include some aspect of reality, of ultimate meaning and of spiritual perfection."[22] But Babin is insistent that all of this "has nothing directly in view as regards catechesis. The cultural development must be considered as an end in itself just like mathematics and not as a means to be able to carry out catechesis at the end of all this."[23]

The practical programme which Babin proposes for this second option is to include group dynamics, discussions on human problems and the attempt at joining in, "from our point of view, the best kind of 'pre-disposing' or 'pre-schooling' on the questions of the realities of the faith. (But deliberately, we will not speak of pre-catechesis. The cultural development will be so much better, even from the point of view of catechesis if there is a complete absence of any 'pre-catechesis' intention or perspective.)"[24]

This last point is of the greatest importance. The development of the faith of these young people depends on their human development, something commended as of the greatest importance of itself. Teachers can help them in doing this, by a climate favourable to this cultural development; it is not simply a means to an end, although as he assumes in his third option, it is only the student who has come into contact with the problems, aspirations of man and so on, who is capable of profiting by his third proposal.

3 — This third direction is entitled: "The search for faith in open structures." It is, as he acknowledges "directly concerned with the catechesis of adolescents. Catechesis will be called 'a quest for

---

20. ibid., p. 420.
21. ibid.
22. ibid., p. 421.
23. ibid.
24. ibid., p. 423.

faith." And it will take place, not in compulsory situations, but in free situations, open and attractive." The contrast with the past is that "the problem is no longer as formerly to learn and to obey so much as to recognize and choose."[25]

Even though it must not be reduced to a system, the basic practice of this quest for faith will be by way of group discussion, instead of a transferring of the revealed given by means of a magisterial pedagogy.[26] Such an approach is distinguished from the cultural development already discussed by the more precise object of the quest. Babin describes it "as an addition to the process of the education of the faith of all the riches and possibilities of a cultural pluralism, so that there is no question of fearing to announce the Gospel but rather of not doing so. The sole requisite of pluralism is not to impose, but to propose."[27]

Babin proposes this course because of its fidelity both to the man of to-day and to his real life situations; for him, it is the essential direction for adolescent catechesis in the future. Furthermore, he considers that compulsory religion courses will have to give way to 'cultural development', and these in turn, will probably lead to three other types of structures, although their existence as structures is less importance than the continuing call to which they give form. Three such possibilities proposed are,

1 — Debates, open to everyone, believers and non-believers alike, on a human or religious problem, presented by specialists in their field and perhaps concluded by some activity in common e.g. folk singing, a meal etc.

2 — A regular meeting, once or twice per week or at determined periods in Lent or Advent, of believers, beginning or at least ending with some topic concerned with the Faith. Such groups will of necessity be small, and may elect for some common action together following discussion.

3 — Week-ends together around a common theme prepared well beforehand, but besides discussion and reflection, attention to life together and to the sharing together of the Eucharist.

Babin stresses the importance of having these three different ideas put forward together and of the invitation being often repeated; they must be made to appear attractive because of the personality of the people who propose them.

The conclusion to the article is an affirmation of the author's faith in the work of catechesis thus renewed:

---

25. ibid.
26. ibid., p. 424.
27. ibid., p. 424-425.

"It is not catechesis which is dead, it is not the putting forward of the gospel which has perished, but only old style language, old style methods—and yet, the spirit of the Resurrection is daring; other forms, other institutions, other languages and methods are in the process of being born everywhere."[28]

(b) *Gabriel Moran*: *"Catechetics R.I.P."*

Moran's article follows the line evident in 'Catechesis of Revelation', 'Vision and Tactics', and 'Design for Religion' but as an article in a popular Catholic magazine, seems to be a somewhat 'raw' version of the thinking which is evident in the third chapter of "Design for Religion." If the title is meant to shock, it is nevertheless faithful to the content of the article itself which argues bluntly:

'Catechetics, a hybrid from theology and a primitive form of education, is dying in the U.S. and this is no bad thing. Owing to the time-lag in its acquaintance with modern biblical study, American Catholicism adopted a style of theology which was going out of favour elsewhere, and catechetics, a European phenomenon was imported, enjoyed a vogue of some importance, but is now moribund. The reason for this is that there is a crisis in the existence, form and function of a Christian church. An 'intramural' word like catechetics, does not mean anything any longer, because as religion courses have been improved they have gradually come to look like something other than religion. It is the breakdown of the self-complacency of the catechetical movement which makes it possible now to try to face the "really enormous problems of religion in education and education in religion." Those faced with such problems, however, in Moran's view, must realise that "if religious education is to be a genuine field of study, and not a cover for indoctrination, it must be born from a combination of sound religion and good education." And this, for Moran, does not necessarily afford Christianity a normative position. Rather, the direction will have to be ecumenical in the widest possible sense and far from individual Christians engaging unofficially in education while their church exists for education in the religious area, Moran claims that the reverse is true.'[29]

Making allowance for the fact that this is a magazine article and perhaps deliberately provocative because of the sharp polarization between 'progressives' and 'reactionaries' in the Roman Catholic church in the

---

28. ibid., p. 427-428.
29. My precis of the article with exact quotation shown.

United States, there are some strong things about this article which deserve closer inspection.

First of all there is a complete rejection of the catechetical movement as he describes it, a breakdown in particular of the complacency associated with the idea that there was *A* catechetical method which could be 'applied' to any group of believers and have the same kind of benefits. But it is precisely this failure of the catechetical movement properly so called which has made it possible, in Moran's view, for people to begin to discover the very different problems which he separates as 'religion in education or education in religion.' Putting to one side this last question which will occupy us in the following chapter, it is significant that what Moran is attacking as the catechetical movement is both the traditional catechism approach as well as the simplistic approaches to the kerygmatic built around the history of the Bible—that faulty view of 'salvation history' which he has attacked in so many of his writings.[30]

Secondly, the contention that, as religion courses are improved, they look less like religion courses, is an important observation, from which one might conclude that these new courses see reality as one thing, not as a convenient division of the world into material and spiritual, sacred and secular. All things are revelatory of God and a true education will find this out. One may add that acceptance of this as an ideal does not necessarily mean that it will be achieved by simply wanting it to happen!

Thirdly, Moran's location of the 'crisis' as in the form and function of a Christian church is important because it is precisely this 'transmission' model which we have criticised in Chapter 2, which becomes meaningless in a society which, in practice, sees the role of the church as irrelevant. As we have indicated in attempting to relate the importance of Vatican II to the task of catechesis, there is such a close relationship that catechesis becomes a useless task — an impossible one — if the church is not an integral part of the society in which it attempts to make the Gospel heard. This is less a question of numbers and influence than of integrity and credibility.

Lastly, there are sharp polarizations in this article to which it is difficult to give an unqualified acceptance. The Gospel *does* need to be preached, the individual finds his revelatory experiences in a *community,* the Church's proclamation does *not* have to be indoctrinatory nor does catechesis have to be *only* the standard model Moran allows it to be here. But as to the ecumenical direction of education in religion in the future and the suggestion as to the non-normative role of Christianity, these are both key issues to be treated more logically in the following chapter.

---

30. e.g. **Vision and Tactics**, Burns and Oates, p. 57 & p. 62.

(c) *Joseph Colomb*: *"Catechesis Contested"* (*1970*)

The matters treated by Colomb in this survey at the end of the most important decade of change in catechesis necessarily recapitulate some of the matters already dealt with in Chapter 1 as well as some dealt with in the articles of Babin and Moran. What seems of value for our purposes is concentrating on the aspects of catechesis singled out for criticism, because it helps us in seeing what is peripheral to the concept and what is central. It is not proposed therefore to deal with all aspects of what is a lengthy article, nor to assume that the criticisms themselves are necessarily to be agreed with, but rather to note how effectively the main lines of the traditional model are rejected as well as some of the superficially thought out substitutes.

The five areas of contestation are those of:

1 — the catechetical method or model;

2 — the content of such catechesis;

3 — the type of faith envisaged by such catechesis;

4 — the language used in catechesis; and

5 — the view of the subjects or recipients of catechesis.

They will be examined in this order.[31]

1—Catechesis as a model is seen at times as remote from reality and dominated by magisterial lessons. Adolescents, in particular, prefer to learn by a process of discovery, not by having faith imposed on them as a form of constraint or obedience. An important insight is that of Le Du when he shows that culture should be thought of as an act of the recipient, not as something imposed by the teacher, who must rather (as Babin points out too) foster such creativity and openness to ideas by the favourable climate of group interaction. The school is condemned, too, where it appears to define and select 'experience' for the pupil or where it appears to impose ideas of 'what should be' prior to the actual experience of the pupil. Besides these latter attitudes on the part of teachers, there is contrast between the roles of the teacher as a resource person and as a witness to the Faith. This matter will occupy us later in this chapter.[32]

2—Concentration on content distinguishes between the true object of catechesis—seen as the promotion and development of faith—and the transfer of cultural forms or values. The former sequence of the catechism which tended to move from the religious to the profane, now has been reversed as catechesis begins from life situations and looks for

---

31. op. cit., pp. 369-370.

32. ibid., pp. 370-375.

the religious values already there, a move which reflects better appreciation of the 'secular' and the 'human' in the light of the Incarnation. From another viewpoint, the same point is made thus: whatever is irrelevant to man should have no part in catechesis. All of this is part of the attitude of the Christian to the world redeemed by Christ. If Christians do not abandon the 'world', it is still important to stress the tension between the discovery of God in the catechesis of the present human situation, without laying so much stress on Immanence as to ignore Transcendence.[33]

3—Faith as the object of all catechesis is stressed, but its formulation in terms of remote absolutes should be avoided. By definition, faith cannot be static so that the recipients of catechesis are always developing, growing in faith, ideally at least, deepening it in face of the new situations in which the world constantly makes them live. This means that there must be in faith, as in other aspects of the human situation, a recognition of a certain 'pluralism' at least *ad modum recipientis*. The controversy over Pope Paul's "*Credo* of the People of God" is instanced as an example of something which must necessarily mean different things to different people according to their diverse backgrounds.[34]

4—The criticisms of catechetical language are considered to be related to the difficulty in attempting to express a sometimes unintelligible theology. The Bible, as the word of God, does not remain uncriticised. Its message will hardly be heard unless it finds ways of speaking to the man of to-day in the language he understands. The same criticism applies equally to liturgy, which, as the expression of profound meaning, must appear so to the participants. Indeed, all religious questions must be capable of being heard and responded to in ordinary language. Catechesis which attempts to engage in dialogue with contemporary man and his problems, must of necessity be adult-centred and meet man in the realities of modern means of communications.[35]

5—As regards the recipients of catechesis, there is strong emphasis on the 'nurture' in the faith of children and in the importance of adult-centred catechesis. There is less unanimity as regards the catechesis of adolescents, some considering that the emphasis here should be on promoting their human development in the fullest possible way as the first task. Put another way, the problem should be problem-centred and subjective so that at a later stage the more objective catechesis of adults may follow naturally.[36]

---

33. passim, 375-378.
34. ibid., pp. 378-380.
35. ibid., pp. 380-383.
36. ibid., pp. 384-385.

If these represent the kind of 'grass roots' problems encountered by those engaged in catechesis, it is possible to look at the changing emphasis in a decade by looking at the sequence of catechetical congresses running from Eichstaett in 1960 to Rome in 1971. These will provide us with our final panoramic view before setting out the central core of catechesis to which our analysis seems to be pointing.

(d) *The Catechetical Congresses* 1960-1971

Our concern here is simply with the event of the Congresses themselves and the extent to which their reports confirm the kind of changes in catechesis which is evident in the writings we have looked at to this point. In much the same way as we have looked at the articles of the previous section, it is considered that the general core of catechesis and its poles is confirmed by the recommendations of these international meetings, particularly in the changing emphasis over the decade.

With regard to the congresses as events in themselves, the following points should be noted as necessary background:

1 — The Congresses were held at Eichstaett (Germany)[37] in 1960; at Bangkok[38] in 1962; at Katigonda (Uganda)[39] in 1964; at Manila in 1966;[40] at Medellin (Colombia) in 1968;[41] and at Rome in 1971.[42]

2 — The presence of many of the same national leaders and of personnel from the leading catechetical centres — Hofinger, Nebrada, Van Caster, Bournique, Audinet, Amalorpavadass — ensured an important continuity.

3 — The fact that the four conferences held outside Europe were held in countries which were comparatively under-developed, where nationalism was either recently acquired or a largely untested element among the local participants, and where there was an element of political instability, resulted in many unforeseen gains. Although it was not stated explicitly beforehand, it could have been envisaged that the European leaders would apply their particular experience to help these developing countries with their special catechetical needs. In the event, something much more radical took place which has helped both to destroy the myth of a standard method of catechesis as well as to further the anthropological emphasis of recent years.

37. Johannes Hofinger, S.J., **Teaching All Nations: A Symposium on Modern Catechetics**, Burns and Oates, London, 1961, contains the papers, discussions and resolutions of the Congress.

38. Reported in **Lumen Vitae**, Vol. XVII, No. 4, 1962, p. 722.

39. Robert Ledogar (ed.), **Katigondo: Presenting the Christian Message to Africa**, Geoffrey Chapman, London, 1965.

40. **Teaching All Nations (4)**, July 1967, pp. 346-350.

41. **Lumen Vitae**, Vol. XXIV, No. 2, 1969, pp. 343-347.

42. **Lumen Vitae**, Vol. XXVII, No. 1, 1972, pp. 103-115.

A broad sweep over the congresses takes us from Eichstaett with its clear support of the kerygmatic movement, to Bangkok where the certainty of Eichstaett was somewhat blunted by the reluctance of the Asian delegates to proceed by a method of history quite foreign to the mentality of the peoples they knew, and where the problems of pre-evangelization were emphasised, to Katigondo where at first tentatively and then with more confidence, it was affirmed that the traditional African attitudes to religion should be retained in the catechesis of these people, to Manila which was faced by the 'kerygma in crisis' and pre-catechesis discussions initiated by Nebrada, to Medellin, dominated by the idea of human development as an ideal in itself and not simply as a means to catechesis, and then back to Europe where in Rome, the whole course of the congress attested to the acceptance of a pluralism in catechesis. In other words the decade which began with catechesis as the kerygma and its stress on God's saving plan in man's history, ended with a firm anthropocentric emphasis, requiring the discovery of God in man and the improvement of man's condition as the first priority inseparable from catechesis. In all this, it is probably important to realize that the real impact of Vatican II which took part in the first part of the decade, was felt more, particularly in under-developed countries, in the later years when the documents were readily available in translation and when the practical implications of much of the theology were being worked out, so that there is much more of Vatican II at Manila and Medellin than elsewhere.

For our purposes, we shall concentrate chiefly on the Medellin congress because of the often startling advances in thinking compared with the evaluation of the traditional model we have discussed to this point, for it was not with the European problem of a post-Christian era, nor with the different mentality of different peoples as in Asia and Africa that the delegates of Medellin contended, but rather with the human problems of illiteracy, exploitation and economic subjection in the same society as a ruling oligarchy or dictatorships in countries in which the Roman Catholic Church was traditionally much more associated with the latter than the former. But our concern is not to itemize in detail what took place at Medellin or to summarize its activities. This has already been done in various journals, and the impetus given to the relationship between catechesis and development has become the focus of attention for much catechetical writing of the past two years.[43] Our attention is rather drawn to try to evaluate how much of this political-anthropological emphasis is central to catechesis as a concept, and how much of it is a

---

43. cf. **Lumen Vitae**, XXVII, No. 1, 1972, which is mainly devoted to this problem and *A Catechesis for Liberation*, Vol. XXVII, 1972, No. 2.

particular need of the world to-day, but hopefully, will be of less importance in the future. This is simply another way of isolating the core of catechesis from its particular manifestations, as well as delimiting the poles of the concept.

The eleventh paragraph of the conclusions of Medellin views the content of catechesis as follows:

"Catechetics to-day, in accordance with a more adequate theology of revelation, realizes that the first place to look when seeking God's design for contemporary man is the area of history and authentically human aspirations. These are an indispensable part of catechetics' contents... To understand the broad meaning of these human realities, it is necessary to live fully with men of our time: thus we will be able to interpret these realities with progress and seriousness, in their actual historical context, in the light of experiences lived by Israel, by Christ, and by the Church's sacramental community, in which the spirit of Christ risen lives and works continually. Understanding man in this way results in a deepening of the Christian message, and this deepening in turn helps us to understand man still better."[44]

Accepting this point of view has important consequences also for the method used because it implies that the starting point is to be man in his present setting. It is here that the revelation of God has to be discovered, rather than introduced from without, as something which helps man to find purpose and meaning in his life. In terms of Babin's article quoted earlier, it is crucial to see such human development as important in itself and not as only a means to something else. Such a perspective is well summarised in the definition of catechesis made by Audinet in his summary of the importance of Medellin:

"Evangelization (catechesis) is the means by which any section of our human society interprets its own situation, sees it, and expresses it in the light of the Gospel."[45] This seems a different kind of emphasis from the concerns of Eichstaett only eight years previously which stated the relationship of the Christian to the world as follows in the seventh of its principles of modern catechetics:

"Catechesis makes the Christian aware of his responsibility for the world and the betterment of its condition... The Christian sees the world as the work and possession of the Father in heaven, and feels responsible for it as 'son and heir.' What is called the

44. (cf. note 41) p. 346.
45. Catéchèse, 34 (1969) p. 42, quoted Erdozain op. cit., p. 27.

'profane' or 'natural order' is not less from the hand of God. If the Christian does not endeavour to restore it to its proper condition in regard to family, professional, economic, civic and cultural life, he is betraying the trust of his heavenly Father."[46]

Hence it is not surprising that concern has been expressed by some commentators that the Medellin attitude runs "a danger of subjectivity and anthropocentrism remaining within human experience, without any transcendental outlook" as Erdozain expresses it.[47] Following his argument further, we find that Erdozain sees catechesis here posing the problem of transcendence and immanence which underlines all theology.[48] The tenth conclusion of Medellin, in stressing the importance of the community dimension of life stated categorically that "Catechetics cannot be confined to individual dimensions of life"[49] and goes on as we have already noted to stress the importance of the present situation and human values, not by being a Christian first (as the Eichstaett quotation suggests) and then a human being later, but being a Christian only to the extent that one is concerned with the present human situation. But if concern for the present as the revelation of God here and now stresses the pole of immanence, the subsequent attention of the Medellin conference through its working parties has been well balanced by the use of the description "a catechesis of liberation," which, with its implications of 'liberation *from*' and 'liberation *for*' has clearly indicated both the limits of immanence as well as the direction towards transcendence.[50] In a debate as old as Christianity, the very vitality comes from the creative tension between these poles, a perspective movingly summed up by Pope Paul VI in these memorable words:

"If we remember that behind the face of every man—and particularly when tears and suffering have made it more transparent—we can and must recognise the face of Christ, and that in the face of Christ we can and must recognise the face of the Heavenly Father, then our humanism becomes Christianity, and our Christianity becomes theocentric, so that we too can proclaim that to know God, one must know man."[51]

2. The concept of "the education of (the) faith."

The concept of catechesis has been most appropriately expressed in recent years by the term used in the French catechetical movement viz.

46. Teaching All Nations, p. 397.
47. op. cit., p. 27.
48. ibid., pp. 28-30.
49. op. cit., p. 345.
50. cf. note 47.
51. Homily at the 9th Session of Vatican II, 7th December 1965.

108

l'éducation de la foi, the education of the faith, for this expression

1 — indicates or implies those involved in catechesis—God and believers in Him;
2 — describes the process by which the believer progresses in this relationship;
3 — concentrates on the one necessary condition for such growth—faith.

(a) *The core of the concept*

In looking for what is central to catechesis, then, we are confronted with the notion of faith, both in the sense of personal faith and in the practices and customs by which 'the faith' is expressed. What is included is everything explicitly stated or implied in the classic theological distinctions of *credere Deum* i.e. to believe in God and His presence; *credere Deo,* i.e. to be confident in trust in God; and *credere in Deum* i.e. to entrust ourselves to God and to seek Him.[52] This faith is clearly the core of the concept of catechesis. As noted already in Chapter 2, catechesis is something different from other aspects of the pastoral ministry such as kerygma and evangelization of which it is the natural continuation. Just how central is this idea of faith to catechesis, a faith which is centred on Christ as the Revelation of God, we shall try to show by considering a series of statements which are descriptive of various aspects of catechesis which have emerged from considerations earlier in this work.

1 — AIM:

Catechesis is the process by which the baptized believer receives instruction and is engaged in the further education of the faith affirmed by him, or on his behalf, at his baptism.[53]

2 — CONTENT:

The content of such 'education of the faith' is the word of God spoken through the scriptures and the history of mankind, especially by the revelation of God in the Incarnation of Christ.[54]

3 — PARTICIPANTS:

Those who participate in catechesis are usually baptized believers who engage in a dialogue in which they mutually influence one another in a fidelity to the graces of their lives as Christians.[55]

---

52. Joseph Colomb, **Le service de l'évangile**, tome 1, Chapter XIX, pp. 597-602.
53. This seems to me an inescapable conclusion from the sequence of this work.
54. cf. Chapter 3, section 5, commentary on Decree on the Bishops' Pastoral Office.
55. **General Catechetical Directory**, Catholic Truth Society, London, 1971, part 4, par. 75, p. 65. Also Margaretha Theis, *The Dialogic Principle inherent in a Catechesis for Adolescents*, in **Lumen Vitae**, Vol. XXV, 1970, No. 1, pp. 69-90.

4 — A CONTINUOUS PROCESS:

Although it has terminal stages (e.g. catechesis preceding first reception of some sacraments), catechesis by its very nature is a continuous process which under diverse forms, deepens the believer's faith through continuing encounter with the word of God in the liturgy, the homily and the events of life.[56]

5 — THOSE RESPONSIBLE:

The responsibility for catechesis in some form or another is that of every believer i.e. it is the task of the believing community, the Church, for if we view Revelation as God's self-revelation to man (as distinct from a more propositional view of revelation as truths *about* God), we will view faith as a meeting, or encounter with God, we shall believe *in* Christ as well as *about* Christ, and be convinced that we should help others to share these beliefs.[57]

6 — A DIALOGUE OF FAITH:

While catechesis i.e. growth in mutual living faith, may be intended by the 'catechist' or one responsible, it would be unfair to the concept to imply that it results simply from the intention of the teacher. Ideally, it constitutes a dialogue between believers in which both are changed. The point is in no way diminished in the so-called 'catechesis of everyday events' because in this, the ability to interpret events in a Christian way, still depends on a perspective or spirit of faith.[58]

7 — DIVERSITY OF FORMS:

If at one level the concept is concerned with didactic teaching of what the true believer should know of the doctrinal and moral teachings of the faith i.e. the official interpretation or magisterium made in the name of the Church by those who have the duty and the authority to offer direction in this matter, at another level it must respect both the freedom and the differing abilities of the 'faithful' in their perception of what is implied by their faith.[59]

8 — DEVELOPMENT AND LIBERATION:

Even where expressions such as catechesis of development or

---

56. General Catechetical Directory, part 5, *Catechesis according to age levels,* pp. 77-97.
57. Paraphrased and adapted from an essay *Modern Theology and Religious Education* by Andrew Hamilton, in **Towards a New Era in Religious Education**, edited by Eastman, Cripac Press, Melbourne, 1972.
58. **The Renewal of the Education of Faith**, E. J. Dwyer for the Australian Episcopal Conference, Sydney, 1970, par. 141, p. 112.
59. Abbott (ed.), op. cit., Chapter II, par. 10, p. 689.

liberation are used as in the description of the Latin American congress at Medellin, the underlying link with faith is preserved, because it is the faith of those involved which expresses itself in concern for others and sometimes elicits their response in faith in return i.e. it acts as a kind of pre-evangelization or pre-catechesis in the classical sense.[60]

9 — LANGUAGE: [61]

The language of catechesis should be simply what is required for believers to share their understanding of the faith. Such language is not necessarily theological in a precise or exclusive sense, although the special nature of the matters described is indicated by traditional expressions which are in themselves theological statements, and because of its close link with the history of salvation, there will be strong scriptural influences. But the more refined theological statements will usually form part of the catechesis at a stage when the participants have had sufficient 'cultural development' for such expressions to have real significance for them. Put another way, faith is not necessarily linked with an exclusively theological language. The point is of key importance when certain forms of catechesis e.g. the 'photo-language' audio-visual series of Pierre Babin, are a necessary form of approach in an 'image' age.[62] It is not necessary for the forms of faith to be recapitulated in orthodox written statements to be learned by heart.

(b) *The Poles of the Concept*

There is another important aspect of viewing the concept of catechesis through the model described as 'the education of the faith' with its central core of faith and its clear indication of the dialogue between partners which its implies. Such a model, being flexible and easily accommodated to the different circumstances of a human society in a constant evolution, manifested in rapid social change as the norm rather than the exception, preserves the perennial relevance of catechesis as continuing knowledge and growth in the Christian life through the diversity of situations encountered. It is also an aid in seeing that although the catechetical model has a central unchanging core of faith, it cannot be limited to a final form without becoming fossilized. The point is well expressed in the twelfth paragraph of the Medellin statement, when it says:

---

60. cf. Erdozain, op. cit., p. 18 and note 47 of this chapter.
61. Joseph Colomb, **Le service de l'évangile**, tome 1, pp. 578-580.
62. e.g. Pierre Babin et *Monde et Foi* Team, **L'audio-visuel et la foi**, Lyons, Chalet, 1970.

"In every situation, catechetics has a fundamental message, which consists of a unifying principle between two poles of total reality. This unifying principle is complex, differentiated, and dynamic.

It excludes dichotomy, separation and dualism, as well as monism, confusion and simplistic identification.

This unifying principle exists:
— between human values and relation with God;
— between man's planning and God's salvific plan as manifested in Christ;
— between the human community and the Church;
— between human history and salvation history;
— between human experience and God's revelation;
— between the progressive growth of Christianity in our times and its eschatological consummation.

For this reason catechetics lives in a permanent tension between continuity and rupture."[63]

At first sight, this may appear simply as a more rhetorical description of the classical theological controversies on subject and object, immanence and transcendence, as Erdozain's article pointed out.[64] It is this undoubtedly, but if in our times the debate has become less academic, it is probably because of the better insights we have already instanced of the meaning for the lives of believers of the idea of an on-going revelation, of the significance of the Incarnation, and consequently of the mystery of the church and of a pilgrim status in it. Expressed in psychological terms, we may better appreciate that the tension between poles of opposition has its own value. It can be productive and creative, while at the same time it reminds us also of the *ne quid nimis* principle of theology, 'nothing to excess.' We have already noted that the use of the term 'catechesis of liberation has its own in-built corrective to the possible materialistic excesses of the 'catechesis of development' concept.[65]

Where this concept of 'education of the faith', thought of in terms of its central core and poles, is particularly valuable is in the insights it affords both to the formal aspect of catechesis in a school situation, and related to this, the particular role of the teacher/catechist. It is to these two aspects that we now turn because both are of central importance to the comparison made in Chapter 6.

---

63. **Lumen Vitae**, Vol. XXIV, No. 2, 1969, p. 346.
64. **The Evolution of Catechetics**, pp. 28-30.
65. cf. note 47.

(c) *Importance of the word 'education' in the concept*

1 — Anticipating the kind of view of education taken in the following chapter, we may say that education is the continuous development of the potential of the human being in understanding and facing up to the demands of life and not simply "the flowering of a settled potentiality" in Michael Oakeshott's phrase.* In this the value of the individual and his freedom is paramount, so that there are no arbitrary norms which regulate the life of the believer by an imposed uniformity, nor is there a kind of "lowest common denominator" approach which is content to reduce the teaching of the faith to rigid formulas adhered to without real understanding.

2 — In not being tied to any particular form of procedure e.g. the teaching and examination of the catechism formulas, the model remains open to the whole range of educational methods. The development of so many of the 'informal' situations for catechesis, as for example in the schema of Chapter 1 and in Babin's article, is a good example of the educational flexibility of the concept.

3 — The notion of 'the faith' does imply a certain set of beliefs and practices which distinguish the believer, but unlike the strictures made on this as a static set of doctrines to be learned in Chapter 1 the full expression, linking 'education' and 'faith', suggests progressive understanding and development in the dialogue of believers which catechesis is. In this sense, the need to 'proclaim', 'transmit' or 'pass on' the faith to others is preserved without the magisterial limitations previously noted. Implicitly too, the combination of these terms does stress the 'community' aspect. As the recent Australian adaptation of the Italian Bishops' statement on this matter observes:

"No one has to make this journey of faith alone. God Himself nourishes and strengthens our reflection and our experience of spiritual things, through His Spirit in the Church. He sustains each traveller as well with the witness of his brothers. . . "[66]

4 — The view of the word 'education' in the concept evidently extends much further than the idea of formal schooling. It is consistent with the idea of terminal stages which require a certain grasp and understanding, although it would have to be admitted in practice, that sometimes (as in the controversy over the age and manner of reception of First Sacraments)[67] the ideal does encounter practical difficulties in situa-

---

*cf. Chapter 5.
66. **The Renewal of the Education of the Faith**, par. 18, p. 8.
67. i.e. Penance and the Blessed Eucharist, or Eucharist before Penance.

tions where the rights of parents, teachers and the official ministers of the Church meet.[68]   But the concept is perfectly consistent with the 'fallow period' and 'cultural development' phases instanced by Babin, thereby underlining the importance of human development as a necessary preparation and concomitant of catechesis.   This is consistent, too, with the theological emphasis of the Christian life as a form of continuing response.

(d) *The role of the teacher/catechist*

As the assumptions underlying the role of the teacher/catechist have already been appraised in Chapter 2, as well as the educational assumptions, what we are concerned to amplify here are those ways in which the concept of 'the education of the faith' is of more importance in achieving these ideals than the traditional model was.   The following statements seem to show this.

1 — The "fidelity to God; fidelity to man" balance seems stronger in the model we are considering because, as already noted, the partners in the dialogue are implied as well as the means whereby man becomes more like God.

2 — Summarizing the assumptions already treated in this new light, the role of the teacher/catechist in the Church (i.e. his 'competence' and 'mission') require him to be a witness to the faith, not simply an intermediary, to be faithful to the nature and content of the message he brings, and to be concerned to produce (with every respect for their freedom) 'believers' rather than 'knowers.'

3 — With the added perspective of the poles of the concept, we may add that the catechist needs to grow in knowledge of what it is to be fully human, with a view which recognises that becoming truly human is becoming truly Christian.   In a view of faith, he appeals to the work of the Spirit in those whom he addresses, without, however, failing to respect the personal mystery of such human development i.e. he does not aim to produce stereotypes, but rather help individuals to accept themselves, their talents and limitations, and their tasks as fellow believers.

4 — In the light of the previous point, it seems crucial in working with adolescent pupils to focus attention on the value of the present and their Christian response to this present.

5 — There are important ways in which the catechesis of children or adolescents in the school community, must relate to the wider community of the church and the world, as an important practical means not only of avoiding the artificiality and self-sufficiency of much school life (per-

---

68. This was highlighted at the Rome Congress of 1971 where the Addendum on this matter in the General Catechetical Directory was strongly contested.

114

haps particularly in boarding schools and institutional care), but also of maintaining that link with reality which has been stressed already. This is not to agree with an uncritical and complacent acceptance of aspects of the local church which are at variance with ideals. For example, the vision of Vatican II in liturgical matters has hardly penetrated many parishes and it has sometimes been urged against enterprising catechists in the extra-school situations of the schema in Chapter 1 or those group situations specifically mentioned by Babin, that their organisation of liturgical and paraliturgical 'happenings' on these occasions, is ultimately pointing up the absence of such informality and participation in the ordinary parish situation. Perhaps the point made in this protest is not without foundation, but it does raise the old age question of whether education is simply intended to produce conformity to what already exists, in an age in which change for its own sake is a common enough view with many young people.

6 — The point made above finds an appropriate comment in a reference already cited to the General Catechetical Directory, which is worth quoting in full because of the other characteristic it requires of the teacher/catechist:

> "(Catechists) are responsible for choosing and creating suitable conditions which are necessary for the Christian message to be sought,, accepted and more profoundly investigated. This is the point to which the action of the catechist extends—and there it stops. For adherence on the part of those to be taught is a fruit of grace and freedom, and does not ultimately depend on the catechist, and catechetical action, therefore, should be accompanied by prayer. That remark is self-evident, but it is nevertheless useful to recall it in present-day conditions, because today much is being demanded of the talent and of the genuine Christian spirit of the catechist, while at the same time he is being urged to have the greatest possible regard for the freedom and 'creativity' of those to be taught." (par. 71, p. 62-63)[69]

First of all, this obviously supports the catechist who gives his fellow-believers a more intense experience of what liturgical life and celebration could be.

But the second point is our main concern. The catechist, while making use of every means at his disposal without infringing the important freedom of his hearers, respects their liberty to respond or not. While proposing the ideal in his own life of what it is to be a Christian, he must be content to pray with and for his fellow believers, that they will have the light and courage to live according to the Christian prin-

69. **General Catechetical Directory**, par. 71, pp. 62-63.

ciples they discover together. The Directory suggests 'accompanied by prayer' from which we may take different meanings, either that the group themselves pray, or that the catechist sees that his personal prayer must be added to his preparation and teaching.

(e) *Interpretation of the concept in practical situations*

These careful distinctions are important both for the words and attitude of the catechist who is striving to maintain that double fidelity to God and to man, which is required of him. The point is of critical importance in the kind of distinctions between religious education and catechesis to be argued in Chapter 6, especially in the approach to problems such as the following:

1 — Since catechesis on the analysis so far presented in this work is by its very nature concerned with the development of the faith by attention to better knowledge and understanding, what are the limits of the catechist's assumptions in view of the kind of matters raised by the conciliar documents previously considered? In practical terms with regard to Religious Freedom —

1—May the catechist presume on the general willingness of his pupils to receive instruction simply because they are baptized and by the wish of their parents attending a Catholic school?

2—To what extent, and on what principles, should catechesis or religious education in such circumstances, be compulsory? In particular, may liturgical worship in the school context be compulsory as regards attendance?

3—In the study of other Christian churches or non-Christian religions, may the teacher distinguish legitimately between his role as teacher and his duty as catechist in the matters already raised above? In practical terms, how does he regard disagreement of opinion at variance with an 'orthodox' position?

4—A position not unlike that mentioned in 3— arises in the actual viewpoint adopted by the catechist with regard to non-Christian religions or indeed to other Christian Churches. As catechist, must he inspect these other positions from *within* the position which he presumes he shares with these other believers with whose instruction in the faith he is charged? Is such a position consistent with his professional approach?

With regard to the first question viz. whether or not the catechist may presume on the general willingness of his pupils to receive instruction and so on, the following remarks are offered in the light of our analysis of the concept of 'the education of the faith':

116

a — On the kind of 'continuum' model discussed in the treatment of indoctrination[70] there is justification for carrying out such instruction with young children as a natural extension of the parental mandate, always assuming the absence of any attempt at indoctrination by method or intention. It is worth noting that the presumption by the catechist in this case, is in favour of the child's being raised in a believing home by believing parents. In these circumstances, there is no difficulty in accepting the compulsory aspects of religious instruction with the same age group, to move for a moment into the second question.

b — With pupils of secondary school age the question becomes increasingly complex. To anticipate the comparison of the concepts of catechesis and religious education in Chapter 6, it can be said that in terms of the analysis of the idea of 'the education of the faith' to this point, the following positions could be posited:

    i — A 'fallow period' or 'cultural development' stage is not necessarily catechetical, nor is it intended simply as a 'pre-catechesis' stage, and valuable only in that respect. Rather than accept the categorical statements of the young teenager who wishes to 'shock' the catechist by declaring his non-belief, the catechist may be advised to proceed with activities which by their general closeness to life etc. may eventually make it possible for situations of the mutual acceptance of a common faith to evolve of themselves.

    ii — A certain objectivity of presentation and appraisal—something more explicit than the 'teaching about' model discussed in the next chapter, allows for a tacit 'suspension of belief' at a time when the teenager is most unsure of himself, while leaving the way open for communal actions (optional) by which faith is expressed, and in the Catholic sacramental tradition, grace received.

    iii — It seems that there are two different positions to be noted. The first, and it is fundamental in the argument of this work, is that many of the situations of this nature faced by the catechist are better identified as situations of religious education rather than of catechesis, a distinction fully argued in Chapter 6.

The second position is similar to the first. It argues simply that the school exists as a religious foundation, and therefore, while respecting the rights of the pupils, it continues to uphold its religious tradition. In this sense while making an assumption of common

---

70. cf. Chapter 2, footnote 60.

belief and practice, it leaves the specifically religious aspects of showing faith viz. worship and prayers, as open as possible.

2 — This last point has answered question 2 with regard to compulsory attendance at worship. Except for special occasions, Foundation Days etc. it is difficult to justify compulsory worship, while at the same time, the concept we are discussing would look to encourage participation in worship; but it would invite not impose, secure in the knowledge that a genuine religious response in faith must above all be free.

3 — Question 3 will occupy us from a different angle in the following chapter. There is a marked distinction between speaking as a believer as does the catechist and speaking objectively, as does the teacher when he is discussing a religion he does not share. But as Colomb remarks in this regard:

"When I speak about hinduism, to which I have no commitment of belief, can I say that I am really informative? It seems to me that I already give a kerygma, in so far as I have penetrated the meaning of this religion and appreciate its values. The informative as such has no sense, it is pure factual presentation."[71] As regards the second point, it is obvious that he is true to his faith when he affirms personally the traditional teaching of the Church's magisterium. This is what is understood when we emphasize that all catechesis takes place in a 'faith context', something different from a simply rational explanation.[72]

4 — Question 4 is not unlike the answer just given. If the question asks whether as catechist, he will pursue his inquiry into other religions only (to exaggerate the point) from the ways in which it differs from the one shared by those involved in this 'faith context', then there is an important failure from the point of view of objectivity. On the other hand, it would be untrue to the position of the participants if at some stages, some bases of comparison were not attempted.

CONCLUSION

This chapter has simply pointed to some of the main aspects of the new vision of catechesis implicit in the idea of "the education of (the) faith." Many further questions, however, are better treated in Chapters 6 and 7, especially by the comparison of the model with the basic models in religious education found in the schools of a pluralist society.

---

71. *Catechesis Contested,* p. 374.
72. This point for discussion occupies us further in chapter 6.

PART TWO

Chapter Five

THE CONCEPT OF RELIGIOUS EDUCATION IN A PLURALIST SOCIETY

INTRODUCTION

The preceding chapters have concentrated on establishing the concept of catechesis as it has developed in the Roman Catholic church to the present day. The concept of religious education to be studied in this chapter is, by comparison, a relatively modern development, associated historically with the growth of public education during the nineteenth century and especially of the movement for a secular form of education which was acceptable in a pluralist society. As the Roman Catholic reaction to this kind of movement was almost invariably to set up or continue specifically religious schools, much of the momentum in developing what was at first some form of religious instruction for the public schools (or indeed of making provision for the lack of religious instruction in such schools) came from the other Christian churches. It seems, then, the development of what the Durham report of 1970 specifically recommended as 'religious education' rather than 'religious instruction' has been a development brought about by the non-Catholic Christian churches. Although not exclusively so, this kind of pattern has been particularly marked in societies which were pluralist and English-speaking, that is, countries where Roman Catholics tended to see themselves as an economically-depressed minority group. Such an historical perspective needs to be kept in mind, because the increasing use of the term 'religious education' by various religious groups of the English-speaking world seems to point towards the evolution of a different concept or at least a development from the traditional idea of religious instruction or any other of the 'traditional' terms referred to in Chapter 2.

This point underlines the main concern of this chapter, for religious education is a broad term applied to such a range of activities that there is difficulty in setting out a normative concept; what is assumed by one group is regarded as indoctrination by another, while from a Roman Catholic viewpoint in its traditional statements on education, the term religious education could be considered a pleonasm.

To do justice, then, to its complexity, religious education will be inspected by four main steps:

1 — Some attempt needs to be made to clarify the meaning of the term, by looking at the origin and meanings of the words which make the conjunction, 'religious' and 'education'. By first looking at the

meaning of each word separately, it may be easier to appreciate some apparent contradictions not necessarily resolved in their conjunction, as well as recognising some of the difficulties in a pluralist society, either of viewing religion only from the viewpoint of education or of viewing education only from the side of religion.

2 — Religious education needs to be distinguished from the more traditional term 'religious instruction' and the whole activity of 'teaching' as distinct from similar activities, needs to be clarified. Activities built around models such as 'teaching religion' and 'teaching *about* religion' are compared with other models, such as 'education *in*' to try to show the wide range of activities which may be subsumed under the general umbrella of 'religious education.'

3 — As a result of the issues raised in the discussion on 'teaching *about*' and 'education *in*', some consideration needs to be given to the controversial issues of objectivity in the teaching of religion, the question of both 'procedural' and 'complete' neutrality, as well as to the already discussed issue of indoctrination.

4 — Finally, four separate models of religious education are derived from the above considerations, to be used as the basis of comparison with the concept of catechesis established in Chapter 4.

1. 'Religion', 'Education' and 'Religious Education'

The fundamental point which is at the root of this analysis of 'religious education' is the assumption that language systems change as language accommodates itself to the changing realities of a society in evolution; the point can be exemplified in the discussion of catechesis and its derivatives in the appendix. If, then, our society is concerned with 'religious education' as distinct from 'religious instruction', 'divinity' or 'religious knowledge', such a change in terminology must not be easily dismissed as pretentious or meaningless.

THE CONJUNCTION OF 'RELIGIOUS' AND 'EDUCATION'

Although it is possible to set out a number of different uses of the term 'religious education' nuanced either towards 'religious' or 'education', it is important to note the difficulty of specifying the concept itself in an exclusive fashion. In other words, the general senses of the words 'religious' and 'education', both broad terms, do not necessarily point towards one single concept of 'religious education'. This is the point of Gabriel Moran's strictures against the "premature symbiosis" of religion and education "as a cross breed that did not originate from two fields of scholarship but from the desire of confessional groups to indoctrinate."[1] Such a view can be supported by reference to the late nine-

---

1. Gabriel Moran, **Design for Religion**, Herder & Herder, New York, 1970, p. 14.

teenth century controversies associated with the growth of national educational systems, especially in English-speaking countries. In a cross-cultural reference, however, an expression such as 'l'éducation religieuse' in French-speaking countries is simply another term for 'la catéchèse' because of the historical position of Catholicism in such countries. But the term, as used in English-speaking countries, reflects a wider religious pluralism.

It seems important, therefore, to look at 'religion' from the viewpoint of 'education' and then at 'education' from the viewpoint of 'religion' to try to establish what the amalgam of the terms really signifies. This, in its turn, requires some explicitation of both terms separately. In view of the fact that many aspects of the concept of education have already been indicated and indeed are implicit in the work as a whole, some leading ideas are offered.

One final comment seems necessary. The concept of 'religious education' can be analysed in terms of what it *should* be by logical derivation but it has already been made clear that in the English-speaking world, at least, such a derivation needs to be related to the restrictions imposed by other considerations, notably those of a wide pluralism. This means that, in practice, the chapter is concerned less with a 'pure' or 'ideal' form of religious education and more with one largely determined by the various balances to be maintained in societies where pluralism has exerted its own restrictions as well as offering its particular advantages.

A VIEW OF 'EDUCATION'

There seems little point in concentrating on the exact derivation of the word 'education' for whether one accepts the "*educere*=leading out" model or the "*educare*= to train or rear" model, the derivation in itself is simply a guideline. In the first case, there is the danger of stressing some kind of 'growth' model in which the person to be educated is expected to arrive at an anticipated ideal state by a mental process akin to biological development; in the second, there is the equally misleading model of looking to the final product, the 'educated man', without paying sufficient attention to the processes by which the individual person is expected to reach this position. R. S. Peters has described education as the "intentional bringing about of a desirable state of mind in a morally unobjectionable manner"[2], and in further elaborating the concept has rightly distinguished between the essentially moral aspect of education as distinct from teaching when he points out that "the achievements of a

---

2. R. S. Peters (ed.), **The Concept of Education**, Routledge and Kegan Paul, London, 1967.

teacher may be morally neutral or pernicious whereas those of an educator cannot be."[3]

Coincident with greater stress in much educational writing on the essentially moral aspect of the process (concern for values and their transmission), there is the explicit view of Michael Oakeshott that "not only is education a moral transaction but it is the transaction on which a recognisably human life depends for its continuance."[4] Noting in passing that such a view of education is not to be regarded as necessarily restricted to schooling in a formal sense, we should repeat his further point noted earlier that "human conduct is not the flowering of a settled potentiality."[5] The potentiality of the human, he argues, is to learn to perceive the world, not of things but of meanings, for "to be deprived of 'meaning' is to be deprived of understanding and to be without this understanding is to be, not a human being, but a stranger to the human condition."[6]

Now the road to such 'understanding' is through response to various forms of communication, principally "to public traditions enshrined in language."[7] This does not mean that education may be defined in a narrow functional way, but rather that it takes on different aspects depending on one's viewpoint. Accepting Peters' description, we may distinguish the *matter,* in which case "education implies the transmission of what is worthwhile to those who become committed to it." If a *cognitive perspective* is adopted "education must involve knowledge and understanding and some kind of cognitive perspective, which are not inert." If the *manner* is emphasised, then "education at least rules out some procedures of transmission on the grounds that they lack wittingness and voluntariness."[8]

To these norms which offer the framework for approaching a formulation of the concept of education, it is necessary to add the following observations which further emphasise that education may not be limited to a simply functional nor uniform role in a pluralist society.

1 — It must be stressed that any theory of education ultimately depends, either implicitly or explicitly, on a theory of man. From this viewpoint, the view of the Christian believer who sees man as a creature of God, must always be different in its ultimate perspective from that of the secular humanist who does not share this religious view of life.

---

3. ibid., p. 40.
4. Michael Oakeshott, **Education: The Engagement and the Frustration**, in *Proceedings of the Philosophy of Education Society of Great Britain,* January 2nd, 1971, p. 43.
5. ibid., p. 44.
6. ibid., p. 45.
7. R. S. Peters (ed.), op. cit., p. 49.
8. ibid., p. 45.

2 — The recipient of education is seen as a whole, so that the educational process may not be restricted to instruction or training, nor indeed to any functional process, although all of these things are important in the whole picture.

3 — While there is obviously a sense in which formal education has a beginning, middle and end, this is not true of education as a whole. Perhaps in somewhat paradoxical terms, it is the "well-educated man" who remains always open to education.

4 — To the extent that education is essentially a process involving the recipient and his fellow human beings, it is influenced by the quality of personal relationships. But in practice, in formal schooling at least, the teacher must balance his respect for persons against his professional respect for intellectual standards, a function recalled by Peters when he quotes Socrates' description of himself as a teacher as "a midwife in the service of truth."[9] This is close to the viewpoint of M. V. C. Jeffreys when he describes the dual nature of the teacher's task as:

"1. To present the truth as he sees it, with his reasons for thinking and believing as he does, and with unremitting effort on his part to examine his own view of the truth.

2. To stimulate his pupils to do their own thinking, and to respect their opinions. To create an atmosphere of honest and responsible thinking, in which it is understood by all that the right to an opinion has to be earned by studying the subject, but that disagreement is legitimate and can be salutary, provided it is untinged by personal hostility. Putting all that more briefly: the teaching situation should be one of love."[10]

As has been already indicated, other aspects of the viewpoint taken on education are implicit in the discussion so that further elaboration is unnecessary. But with this explicit statement of some principles, it is possible to turn to the viewpoint of religion seen from education.

RELIGION FROM THE VIEWPOINT OF EDUCATION

A starting point which may help to indicate some of the practical difficulties in the relationship between religion and education is the fairly widespread contemporary opinion that much religion is better taught in schools not as religion but as literature or art, social sciences or music. Moreover, the interest in English education in such matters as moral education and the development of values (a term widely popularised in the United States through the work of Simon, Howe and Kirschen-

9. ibid., p. 59.

10. M. V. C. Jeffreys, **Truth is Not Neutral**, Religious Education Press Ltd., Oxford, 1969, p. 66.

baum) apart from a specifically religious context, is close to that other interest in religion as part of a school humanities programme or the recent symposium entitled **Religious Education in Integrated Studies**.[11] One of the key essays of this symposium, is that of Edwin Cox, who, in outlining the aims of religious education, writes as follows:

> "Religious education differs from other school subjects in that the teacher's concept of what he is doing may vary at different times and in different environments... In an age such as the present one, however, with pluralistic religious beliefs, and doubts about the veracity of all of them, such an aim (i.e. in context, the passing on of religious truths and instructing in a moral code) would be regarded as improper indoctrination."[12]

But if this represents a possible source of conflict, an analysis of education and religion simply as forms of activity also shows a certain amount of common ground, faithful to each concept.[13]

In his **Education in Religion and the Emotions**, John Wilson is interested in aspects of convergence between religious education, moral education and education in the emotions when he writes:

> "We have tried to argue that religion is *Centrally* concerned with questions about the appropriateness of various objects of awe and worship, and with other human emotions. Hence the larger and important part of anything we could sensibly call 'religious education' would fall within the sphere of the education of the emotions, and hence of moral education."[14]

It is this kind of convergence between religion and education which has led some writers towards considering the term 'religious education' a pleonasm, for where both words are given a broad significance, it seems that true education is faithful to seek out the particular aspects of religion as a distinct form of thought and expression, and religion in its turn respects above all, the importance of the freedom of the individual as essential for a true religious response. The point is reinforced when it is considered that for many centuries of European history, the disjunction of religion and education would have been inconceivable. There is evidently much common ground shared by the concepts but the question which remains is whether such common ground is the really important point in this kind of discussion. It is what is distinctive about religion as distinguished from education which may have more relevance for this present section.

---

11. Ian H. Birnie (ed.), **Religious Education in Integrated Studies**, S.C.M. Press, London, 1972.
12. Edwin Cox, **The Aims of Religious Education**, in Birnie (ed.), op. cit., p. 27.
13. ibid., p. 29.
14. John Wilson, **Education in Religion and the Emotions**, Heinemann Educational Books, London, 1971, p. 164.

Paul Hirst argues for the recognition of "distinct disciplines or forms of knowledge", the latter referring to "a distinct way in which our experience becomes structured round the use of accepted public symbols."[15] Religion, considered as one of these distinct disciplines, has therefore its own central concepts and terminology which are peculiar to it as a unique and irreplaceable form of thought and experience. In these senses, it is worth noting the specific character of religion compared to the more general character of education so that if we ignore the common ground relationship between the two, we may rightly concentrate on the various ways in which religion (as a distinct form of knowledge) may be better taught by the application of educational principles. But before doing this, it is necessary to indicate some of the distinctive aspects of religion, understood principally for this section, as traditional European Christianity.

Putting to one side, then, that magical view of religion which in a more primitive age supplied forms of explanation for events beyond human control, religion is better understood as providing some kind of answer to man's questioning of the cosmic mysteries which surround him, the irreconcilable contradictions of life manifested as good and evil, pain and suffering, joy and sadness. In Lonergan's analysis of religion, there is man's questioning of his very questioning:

> "It follows that, however much religious or irreligious answers differ, however much there differ the questions they explicitly raise, still at their root there is the same transcendental tendency of the human spirit that questions, that questions without restriction, that questions the significance of its own questioning, and so comes to the question of God."[16]

The Christian glossary of terms such as sin and redemption, sacrifice and sacrament, and all they stand for, are explicable only in a view of faith, here thought of as a special form of knowledge "born of religious love."[17] Understanding such concepts requires not a suspension of human rationality and judgement of the factual, but rather a positive commitment to a searching for an understanding of life. The distinctiveness of religion in this regard is perhaps best seen in the whole notion of worship, about which Miller observes:

> "The liturgy, from whatever tradition—the mystical Orthodox, or the redemptive Catholic, or the Quakers' use of silence, or the Protestant reliance on the Word—is a cultic act by which the

15. Paul H. Hirst, *Liberal Education and the Nature of Knowledge,* in Archambault (ed.), **Philosophical Analysis and Education**, Routledge & Kegan Paul, London, 1965, p. 128.

16. Bernard Lonergan S.J., **Method in Theology**, Darton, Longman & Todd, London, 1972, p. 103.

17. ibid., p. 115.

125

worshiper recovers the reality that all things are in God, even the most uncanny, the terrible, like pain and death."[18]

What is important to note about this aspect of religion in comparison, say, with education, is that a merely factual presentation of material describing what people do or feel at such religious ceremonies is only one aspect and that not the most important to a religious believer. Perhaps the separating point here is that while an objective education may concentrate on searching out knowledge and helping towards vicarious experience of the religious act of worship, this is still quite different from that personal assent to the numinous which is the basis of religious faith. It is not that vicarious experience is unimportant nor is it implied that understanding is possible only to the believer. But the uncommitted observer and the believer often stand on either side of a religious or metaphysical divide, so that while it is clearly important to know what common ground can be shared or experienced even vicariously, it is even more important to know what separates them.

This is where religion viewed only from education is likely to fall short of the ideal because of the tendency to concentrate on the factual and the objective, both, admittedly, important enough ideals in a pluralist society. But as has been illustrated again and again in the disputed question of religious language, attempts towards a form of reductionism which would enable religious utterance to satisfy the claims of a purely scientific objectivity, fail to appreciate the distinctiveness of religious thought and expression. Attempts at reducing basic religious terminology are no more successful than reducing poetry to the simplest and most straightforward expression, for whatever else is achieved, there is a fundamental loss of explicit and implicit meaning. Perhaps the reason for this is well conveyed in Samuel H. Miller's observation:

> "The 'part-whole' structure of religion is communicated not, in the first place, by ideas but by symbols... Symbol, rite and myth are the constituent elements by which religion transmits its wisdom, witnesses to the revelation of what is beyond the 'trance of ordinary experience' and celebrates what it cannot explain."[19]

Where education and religion are often found close together, as has been noted earlier, is in certain aspects of aesthetic education whether in literature, art or music. It is easy to see some basic resemblances which make this likely.

Primarily, it is in the attention paid to the *education* of the emotions. If the measure of being successful, in having fifteen-year-olds listen attentively to Beethoven, is either the authority of the teacher or the

---

18. Samuel H. Miller, *Oppositions between Religion and Education*, in Theodore R. Sizer (ed.), **Religion and Public Education**, Houghton Mifflin Co., Boston, 1967, p. 114.
19. ibid., p. 115.

authority of the composer — "You ought to like this because Beethoven was a great composer" — it is possible that something worthwhile is achieved. But genuine education, while providing both the opportunity and the explanations, would be more concerned with developing the kind of sensitivity which is necessary for real appreciation to be learned. From a practical point of view, much of this requires a certain background and atmosphere, to provide the objective criteria for forming personal judgements. A Strauss waltz may not be the highest form of classical music, but its appealing rhythm and melody may attract the young listener and provide a transition towards the appreciation of a more complex work. As the learner progresses, it is the establishment of a background of reference works which enables him to reach the maturity of appreciating the enduring art forms where repetition is felt to be more valuable than novelty.

Part of this development is obviously that of the emotions. It is not to the point to try to categorize all those involved, but certainly awe, pity, fear, anger, joy, guilt and so on may be variously experienced in music and drama, as indeed they may be in religion. One thinks of the catharsis — "mingled emotions of fear and pity" — to which the audience was invited by the chorus in the Greek drama. The learning of these emotions — or better the identifying of them *as* they are experienced — is central to education, whether it be in the formal literature or music or drama workshop, or in the initiation in home or church to the expression of worship together, the mysterious elements of the religious service, the beauty of the singing, the special quality of reverence of those present.

Education, formal and informal, proceeds in aesthetic subjects by the development of the pupil's emotions and to the extent that religion has a strong emotional content, it is certainly appropriate to speak of education in religion. As will be looked at in the next section, the term would hardly be applicable in the same sense if the model of teaching was restricted to "teaching that" and the subject matter consisted of objective statements of doctrinal beliefs and moral obligations.

But the kind of evidence supplied for regarding Bach and Beethoven as more important than, say, Rodgers and Hammerstein, would be qualitative rather than quantitative, based on growing perception rather than authority alone, and whatever measure of freedom was ultimately extended to pupils in their choice of favourites, there would have been reasons given why the former composers could be viewed more seriously. This giving of reasons is important; it is more than a kind of objective cafeteria-like presentation, followed by an invitation to free choice. One could specify it more as an informed choice, for which reasons can be given.

Applied to the idea of education in religion, it is important to underline the particular nature of religious faith with its commitment to

127

a life style and to a certain specific view of the world. This basis of religious faith, not of empirical knowledge, ensures that the criteria of acceptance are necessarily different say from mathematics. But as poetry makes use of symbol and metaphor to indicate what is felt by the emotions rather than deduced by attention to literalness, so too does religion make use of symbol and ritual in its liturgy, so that it is not simply a question of rational perception of the reasonableness of doctrine and morality, but perhaps equally the experience of the believing worshipping community and the emotions of awe, reverence and wonder. It has been well noted that the educator as well as the minister, priest and rabbi, is confronted with the same challenges as those with whom he is associated.

It is precisely the absence of this last factor, on the grounds of non-partisan presentation of belief, of impartiality, and of fear of indoctrination, which raises the most serious questions with regard to the limitations of education in the service of religion in the state school. As this issue is central to the next two sections of the chapter, it suffices to say here that the real dilemma is not so much the old bogey of proselytising or indeed of indoctrination, but the much more serious limitation to the true nature of religious belief and its communication which this attitude supposes.

In summary, the following points should be noted about the perspective which would look at religious education principally from the viewpoint of education.

1 — That view of education which stresses rationality and the giving of reasons as the basis for perception of the truth, is both legitimate and commendable, provided that it does not impose these criteria in isolation on the notion of religion in a way that restricts its distinctive scope, e.g. by subjecting it to the criticism of criteria such as empiricism, which are inappropriate for the form of knowledge which religion is.

2 — As a distinct form of knowledge, religion has its historical bases and manifestations which may be studied objectively in education under the aspects of its history, sociology or psychology. But these are not the essence of religion. It is doubtful in a pluralist society whether education by the State can do much more directly than point the way towards showing the kinds of questions with which religion is concerned, as education in religion in a more profound sense can only take place where metaphysical and religious questions or the experiences of worship can be explored in the company of believers or perhaps, in a more profound fashion, with fellow-believers.

3 — In an indirect fashion, however, education and religion occupy important common ground in the education of the emotions. This

means that attention to awareness, to ultimate questions, which are confronted vicariously through literature and aesthetics generally, offer an easily reversible process for deepening both education and religion. Education here raises the questions which lead ultimately in the direction of metaphysical, if not religious ideas. In these senses, the attention to religion in integrated studies has much to commend it, although it would be naive to regard this as an innovation; good education has always touched the religious element in diverse ways.

It is necessary, at the same time, to see this development of sensitivity and awareness as important in its own right: those things which lead towards a more rounded human development are to that extent facilitating the all round realisation of a fully human being, but they are not in themselves religious, nor is their importance solely because of the direction they lead. Perhaps in terms of the discussion of the notion of pre-catechesis in the appendix, the same point might be made: the development of the human towards greater completeness is important in itself, not simply as a means to an ulterior end.

4 — Religion as an autonomous form of thought is served by education which, unlike religion, is not a separate form of knowledge, but a general description of the principles which should generally underlie the approach to separate disciplines.

5 — Education, regarded as the development of rationality via initiation into society and into forms of knowledge, should ideally at least, discover the religious dimensions which lie outside the merely factual and the immediately obvious. In a pluralist society, it is as much as it can do in the state school but ideally at least, is successful if it leaves its recipient open-minded, flexible in outlook, and potentially open to the personal discovery and exploration of the religious element.

EDUCATION VIEWED FROM RELIGION

Education, viewed from religion, is the traditional standpoint which has been the historical basis of the development of formal education in Europe due largely to the efforts of the Christian church. This viewpoint can be expressed simply: man should be educated with regard to his nature and his final destiny, as the following statements indicate in various ways:

1 — "Our views about the nature of education, its aims and content and method, depend very closely upon our views of the nature of man and the purpose of his existence."[20]

---

20. **Christian Commitment in Education. Report of the Methodist Conference Commission on Education**, Epworth Press, London, 1970, par. 6, p. 16.

2 — "But Christians will see education — as they see life — in the light of an ultimate reference."[21]

3 — "For if the whole purpose of education is so to shape man in this mortal life that he will be able to reach the last end for which his Creator has destined him, it is plain that there can be no true education which is not strictly directed to that last end... there can be no complete and perfect education other than that which is called Christian education."[22]

It would be wrong to leave these statements, however, without pointing out that they must not be read in a narrow way simply stressing individual salvation. The man to be educated is not alone: he is a member of a number of different communities so that his education must take place only with regard to those others with whom he shares the world:

"For a true education aims at the formation of the human person with respect to his ultimate goal, and simultaneously with respect to the good of those societies of which, as a man, he is a member, and in whose responsibilities, as an adult, he will share."[23]

Another author notes the importance of "the integration of Christian education into the whole pattern of human life in all its aspects."[24]

An over-simplification of the traditional Christian Education position must be guarded against. The education commended is not simply basic instruction in religion but a total view of the world, of life, and of the relation of the Christian to other realities:

"Therefore Christian education embraces the whole sum total of a man's activity, sensible and spiritual, intellectual and moral, individual, domestic and social; not with a view to attentuating that activity, but in order to ennoble it, guide it, and perfect it according to the example and teaching of Jesus Christ."[25]

If this attitude to education could in the recent past sometimes appear as an advocacy of a return to the mediaevel synthesis of religion in daily life, it is certainly not the spirit of the recent Second Vatican Council. In a comment on the "Declaration on Christian Education," Bishop Emmet Carter notes that the document calls for "the integration

---

21. ibid., p. 17.
22. Pope Pius XI, in *Divini Illius Magistri* (1929), Catholic Truth Society, London, par. 7, p. 8.
23. *Declaration on Christian Education,* in Abbott (ed.), **Documents of Vatican II,** p. 369.
24. Bishop Emmet Carter in Abbott (ed.), op. cit., p. 365.
25. Pius XI, op. cit., par. 119, p. 44.

of Christian education into the whole pattern of human life in all its aspects."[26]

He continues:

"...Christian education is *in* the world and, in a sense, *for* the world, since man must always work out his salvation in the concrete situation in which God has placed him and must achieve this not by protection but by contributing to the whole human community of which he is an integral and inseparable part."[27]

It is evident that this view of education is much more fundamental than "instruction in religion" or even "schooling in religion". The educational process is considered in a context much wider than formal schooling but there are two underlying ideas which need to be made explicit:

1 — The first of these ideas is that education is a broader term than schooling, for the school is regarded as continuing what was begun already in the home and indeed there is much emphasis on the juridical status and authority of the school as coming ultimately from the delegation of parental rights. Hence we read that "The Church praises those authorities and civil societies which take into account the pluralism of modern society, and support due religious liberty "helping families so that the education of children in all schools may be given according to their own moral and religious principles."[28]

2 — The second of these ideas, much stressed in traditional Roman Catholic claims for separate religious schools, is what is called the "religious atmosphere" of the school. The classic statement is again that of Pius XI in 1929:

"For the mere fact that religious teaching (often very meagre) is imparted in a school does not make it satisfy the rights of the Church and the family, nor render it fit to be attended by Catholic pupils. For this, the whole of the training and teaching, the whole organization of the school—teachers, curriculum, school books on all subjects—must be so impregnated with the Christian spirit under the guidance and motherly vigilance of the Church, that religion comes to provide the foundation and the culminating perfection of the whole training."[29]

---

26. Abbott (ed.), op. cit., p. 365.
27. ibid.
28. *Declaration on Christian Education of Vatican II*, translated by Catholic Truth Society, London, par. 7, p. 10.
29. op. cit., par. 98, p. 38.

In this summary inspection of education from the viewpoint of religion, two further points should be noted before an attempt is made to draw some conclusions from what has been set out. It should be obvious that the foregoing principles are based on the assumption of a common belief between those educating and those educated, or if this is too strong, that one of the tasks of education is to prepare the human subject for the acceptance of faith by presenting it gradually in a way that will ensure its acceptance as the principle upon which a commitment to a particular religious way of life is made. This may well take the traditional form in Christianity of infant baptism and the later development of the *habitus fidei* through instruction and the discipline of a Christian life.

The last point that needs to be made concerns the kind of pedagogy which is traditional to this approach. This matter, already discussed in Chapter 2, made the point that proclamation of the Christian message and Christian education were ideally simply two aspects of the one reality. This meant a strong reliance on authority, the source of which was the parental mandate transferred to the religious school of the parent's choice. The teaching model was therefore principally regarded as "teaching *that*".

Some observations on this view of education need to be made to be set against the conclusions of the preceding section, for it must not be concluded that the foregoing summary represents a static and completely acceptable view of education for all who are in favour of education being determined on religious principles, let alone for those responsible in a pluralistic society for the schools of that society. The question does assume different aspects depending on the starting point so that for some it may be surprising to find modern Roman Catholic theologians endorsing the following statement:

> "If 'education' secures the free human person his own place in the world, then a system of schooling that teaches a particular world view clearly fails to educate: instead of education we have a narrow philosophic formalism."[30]

These traditional ideas of education from a religious viewpoint need to be balanced against the following observations.

1 — The controversy as to whether or not human learning has intrinsic value or whether it is valuable only in helping man to see his religious destiny, has continued since Renaissance times. There is danger of an implicit denial of the autonomous status of various forms of knowledge, as referred to above. Christian faith has

---

30. **Sacramentum Mundi**, Vol. 2, p. 213.

nothing to fear from the serious pursuit of what are now autonomous disciplines: history, the critical study of literature, the natural and social sciences.

2 — Education in the service of religion is one thing, but the strong thesis seems to accord education only a functional aim, i.e. education is not regarded as a valuable product but rather as a process to achieve the ends of religion; it exists as a means to attain the ends set by religion.

3 — If the above view is accepted, then indoctrination in its most pejorative sense is the very type of successful education, a situation completely opposed to that described in the first section, for such indoctrination respects neither the criteria for true education nor the nature of the recipient.[31]

4 — Parental rights in education are primary but they are not absolute and it seems that, practically speaking, the real educator in the secondary school must accord greater opportunities for the development of autonomous behaviour (and its responsibilities), thereby running the risk of appearing at times to side more with pupils than with parents.

5 — It is difficult to prove empirically that the kind of 'atmosphere' traditionally commended is actually a positive help to pupils in leading them to a life-long commitment to their religion, however much it may appear so in school years by the exercise of a strong authority and discipline.[32]

6 — In the actual (as compared with the theoretical) situation of many religious schools, a number of teachers no longer wish to indicate their own beliefs and religious attitudes, on the grounds that this is outside their professional obligations as teachers employed in view of their academic competence and training. This attitude may be based on respect for their pupils' freedom, or on their own right of freedom of expression.

7 — While respecting the historical reasons for the establishment of separate religious foundations especially at the height of the secular movement of the last century, it is important to note that the reasons were historical to meet the particular situation then prevailing. There is nothing for example, in a philosophy of education based on Catholic principles which makes the continuation of such schools strictly necessary.

---

31. cf. Chapter 6 and Section 3 of the present chapter.
32. A. M. Greeley and P. H. Rossi, **The Education of Catholic Americans**, Aldine Publishing Company, Chicago, 1966, pp. 112-113.

2. Religious education or religious instruction?

'EDUCATION' OR 'INSTRUCTION'?

The deliberate polarizations of the arguments from either side in the preceding section has still left quite a deal of harmony between the separate concepts of religion and education, although the extent of any common ground varies with one's change of viewpoint. If we make the conjunction of "religious education", we do not so much resolve the inherent contradictions but rather counter-balance one concept against the other. But, as has been the consistent viewpoint on changes in terminology throughout this work, changes in language indicate changing views of reality, a point implicitly acknowledged by the Durham Committee Report when it begins its list of recommendations by stating:

"The term 'religious instruction' should be replaced forthwith by the term 'religious education'."[33]

What was envisaged by the Durham Committee by the latter term may be gauged from the following excerpts.

1 — "Religious education... is not the inculcation of a system of beliefs which pupils are required to accept. The question is no longer one of handing out doctrinaire blueprints... religious education has a place in the educational scene on educational grounds, where education is understood as the enriching of a pupil's experience ..."[34]

2 — "... (The Christian's) proposals for religious education will therefore emphasize the exploratory aspects of a discipline whose task of interpretation is never complete nor rounded off in a neat system..."[35]

3 — "The Christian unequivocally accepts the necessity of reasoning, even if he takes the liberty of doubting its ultimate sufficiency..."[36]

The concept of religious education envisaged in these excerpts is something much broader than that implied usually by the term 'religious instruction' as the following analysis indicates.

In its simplest sense, 'instruction' refers to the handing on of factual information or to the training of someone in a series of techniques or routines. For example, in traditional Army training, instruction in the care and use of small arms is the subject of exactly worded pieces of

33. The reference here is to the term 'religious instruction' as used in the 1944 Butler Act in Britain. **The Fourth R: The Durham Report on Religious Education,** S.P.C.K., London, 1970, par. 571, p. 274.

34. ibid., par. 115, pp. 58-59.

35. ibid., par. 113, p. 58.

36. ibid.

134

information, accompanied by practical work which involves carrying out the actual movements and procedures specified by the instructor's manual.

As an educational method, instruction has an important but limited scope? It is the basis of the traditional apprenticeship system, with the master craftsman ideally developing the apprentice's intellectual as well as his practical skill in the craft he is learning. In as much as instruction is related to teaching, it has always relied heavily on the idea of authority. The one charged with the instruction was *an* authority even in his limited knowledge of the theoretical and practical aspects of his trade, skill or profession: moreover he was frequently *in* authority over those whom he instructed, with the result that he could back up his position by some appeal to his authority or simply by recourse to corporal punishment or the threat of its infliction. There are obvious similarities with the traditional picture of the schoolmaster of many centuries.

Now, it may be argued (following Morton White's distinction[37]) that there is an important distinction between the notions of "instruction *in*" and "instruction *on*". To use his own example, instruction *on* Communism would be regarded as a necessary piece of information in western society, given the balance of world powers and so on, whereas instruction *in* Communism might be subversive. Certainly the application of the distinction illustrates a critical difference: instruction *in* religion suggests that the one being instructed has already indicated his willingness (or perhaps the intentional aspect is that of the instructor!) to adhere to this religion (as for example with the catechumens) so that there has been some first expression of faith. It is precisely this assumption of common faith and the desire for instruction which is, of course, not possible in the ordinary state school. But instruction *on* or *about* is possible. Whether, on another score, such a form of instruction is altogether fair to the nature of religion is a separate question to be looked at later.

Three distinctions which might be made between instruction and education could be made with equal validity with regard to separating religious instruction and religious education along the lines of the quotations given from the Durham Report at the start of this section:

1 — Instruction is more limited than education. In the apprenticeship examples, the knowledge content is closely and practically linked with the skill and the techniques to be employed so that instruction could usually be regarded as having a functional approach to knowledge. Moreover, it is presumed that the 'instructed' person

---

37. Morton White, *Religion and the Higher Learning* in Scheffler (ed.), **Philosophy of Education,** op. cit., p. 316.

has acquired a certain skill which he did not possess previously for instruction has a beginning, middle and an end.

2 — As a corollary from this, the well-instructed person might possess a limited knowledge and skills but may not have either ability or inclination to see further than the practical application.

3 — Successful instruction is different from conditioning which is more of a physical thing, but it is not far removed from indoctrination in that the emphasis may be the authority of the instructor and successful performance according to his advice or commands, rather than on the appraisal of things on rational grounds as part of the development of rationality. Obviously, this does not have to be true of all instruction, but it is possible (and still successful instruction) where it could not be regarded as successful education.

It is evident that religious education and religious instruction are broadly different activities but this is not to say they are not related. Instruction is properly seen as an important part of the content of education but at the service of education; the instructed person who has absorbed certain intellectual information and skills is not necessarily educated, whereas the properly education person has developed both his knowledge and skills past the stage of merely passive acceptance of instruction.

For the purposes of this chapter, then, religious education includes all that is implied by religious instruction but its horizons are broader and its potential unrestricted because as already noted "its task is never complete nor rounded off in a neat system". This is why the Durham Committee described their task as follows:

"We recognise that 'religious education' in the schools of England and Wales has two essential components:

1—Religious Teaching, i.e. what pupils learn about the subject through curricular and extra-curricular study and activity.

2—Worship, i.e. what pupils experience through participation in acts of worship in school..."[38]

It is to the first of these aspects that we now turn viz. the idea of teaching religion or teaching *about* religion.

TEACHING RELIGION

Before proceeding to an analysis of this expression it is necessary to establish some broad lines of agreement on what is understood by the concept of teaching. The approach taken is mainly based on the

---

38. **Durham Report**, op. cit., par. 191, p. 195.

136

distinctions made by Scheffler beginning with his separation of 'teaching' from 'telling.'[39]

The first set of nuances to be distinguished may be set out as follows: teaching, rather than telling, is usually the more *purposeful* activity.

Secondly, it is worth noting the force of "teaching" as a goal-oriented activity, for unlike "telling", "Teaching is engaged in, it is directed towards a goal the attainment of which normally involves attention and effort, and provides a relevant definition of success."[40]

This aspect is interesting to consider in regard to the jingle which says that "Religion is caught, not taught", for it may be pointed out that teaching being what it is, it may be more true to suggest that "Religion is caught *because* taught!"

Thirdly, with regard to the relationship between teacher and pupil, Scheffler makes the important point that "to teach, in the standard sense, is at some points at least to submit oneself to the understanding and independent judgement of the pupil, to his demands for reasons, to his sense of what constitutes an adequate explanation."[41] More than this, if the ideal is to have the pupil accept what is taught according to his capacity to receive, it is necessary (to avoid his acceptance of things simply on the authority of the teacher) for the teacher to put forward reasons "and, by so doing, to submit them to his (pupil's) evaluation and criticism."[42]

When the expression "teaching religion" is reduced to its equivalent form, "the teaching *of* religion", there are, to follow Morton White's analysis of the term,[43] two different meanings, e.g.

1 — X teaches Y that religion is such and such (factual information, doctrines, historical religion, moral attitudes etc.)
2 — X teaches Y to be religious by describing (and encouraging?) what are religious attitudes, how to take part in worship etc.

The point is that one may accept both of these ideas as worthy aims for teaching religion, but in a pluralist society it is likely that many who accept (1) would not accept (2) on the ground that it could constitute indoctrination in the most literal sense even of that term.[44]

---

39. Israel Scheffler **The Language of Education**, Charles C. Thomas, Springfield, U.S.A., 1960, Ch. V, pp. 76-101.

40. ibid., p. 76.

41. ibid., p. 61.

42. ibid.

43. op. cit., p. 318.

44. Of course, 'teaching religion' is a very general term which may stand for such diverse activities as 'teaching Scripture', 'teaching dogma' and 'teaching the catechism'.

If one accepts the first term but not the second, one subscribes to a notion which will be called "teaching *about*" and it is to be an analysis of what this means that we now turn. It may even be that 'teaching' is perhaps not the word which should be used for this activity; does it appear better suited by the expression 'telling *about*?'

TEACHING ABOUT RELIGION

The basis of this section is largely by way of a commentary on a contribution to the Religion and Public Education Symposium of 1966 edited by Theodore R. Sizer of the Harvard Divinity School,[45] in which Frederick A. Olafson expresses his own misgivings in an article entitled *Teaching about Religion: Some Reservations*.[46] Broadly speaking, his chapter is concerned with attempts to maintain the distinctive aspects of religion as a separate form of thought and experience, while at the same time maintaining the objectivity and neutrality demanded in public education in a pluralist or secular society. The key paragraph of his article is as follows:

"...I wish to make a number of points that have a bearing on the desirability and feasibility of two somewhat different kinds of academic work concerned with religion. One of these would consist of courses devoted, either partly or wholly, to the imparting of information about the major world religions; and I am assuming that both the doctrinal content and the history and sociology of these religions would be taken up in such courses. The other would be primarily designed to enable students to develop a measure of understanding of what might be called the religious aspects of human life, i.e. the features of our situation as human beings that perennially inspire one form or another of religious affirmation. Such an understanding would presumably be gained by analyses of typical expressions of religious thought and feeling which might be drawn from a variety of sources, among them imaginative literature, biography, and the literature of devotion."[47]

The wording of Olafson's first point might suggest that the providing of information as suggested could be more aptly described as an instructing or telling activity rather than teaching, were it not for the question he himself raises as to whether or not this kind of study, with all its related disciplines, is suitable for primary or even secondary schools for he asks: "Are we also prepared to have religion discussed there with the same degree of objectivity and freedom we expect and often achieve in our colleges?"[48] One might question whether his question should not

45. op. cit.
46. ibid., pp. 84-99.
47. ibid., p. 84.
48. ibid., p. 86.

be amended to consider whether such objectivity and freedom can be attained at all by primary children, and to what limited degree only by secondary pupils. And if this is not attainable, what kind of comment should be made on this kind of activity which speedily becomes reduced to the provision and sampling of a great deal of information outside pupils' experience?

Certainly, the mere accumulation of facts is not necessarily an educational activity, whether the facts happen to be "religious ideas" or simply "inert ideas". What is being achieved, it must be suggested, is certainly not education. If it becomes instruction *in* religion it offends against the objective and neutral principles; if it is so narrowly objective that it is better described as "telling" rather than "teaching", it seems to lack that purposefulness which should be characteristic of a teaching activity. For example, in terms of Ninian Smart's analysis of the dimensions of religion, it is difficult to escape feeling that a mere catalogue of myths, doctrinal and moral beliefs, descriptions of worship on a personal or communitarian basis, with the positive exclusion of the experiential, describes much of the outward shell of religion without ever coming close enough to the core to make the exercise worthwhile. If the comment is made that this is surely better than nothing, one would be implying that such distortion and inadequate presentation had some validity because of the inherent 'goodness' of the subject matter which supposedly might lead the recipients to become more disposed towards religion. Even granting the highest possible success by such procedures, this is a vague, haphazard approach at best and deserves Morton White's evaluation:

> "But teaching *about* religion, or communicating moral feeling and aesthetic appreciation while one teaches philosophy, literature and history, no more constitutes people to be religious in any sense of that word, than teaching *about* Communism amounts to propagating it."[49]

A similar reservation is felt with regard to Olafson's idea that "we must be prepared to look at religion as a human and historical reality through secular glasses and without ulterior motives of prettification or edification."[50] The difficulty here is not in accepting such a viewpoint in a pluralist society, but rather in accepting that such a viewpoint is consistent with the distinct thing that religion is. This is not to deny or underestimate the historical basis of the secular movement which was strong at the time when the secular education Acts were brought down, but to limit religion and its teaching to such a position is to try

---

49. Morton White, op. cit., p. 314.
50. Frederick A. Olafson, **Teaching about Religion: Some Reservations**, in **Religion and Public Education**, edited by Theodore R. Sizer, Houghton Mifflin Company, Boston, 1967, p. 86.

to obviate the complexities of the debate by some kind of prescriptive definition of what religion is allowed to be in the secular society. This is certainly changing the question with which Olafson concerns himself in this article but to agree to accept the matter as he suggests seems to confuse two issues: firstly, if religion "as a human and historical reality"[51] may be studied with the greatest objectivity without those involved being required to do more than (1) study *what* is believed (2) find out at secondhand *how* religious adherents worship, and (3) consider *why* the religious believer sees reality differently, the so-called objectivity succeeds in secularising religion for the sake of the uncommitted viewer, but this is still a long way from the believer's view of religion; secondly, the restrictions of "ulterior motives of prettification or edification" of which Olafson speaks, may be simply a warning against any attempt at proselytising (a judicious warning in the circumstances), but if this simply limits the intentionality of the teacher, it is difficult to see what else is being said. Are "prettification and edification" — and the first term suggests a falsification which is not true of the second — a limitation on the kind of inspiration which Christians, for example, have always found in the lives of Christ and his saints? Certainly, if we dismiss the proselytising aspect as outside the true objectivity demanded in the secular society, the believer should not be required to deny the inspirational value (edification?) which religion has aroused in its adherents when they have considered Christ and their fellow humans who have tried to imitate his example. This, surely, is precisely what even an objective study must show about the very thing that religious belief, and adherence to it, mean in our society or have meant at different times in the past. Objectivity is not a value in itself; it is a safeguard against something else.

It is worth quoting another section of Olafson's essay to add to the comments just made. He is arguing for objective presentation of material:

> "The point is that the story of the religious life and development of a people is deeply interesting simply in human terms without raising questions about the ultimate claims to truth of specific religious doctrines; and it seems perfectly feasible and legitimate for a teacher to limit his considerations of religion to the aspect of it that can be made intelligible in these terms."[52]

Two comments are in order. Accepting the point that Olafson is making, could it not be asked whether it is truthful to the inner nature and logic of the subject to restrict it within such an explanation?

---

51. ibid.
52. ibid., p. 87.

Harvey Cox has commented that "all good teaching requires fidelity to the phenomenon being taught, and it is of the essence of the religious as such that one really knows about it only through some empathic identification with it. Religion, like chemistry or drama, is taught badly if people are not encouraged to act it out."[53] Now to be faithful to this particular aspect of religion, a teacher must be prepared to show what believers themselves claimed was true about their religious beliefs as well as the particular shape and meaning which these beliefs gave to their lives. This is not to imply that it was true because they believed it. In passing, Olafson's wording of his sentence seems unfortunate if it implies that one can tell the story "in human terms" without at the same time seeing that religious beliefs and activities are part of what it was for them to be human!

Secondly, it should be asked just what the teacher is supposed to do when his explanation along these narrow lines leads to more fundamental questions from his audience? It is certainly true that many aspects of religion may be met with in the study of other disciplines. How, for example, could one deal with the history of architecture without some study of churches and their symbolic as well as their practical purpose? But it seems curious, and certainly opposed to what would be understood by education, to have the teacher limited his considerations "to the aspect that can be made intelligible in these (human) terms"[54], for the reason that this is what one cannot do with religion without falsifying it as a phenomenon. Moreover, if one envisages an even moderately open teaching model (as distinct from the kind of teacher-controlled situation implied by the quotation), it is impossible to see successful education taking place except by the realisation that education in religion cannot be confined to arbitrary limits by considerations apart from the discipline itself.

A continuing reflection on the whole historical origin of the secular school shows that its pre-suppositions can be challenged. But this exclusion of the controversial is a serious question for our age which resounds with so much criticism of the stultifying approaches of so much formal education and has seen the growth of a significant de-schooling movement. In other words, has sufficient weighting been given to the "education" aspect of "religious education" instead of the emphasis which the "teaching about" model suggests?

But the moment we suggest the term "education *about*" instead of "teaching *about*" some other weaknesses suggest themselves. First of all, the idea of "education *about*" is nonsensical if it means the artificial construction of education within arbitrary bounds, the very

53. Harvey G. Cox, *The Relationship between Religion and Education,* in Sizer (ed.), op. cit., p. 101.
54. Frederick A. Olafson, op. cit., p. 87.

141

imposition of which is a contradiction of that free enterprise and search for truth which education is. This is not to deny the tensions between indoctrination and education, but rather to suggest that education has to be seen as a process which continues through the dialectic of opposing viewpoints. Using the comparison with the preparation of scientists, Morton White argues that no number of courses in the history and methodology of science will help in compensating for laboratory experience and study of techniques for "no amount of methodological tourism will make him a scientist or scientifically minded." The application of "teaching *about* religion" he makes as follows: "But if it should be said after all this that religious instruction is not supposed to make people religious, but simply to give them some understanding of the religious life, that, of course, can be achieved by teaching *about* religion, not by teaching students how to feel and act, in a religious way, but by teaching them what they should know about religious feeling, action and belief. If in absorbing this knowledge students develop deep religious feelings, it will happen per accidens, as it were, and not as a result of the concerted efforts of the professors of feeling and willing."[55]

This quotation contains an important distinction not always recognised in this kind of discussion: much of the "teaching about" model over-emphasises the intention and evaluation of the teacher in what has already been described as a "purposeful activity." But from the viewpoint of the recipients themselves, the situation which results can hardly be attributed simply to the work of the teacher. We have noted earlier that the role of the teacher in this regard may be appreciated in amending the slogan about religion teaching to "Religion is caught *because* taught!" We may well conclude, then, that the teacher of religion has to maintain his balance between respect for his pupils' freedom and respect for the form and discipline of his subject. Ideally, a resolution is achieved between these ideals where they are in potential conflict, when the teacher presents his material in an objective manner ("teaching *about*?") but accompanies the whole process with a breadth of approach and a concern for deep reflection by his pupils which raises the process above instruction to education. Perhaps the best name for this process is "education *in*", our next model to be examined.

EDUCATION IN RELIGION

This model may be considered a stronger form of the "teaching *in*" model discussed briefly in the application of the word "teaching" in an earlier section. It is an improvement on the more functional "instruction *in*" (and the more teacher-oriented "teaching *in*") because

---

55. Morton White, op. cit., p. 315.

142

of the amplification and moderation suggested by the word "education".
As distinct from these other models, it lacks the result-directed sense
implied by "teaching" and, ideally at least, avoids the most controversial
aspects of the teaching of religion in its second sense of "teaching for
commitment," "teaching for life" in the state schools of a pluralist society.

The most important thing about this model is that it seems to offer
a further possibility to the list of attitudes towards religious education,
such as those suggested by Harvey Cox:

1 — "avoiding religion in education as much as possible and thus pre-
   venting pupils from exploring a range of human thought and activity
   which no one can deny is a part of the historical and contemporary
   world;

2 — looking at religion entirely 'objectively' and discouraging any sort
   of participation—and thereby falsifying the phenomenon of religion
   as such; and

3 — involving pupils in religious activities, rituals, and the expression of
   various kinds of religious activities, rituals, and the expression of
   various kinds of religious beliefs, thereby running the risk of creating strife and division."[56]

As expressed, the first is no solution, the second is unfair to the
form of thought being studied and the third seems possible only in a
religious school, i.e. one run by a religious denomination for the instruction of pupils of that religion.

Perhaps the model of "education *in*" manages to avoid the extremes
of (2) and (3) by working within the limits set by these as extreme
positions according to the following norms.

1 — "Education in religion" is linguistically closest to "religious education" for it respects both the adjectival force of 'religious' as a
   distinctive form of education, and at the same time limits the scope
   of 'religious' by considerations imposed by the general principles
   arising from the particular activity which 'education' is. For
   example, if 'education' is, in R. S. Peters' phrase "the intentional
   transmission of what is worth-while,"[57] then 'religious education'
   must follow a careful course, neither imposing one limited viewpoint and claiming it as the only one worth considering, nor on the
   other hand, providing a kind of smorgasbord of religious beliefs and
   attitudes which implies that the whole subject is relative.

2 — Religion is regarded as a distinct form of knowledge which may
   not be replaced by any other form of knowledge, nor by any combination of such forms.

---

56. Harvey Cox, op. cit., pp. 101-102.
57. R. S. Peters (ed.), op. cit., p. 35.

Therefore, the following gradations of the subject 'religious education' seem justified by the sense of "education *in* religion."

1 — In an evangelistic or confessional sense of the term, it is the initiation of the young into the teachings and practices of a particular religious community;
2 — More objectively, it is an attempt to help pupils understand the religious elements encountered in human life, the particular nature of religious claims to truth and the viewpoint which the acceptance of religious beliefs gives to human life and and its living;
3 — More narrowly, it could be taken as an introduction into the lives of pupils of those elements which have been the traditional framework of western society, particularly in the formulation and growth of ethical and legal codes.

If, in a pluralist society, (1) must be avoided, it is difficult to see how the sense of the word 'education' can be retained without (2) or at least (3). Even if the mandate is regarded simply as encouraging the exercise of reason within the area, i.e. subjecting religious statements and propositions to the scrutiny of reason, this must not be interpreted in too narrow a way. While agreeing broadly with the following opinion that "any examination of the many attempted definitions of religion makes it abundantly clear that the most we can hope for in this (as in other cognitive fields such as morals, aesthetics or personal knowledge) is the exercise of reason within this area", it must be made clear as our earlier discussion of the relationship between religion and the education of the emotions indicated, that this 'exercise of reason' should not be limited to a simple logical examination in too formal a sense of the term. The criteria for appraisal must be closer to those suggested for the evaluation of aesthetic experiences, because this is the distinct form of activity which comes closest to religion.

Perhaps the kind of balance which must be maintained is that suggested by the famous distinction of Pascal when he remarks:

> "If one subjects everything to reason our religion will lose its mystery and its supernatural character. If one offends the principles of reason our religion will be absurd and ridiculous... There are two equally dangerous extremes, to shut reason out and to let nothing else in."[58]

Very close to this model of 'education in' is the model proposed by Ninian Smart when he suggests 'teaching *how*' as an appropriate form of activity to bridge the gap between the extremes of 'teaching that' and the activities we have described as 'teaching *about*'. Its particular

---

58. Quoted in Translator's preface to **The Idea of the Holy**, by Rudolf Otto, Oxford University Press, reprinted 1971, p. xviii.

advantages will be discussed in our setting up of four models in the fourth section of this chapter.

The discussion of different models of religious education to this point has continued to bring us up against the questions of 'objectivity', 'neutrality', and 'indoctrination'. Even though each of these has had some interim treatment, it seems necessary, before setting out the boundaries of the concept of religious education to examine each of these ideas in some more detail.

3. Objectivity, neutrality and indoctrination

Some consideration of the first two of these issues has been implicit in aspects of this chapter, especially in considering the "teaching about" model, and the third, indoctrination, has had some relevant treatment in a previous chapter. The attempt here is to provide some selective consideration of what are in themselves important philosophical questions, the perspective being their relevance to a formulation of a normative concept of religious education. Hence, although the treatment is according to the above sequence, each term is implicitly being considered in relation to the other two as well as in relation to religious education. The inclusion of the closely related 'objectivity' and 'neutrality' separately is in deference to the use of the terms differently, at least as regards historical circumstances. For example, the concept of 'neutrality' was closely related to the establishment of secular schools in the late nineteenth century, but the term has enjoyed a new publicity in Great Britain since the work of Laurence Stenhouse in the organisation and running of the Humanities' Project of recent years.[59] In legal circles in the United States, the term has been much used in various attempts to test the validity of various State laws referring to the teaching of religion in state schools (or its absence), against precedents established in test cases brought under the First Amendment. But it is especially that sense of neutrality which approximates to 'impartiality' which describes at least the negative aspect of 'objectivity' which warrants its separate inclusion. Finally, the main locus of this discussion is that of the State schools of a pluralist society.

As has been stated earlier, 'objectivity' is not a value in itself but simply a safeguard against extremes of excess or defect. It is related, then, to a central position affording a non-partisan approach which resists no less the dangers of non-involvement as well as those of direct indoctrination, and balances the traditional aspect of parental rights in education against the educator's task of respecting the development of a genuine autonomy by his pupils.

---

59. Nuffield Foundation and Schools Council Humanities Curriculum Project (1965-1972).

Objectivity, then, is essentially an adult ability. Its development in pupils is a task of education and hence something which requires a certain degree of mental development for its perception by pupils as well as a certain exercise of one's freedom in its use. This aspect of weighing evidence and balancing ideas against one another is particularly associated with the objectivity which has characterised historical studies in the past century. This, in itself, however, is an application to a different field of that empiricism and development of scientific method which has been the hallmark of the advance of science. The idea is much more elusive when applied to aesthetics. If the historian can balance, say, the patriot's or the novelist's view of the 1745 Rebellion by careful recourse to the evidence provided by documentation, this is not much help in music, poetry or drama. Objective linguistic analysis of the words of a poem, for example Hopkins' "The Windhover", may be the form of dissection best calculated to miss the point of the poem altogether. Nor will the merely factual narration of the chordal and melodic sequences explain why Beethoven's "Eroica" is a masterpiece. Responses to the questions 'What?', 'Why?', and 'How?' may never produce the kind of aesthetic understanding which, while it includes these aspects, is much more closely related to forms of emotional response. Now, it is precisely to the kind of emotional responses suggested by words like anger, prejudice and pity, that objectivity may be regarded as the counter because of its concentration on other factors of a more rational nature. Such objectivity may be exercised in the field of aesthetics with regard to the incidental factors such as the hall in which new music is heard, the qualities of performance in technical terms attained by the performers and so on, but just as important, by the exclusion of arbitrary criteria for evaluation, so that any idea that all new music was judged according to its resemblance or divergence from Beethoven's music, would be most unfair, precisely by denying the value of the subjective views of the composer and his mode of expression.

The bearing of this point on the question of objectivity and the teaching of religion may be expressed as follows. First of all, although much attention is naturally directed towards the actions and attitude of the teacher, objectivity must extend more widely than this. As has been shown already, consideration needs to be given to the age and ability of the pupils themselves. A most objective presentation to young pupils or slow learners may effectively result in a distorted view of religion and its practice, or a reduction of it to factors that are really quite unimportant, as was shown by so much of Ronald Goldman's research.[60]

The central criticism is that if one applies either the objective criteria which go with scientific investigation or the canons of historical

---

60. op. cit. **Religious Thinking from Childhood to Adolescence** and **Readiness for Religion.**

146

research to an activity such as religion, the methods used will tend to stress elements which are primarily factual or descriptive, in other words only partial aspects of religion. As has been indicated elsewhere, these criteria leave one still in the realm of *knowledge* or belief whereas religion needs to be complemented by a view of religious *faith*. Such a viewpoint is one that stresses 'belief *in*' rather than 'belief *that*' in the common sense of 'knowing *that*'. Furthermore, a simple description of the inspirational aspect of a religion such as Christianity with its stress on a 'Revelation' does not seem capable of itself in leading to that understanding of the believer's view of a fundamental consent to be given to the authority of the 'Word of God' or that of the 'teaching Church'.

These points have already been treated by implication, at least, in an earlier section of this chapter,[61] but it is well to consider some of the attempts made towards objectivity in activities such as teaching the Bible as literature or history, or in the study of comparative religions because these frequently show how the kind of activity undertaken is sometimes ambiguous in its intention (teaching the Bible as literature will possibly lead to appreciation of it for what *more* it is) as well as false in its scholarship.

To justify this treatment of the Bible as literature in the schools of a traditional Christian society, the following argument is sometimes advanced. The Bible is such an important book in the history of western civilization that no one can claim to be educated who is ignorant of its contents. As the Bible may be viewed from different partisan positions by Jews, Protestants, Roman Catholics and secular humanists, it is practically impossible for it to be presented in any one of these religious senses in the schools of a pluralist society, so that knowledge of the Bible and its contents can only come about through study of it as literature.

But this compromise must then face the following objections:

1 — To treat the Bible as literature only, is to confuse a pragmatic working compromise with objective scholarship, for its reduction to these considerations is a falsification of what it generally means. This is obviously a different position from that of the mature student of 16th-17th century English language and literature who has these limits to his scholarship set by the nature of his study.
2 — The Bible may be evaluated as either literature or history but the assumption is that this is a deliberate limitation of one's study of these selective elements and this is the work of a reasonably mature student. M. V. C. Jeffreys would add that "the Bible can be

---

61. Especially the opening section.

147

understood only as the record of religious experience and insight. And to understand experience, we must share it."[62] This last point seems a little doubtful, but the main contention is valid.

3 — An American Jewish writer, with the U.S. situation particularly in mind says:

"Reading the Bible as literature rather than as revelation is worse than not reading it at all. In the latter case, at least, the word waits for us without a superimposed secular construction. Yet to read it as literature but really hope it is heard as revelation, which is probably the hidden agenda of most religionists advocating this practice, is as immoral in its deception as it is illegal in its substance."[63]

A different kind of objectivity is that advocated by those who, wishing to acknowledge the importance of some encounter with the religious elements of life as part of formal education, consider that a comparative study of religion may well satisfy both sides of the debate.

Contrary to this view, and to the traditional view with regard to Agreed Syllabuses in some areas, a whole range of arguments may be advanced of which the following seem most appropriate with regard to the aims of this chapter:

1 — "Examination of any belief, as distinct from the mere holding of it, demands a high level of abstract thinking"[64] as the Schools Council pamphlet states. This kind of study, it seems, would be suitable only at a sufficiently advanced stage of the secondary school. While agreeing with the main contention put forward, perhaps we may add it is important in this question not to equate some understanding and appreciation of different religions with the ability to express oneself with regard to them.

2 — A variation on this first position might be expressed as follows. If the aspects of understanding and appreciation of (1) are sometimes encountered in young children, they are still debarred on their age alone from being capable of exercising any great objectivity with regard to what they have encountered. This is certainly the view of the U.S. ADL committee which "believes that the study of comparative religion is best undertaken only when students have achieved a degree of maturity."[65]

---

62. M.V.C. Jeffreys, op. cit., p. 43.
63. Eugene B. Borowitz, *Judaism and the Secular State* in Sizer (ed.), op. cit., p. 280.
64. Schools Council Pamphlet, **An Approach through Religious Education**, Evans Methuen Educational, 1969, p. 50.
65. i.e. the Anti-Defamation League; cf. Sizer (ed.), op. cit., p. 48.

148

3 — A much more fundamental question, however, is raised by William B. Ball when he questions in the United States' situation:

"A parent, in the exercise of parental and religious rights, may desire to raise his child *to believe that a certain religion is true.'* May the *public school* which that child attends compel him to learn that there are many differences with the beliefs his parents or church have taught him, many different ways of interpreting these beliefs, many beliefs that he might entertain instead. Assuming the strictest observance of the strictest canons of objectivity by the most perfect of teachers, the answer can scarcely be in the affirmative."[66]

This last point of view raises the fundamental issues which provide the tensions of this 'objectivity' discussion—the meeting point of fundamentally different rights and duties—those of the child, of the teacher, of the parent, of the state and of the church, which give rise to the following questions:[67]

1 — May the State in the name of compulsory education proceed as Ball has suggested above without overstepping the limits of its mandate and thereby infringing the rights of its other citizens? As has been said earlier, not everything that is to be learned is necessarily to be learned through formal schooling.

2 — Is not the gradual development of the autonomy of the pupil a succession of personal decisions, frequently involving successive 'alienations' from the 'mores' held previously on the authority of the parents (or teachers)? In other words, does not the teacher who answers Ball's point affirmatively proceed no differently here than he does in modern mathematics and physics (or in certain classic cases, in the discussion of evolution in biology), when he is responsible for the pupil forming different judgements and evaluations from those that satisfied his parents? Or is it more to the point to remind ourselves that religion is such an all-embracing activity, that a change in belief is likely to lead to a change in what are seen as worthwhile or ultimate values? In Ninian Smart's phrase, religious teaching "must transcend the informative"[68] so that the teacher who proceeds along the lines suggested by Ball's quotation, is influencing both the beliefs and actions of his pupils, thereby arrogating to himself and the school matters outside of this teaching mandate.

---

66. ibid., p. 159.
67. cf. especially Chapter 4.
68. Ninian Smart, **Secular Education and the Logic of Religion**, p. 105.

It is obvious that this whole question is surrounded by many inter-related considerations which complicate any attempt to formulate a simple, normative form of objective teaching of religion.

Nor is there any greater clarity shed on the resolution of these differences by recourse to the word 'neutrality'. From a philosophical point of view, it is at least extremely doubtful whether 'neutrality' as a concept can be considered as 'value free' even if one surrounds it with a specification such as 'procedural'.[69] In the first place, there seems to be an arbitrary limit imposed on the activity of the teacher and the positive thing that teaching is, precisely at that point where the teacher *qua* teacher can do what the teaching machine cannot do, viz. enter into a relationship with pupils in the appreciation of truth. If it is claimed, however, that 'procedural neutrality' throws the onus on the pupils to do their own thinking, the point may have some value as a limiting principle on either the dominating or "spoon-feeding" teacher.

Perhaps, too, a slight alleviation of the interrelated tensions may be obtained by considering the function of 'neutrality' in a procedural sense, as something which, in conjunction with objectivity in the preparation of the material, ensures that those forms of indoctrination which result from the selective emphases of the teacher or appeals to implicit or explicit authority, are at least minimised or kept in healthy balance. But two points should be made with regard to this.

1 — It is important to consider that a 'negative' indoctrination, or indoc-trination by neglect, may also take place by the absence of a positive viewpoint. Neither objectivity nor neutrality should be taken as synonymous with a complete relativism in values arising from the fact that the very absence of an affirmation of certain beliefs or attitudes may give a false picture by this very omission.

It is one thing to put forward only one point of view, but it is quite another to pretend that by putting forward no viewpoint at all, we do anything better, for surely the choice of the teacher is not between teach-ing and not teaching, but between teaching in an open way according to the age and intelligence of those taught, and teaching only one view of life or one manner of conduct. Speaking of moral education, R. M. Hare remarks that "it is no use merely leaving children as free as possible from external moral influences, and hoping that the thing will just grow. It WILL grow in most cases, but only because the seed is there *in our own way of thinking* from which it is well nigh impossible to isolate a child.."[70]

69. i.e. referring to the way in which the teacher acts in the classroom.
70. R. M. Hare, *Adolescents into Adults*, in T.H.B. Hollins (ed.), **Aims of Educa-tion**, Manchester University Press, 1966, p. 61 (my emphasis).

R. S. Peters shares this viewpoint when he writes:

"This generalized agnosticism about moral matters leads to a lack
of firmness in handing on rules to children. Children, it is proclaimed, must decide these things for themselves. As if anyone—
let alone a child—decided for himself lying and cruelty are wrong. . .
In the early stages, they (children) have to learn to do what is right
without properly understanding why. . . One of the palpable facts
is that most things in life have to be learned before they are properly
understood."[71]

2 — From another perspective, it can appear that neutrality with regard
to any shape or form of religious teaching as exemplified in the
secular schools controversy, can impart an ideology of "secularism"
which, far from being neutral, is a positive disservice to religion.
This matter, which has been the subject of litigation in the U.S.
Supreme Court may be expressed in various forms such as the
following opinions:

   1 — "In an effort to remain" neutral, the educational process in the
       public school became completely 'secular'. . .[72]
   2 — "It is insisted that unless these religious exercises are permitted,
       a 'religion of secularism' is established in the schools."[73]

The root source of the ambiguity in the 'objectivity-neutrality'
debate seems to be arising from a confusion of teaching methods with
the inherent nature of certain kinds of subjects. It is probably possible
to teach scientific concepts, perhaps even more so mathematical concepts,
in a completely objective fashion but part of the reason for this is that
the nature of the subjects themselves involves forms of activity which
are little influenced by the personal qualities of the teacher except in
requiring that he teach his material clearly. But part of the nature of
a subject like religion is that it postulates a world view, it takes a
definite position towards other people and their mutual involvement, and
most frequently it leads towards some form of external commitment by
the believer in forms of worship.

M. V. C. Jeffreys remarks on this difference:

"The difference between religion and other branches of knowledge
is *not* that religion involves personal participation and others do
not. The difference is that, in religious understanding, a man

---

71. R. S. Peters, *Moral Education-Tradition or Reason,* in Macy (ed.), **Let's Teach
    Them Right**, Pemberton Books, London, 1969, pp. 104-106.
72. Neil G. McCluskey S.J., *The New Secularity and the Requirements of Plur-
    alism*, in Sizer (ed.), op. cit., p. 237.
73. George R. La Noue, *The Conditions of Public School Neutrality,* in Sizer
    (ed.), p. 22.

attempts to discover his relation to the whole of reality, and not only to a section of it. It is the totality of the undertaking (involving the whole of reality and the whole of the man) which distinguishes religious understanding."[74]

It is clearly possible for someone to use indoctrinatory procedures in teaching mathematics or physics if he simply provides pupils with methods of arriving at correct solutions without having to give reasons for what they are doing. Eventually, however, such teaching reaches a limit precisely because the nature of the subjects involved requires pupils to learn to exercise their reason according to the principles they have learned.

Put another way, indoctrination takes place when teaching models such as "teaching *on*" or "instructing *on*" are so used that there is no consideration for the development of the capacity of the learner himself to learn how to solve problems. This may occur by emphasising techniques of obtaining right answers rather than reasoning, or by unwarranted appeal to authority as the basis for passive acceptance. In such cases, there is respect neither for the learner engaged in the process nor for the special nature of the subject matter itself; and it is this double failure which constitutes the worst kind of indoctrination. But as this chapter has emphasised, the use of 'objectivity' and 'procedural neutrality' must be regarded as means of avoiding the undeniable disservices brought about by indoctrination, rather than as ends in themselves; and in the nature of a subject such as religious education, they are to be balanced against the nature of the subject itself and the particular forms of thought and awareness which it involves.

4.   A normative concept of religious education in terms of models.

As has been suggested at the beginning of this chapter, the derivation of a normative concept of religious education cannot be satisfied by a definition, something even more evident from the considerations already made in this chapter. Another restriction needs to be made: the concept of religious education which may be acceptable in the state schools of a pluralist society, is not necessarily one that is acceptable in all circumstances. In practice, religious education even in its most formal schooling sense, will be viewed much less generally by religious minded parents who believe that their duty lies in the instruction and upbringing of their children in their particular religious tradition, and the same point often goes for those who support private schools as religious foundations.

Another related issue in a pluralist society is whether or not Christianity is assigned a normative role for the schools of a pluralist

---

74. M. V. C. Jeffreys, op. cit., p. 68.

society (assuming that they have religious education).[75] Historically, the question may seem to be unnecessary. The countries being considered are predominantly those with a European tradition synonymous with the growth and development of the Christian church, so that on an ordinary assumption, Christianity claims a majority of adherents and represents the main religious traditions of the country. But it seems that there is a gradual movement away from the position of Christianity as the unexpressed assumption of all religious education. This is obviously so in tertiary education where the academic study of religions is carried out with proper scholarly objectivity, but increasingly in secondary schools, the approaches to religion which include study of world religious seem by a combination of subject matter and the requisite objectivity in the state schools of a pluralist society, to be tending towards removing Christianity from a normative position. In the United Kingdom, it seems the increase of migrant people from other religious traditions has been an important factor in this trend, for representatives of many different non-Christian regions are to be found in many schools.

This point needs to be faced firmly. The traditionalist Christian does not believe that any one religion is as good as another. Moreover, his religion has an evangelical element which requires him to try to spread it for the sake of others. He does regard other religions as less important than his own; he appreciates the fact that both on principles of orthodoxy and freedom to worship, various great Christians of the past were prepared to lay down their lives. And so on—the argument could be continued. In short, traditional Christianity is associated with a fundamental view of life which regulates what may be done and what omitted, and although Christians have always found their compromises, the ideal remains. The tensions between Christian and Moslem and between Catholic and Protestant may be generally alleviated in our times in comparison with even the recent past, and in public education over the past century there has gradually evolved the important principle of the withdrawal clauses and their equivalents. But there is a marked difference between objectivity and detachment of the academic study of religion possibly to the inquiring adult mind, and the perception made by the primary school child, who, in being taught about various world religious, may at best derive an attitude that the whole thing is simply relative or at worst come to the conclusion that it hardly matters. We have already noticed earlier the point made by Ball with regard to the teaching of comparative religion in primary schools.*

Now it seems that in the general movement towards tolerance and genuine respect for religious freedom, this question of the normative role of Christianity is no longer in practice the clear-cut assumption first

---

* cf. note 66.
75. cf. Durham Report, par. 123, p. 63, where this question is discussed in a balanced way.

imagined. This point may be confirmed in part at least by noting the movement away from the Agreed Syllabus approach. Two recent Local Authority publications illustrate the point.

1 — "In the secondary school the material is therefore selected and arranged in such a way that the pupils may grasp what the Bible is about, what Christian believe, the principles of Christian conduct and the growth of Christian activity in the world... During the first two years of secondary education a Common Syllabus should be followed. Alternative schemes for use at the teacher's discretion are provided, but generally the aim has been to provide an essential foundation irrespective of the child's natural ability."[76]

2 — "The capital (London) has always been cosmopolitan but never in the past has immigration brought so many pupils from so many different countries within its schools. Religious education must be considered in relation to the many cultures represented by these pupils. It must also be seen in the light of current religious beliefs and attitudes in this country, the changing pattern of Church attendance and increasingly vocal hostility towards religion in school...

...This Syllabus, therefore, is not only concerned with Christianity as an abstract concept, but with what it means in every sense to be a Christian and to be religiously committed."[77]

The marked differences between these quotations is not only in the explicitly 'transmission, foundational' aspect of the first when compared with the much more 'life-centred' approach of the second. More relevant to the point being considered is the closer attention to religion as a phenomenon in the second; it is not so traditionally 'orthodox' as the first. This, in itself, may appear to some to be a 'dilution' of the Christian message for the sake of some agreement, but whether or not this is so, the question about the normative role of Christianity still remains an important one. If any compromise on this ground represents betrayal for some, for others it may be understood simply as limiting the word 'religious' by the word 'education'.

Pressures for change in the content and manner of religious education have come from the basic dissatisfactions expressed by many teachers working in the subject, especially when the general staff-room misgivings have been supported by the kind of empirical and theoretical evidence which Loukes, Goldman, Alves, Rees in this field, and Piaget and Kohlberg in the related field of moral education have brought into prominence in the past decade. If one aim of religious education was ideally an understanding of a religious view of life if not actual commit-

76. Life and Worship—Agreed Syllabus (Senior Section) for Northamptonshire Education Committee. Aims and Introduction, pp. 10-11.
77. Learning for Life—Inner London Education Authority Syllabus, 1970, p. 9.

ment to it, it seemed that the aim was not being attained. Evaluation by those engaged in the process was matched by the concern expressed by those who, for one reason or another, were opposed to anything except the broadest descriptive approach. Their arguments often included the important observation that the grouping of pupils together in a school was for the purposes of formal schooling as distinct from the total educational process that life presented, and that formal assemblies which included group worship and spoke of God in traditional Christian terms, constituted a tacit acceptance of Christianity beyond the mandate of the school in a pluralist society. For the believer, it was suggested, an alternative to the statutory religious teaching, minimal as it was, always lay at hand in the specifically religious foundations where the majority of the pupils were of the same religion, or required by the terms of entry to the school, to follow religious instruction and attend chapel services. Increasingly, however, many Christians have been less and less convinced of the efficacy of such schools especially where it has meant, in practice, that there has been a notable lack of involvement by a particular church in the ordinary schools of a society, a constant criticism of the role of the Roman Catholic church in the United States and most other English-speaking countries. In the many arguments deployed, there has been the questioning of the evangelical consistency of a religious group claiming to possess the truth, failing to be concerned with the ordinary schools of the society. More of a family argument has continued around the question as to whether or not such isolation of a group of believers from other viewpoints on religion in the society has not resulted in an "inward-looking" policy, which, besides implicitly denying the importance of proclaiming the Christian message to all men, has little empirical evidence to prove that such a policy results in the production of committed believers.[78]

What many sincere religious believers sometimes failed to see was that concern about wrongful indoctrination was not, or should not have been, simply the concern of those opposed to religious teaching in schools, for any true religious response was worthwhile only to the extent that it was consistent with the nature of the recipient and his freedom as an individual. The basic lack of respect for the individual constituted by indoctrination in a pejorative sense, was hardly consistent with that "freedom of the children of God" which was to be the hall-mark of Christianity. On the other hand, the Christian could, for his part, rightly claim that education without some form of religious understanding lacked one of its fundamental dimensions. The dilemma to be resolved is that proposed by Paul Hirst when he contrasts the view of

---

78. **The Future of Catholic Education in England and Wales,** Catholic Renewal Movement, London, 1971; also J. M. Cameron, in **Images of Authority,** Burns and Oates Compass Book, London, 1966, pp. 107-113.

the person who believes that an understanding of the Christian faith should be part of education "but bringing up a child in any particular faith is not what education is about," with the attitude of the parent who wants his children brought up in the same faith as himself, an attitude which Hirst finds unacceptable as true education. As has been discussed earlier, this is a question which is based on a divergence of opinion with regard to the extent of parental rights in education, both as regards their scope and duration, and perhaps at the root of the divergence, is a difference of opinion with regard to the nature of man and his destiny.

With these reservations in mind, it is proposed that the concept of religious education may be best described in terms of four models, three of which have already been discussed at length in the previous section. As it is important to consider each of these models in relation to the others, a schematic presentation is offered* prior to some further summary and discussion of each. In a general way, it is evident that the movement from the most 'closed' to the most 'open' is clearly related to the view taken of 'religious' and 'education', so that as one moves from the first to the last, there is progressively less emphasis on Christianity as normative and more stress on 'education' rather than 'religious.'

1 — Model A: "teaching that" or "the teaching of" (first sense)

This model, already discussed in both its aspects, is obviously close to the magisterial model of catechesis of the schema in Chapter 1. Here, however, it is to be regarded more as an example of the kind of neo-confessional teaching in county schools which originated with the Agreed Syllabuses, and which has been the basic model in most of the Agreed Syllabuses until the late 1960's when the "Learning for Life" syllabus of the Inner London Education Authority attempted to come to terms with the particular changed emphases which had come about in the twenty-five years following the 1944 Butler Act.[79]

It presumes that all are Christians, or should be so, and while respecting the possibility of doctrinal differences, concentrates on the teaching from the Bible of what would be called the fundamental truths of Christianity. In this sense, it is 'neo-confessional' while at the same time, perhaps, fairly fundamentalist.

Morality is derived from the Bible and from the traditional practices of the country as it is assumed to be a Christian country and acts of worship, hymn-singing and so on, are shared by teachers and pupils although of course, there is also provision for withdrawal on conscientious grounds.

---

*See page 157.
79. cf. note 77.

FOUR MODELS FOR RELIGIOUS EDUCATION

MODEL	A "Teaching that"	B "Educating in"	C "Teaching how"	D "Teaching about"
Aims	Instruction of *believers* or those assumed to be believers in Christianity.	Awareness of religious truth through forms of instruction and experience.	Understanding and sympathetic view of religion and its relation to life.	Knowledge and some understanding of religious claims from an objective treatment.
Description	Authoritative, dogmatic and confessional or "neo-confessional".	Open to all forms of religion but especially keen to have religion appreciated *within* its own tradition.	Open to all dimensions of religion, especially understanding and appreciation of its elements as distinct from doctrinal and moral statements.	Descriptive and evaluative rather than authoritative; intellectual and cognitive appeal but little attention to experiential except in vicarious way.
Role of Teacher	A believer and worshipper; endowed with parental and church's own mandate.	A fellow seeker after truth; open to all aspects of religious thought and life.	May be committed but does not restrict understanding and choice.	Objective presentation of material; care not to offend religious viewpoints of group.
How viewed from within pluralist society	Unacceptable in state's own schools; for some, not acceptable in *any* schools.	Not acceptable to all because of stress on understanding *from within*; fair balance of both religious and education.	Acceptable for its stress on both objectivity and understanding; non-confessional in its approach but attentive to the cognitive aspects as well as the rest.	Respects differences of society but may be unacceptable to groups at extremities of belief and non-belief.
Religious commitment	The logical proof that the teaching has been successful is the close fidelity to the faith so learned by practice of one's religion.	Open minded and tolerant, so not pressing for a precature form of commitment, but aware that some aspects of faith in a religious sense *follow* reason.	Free choice of the individual is more important and may have to await the individual's own development.	Descriptive approach makes no demands for acceptance or rejection, except from the kind of examples given.

157

There is close attention to the idea that a religious commitment to life should be pressed for without actually infringing the liberty of the pupils themselves.

2 — Model B: "education in"

The full discussion of this model in the early part of the chapter may be summarized around the following points:

a — It retains the 'initiation' and 'transmission' ideas of the former but subjects the whole process to the critical appraisal of educational principles.   Ideally, at least, it concerns itself with all the dimensions of religion, not only with the doctrinal and prescriptively moral.

b — It postulates that profound understanding of the very important thing that religion is, can only come from *within* the religious tradition.   It is therefore concerned with the purpose and meaning of life in Christian terms, but does not equate mere conformity or conditioning with the free religious commitment it tries to encourage. It aims for the development of a genuine, if limited, autonomy.

c — It also makes its own critical appraisal of tradition, not necessarily accepting literal tradition as such but appraising the values it seeks to preserve.   In this sense, it respects the authority of the teaching church wihout necessarily accepting its pronouncements uncritically.

3 — Model C: "teaching how"

This is the description of the teaching model based on the ideas of Ninian Smart as a conclusion to the Heslington Lectures of 1966 at York, and subsequently published under the title of **Secular Education and the Logic of Religion**.[80]

"Teaching how" as an activity is characterised by the fact that the more it stresses understanding and choice based on that understanding, the less teacher-oriented it becomes (see earlier discussion)[81], and the more it encourages the importance of the properly informed choices of the pupil, the more it approaches the ideal of education set out in the first section of the chapter.   In these aspects it is markedly superior to "teaching about" in those very aspects where the latter is easily reduced to supplying factual information.

Perhaps more than the other models, it attempts to span the apparently unbridgeable gap between the extreme positions, or simply the two positions set out by Hirst above.   It is based on five main ideas, each of which will first be stated and then commented on where necessary.

---

80. op. cit., as referred to in Chapter 1.
81. Especially Chapter 2.

a — "Religious education must transcend the informative."[82]

b — "It should do so not in the direction of evangelizing, but in the direction of initiation into understanding the meaning of, and into questions about the truth and worth of, religion."[83]

This is certainly in according with the view of Hirst when he writes: "To understand beliefs or actions does not necessitate that one either accepts or approves of them and to teach for such an under-standing demands acceptance or approval of them by neither teacher nor pupil."[84]

Perhaps the difference between this approach and the "education *in*" model is the position afforded to the giving of reasons. "Education" can claim rational justification in the sense that the claims it supports are neither un-rational nor irrational; it simply places the religious tradition it supports as something transcending reason, the distinction being basically that made earlier between "knowledge" and "faith". But "teaching how" is particularly con-cerned with the rational inspection and appraisal of beliefs so as to lead to understanding; it makes no attempt to lead pupils to acceptance of these beliefs.

c — "Religious studies do not exclude a committed approach, provided that it is open, and does not artificially restrict understanding and choice."[85]

This is both realistic and a proper evaluation of what is involved in the action of the teacher when he teaches, but the question takes on another aspect, perhaps, if one suggests as a corollary that one who is not a believer may yet teach religion. This raises again the question of the objectivity of the teacher. Those who doubt whether the non-believer can teach religion, point to the purposeful aspect of the verb "to teach" and claim an apparent inconsistency between presentation of religious claims and their personal non-acceptance. This is really a comment about the nature of religion. While it is true that religion may be "got" with as little effort as catching a cold, it would be untrue to suggest that it is simply a matter of being exposed to it. It would be different if the non-believer, in teaching religion, emphasised why he was not a believer himself, but to imply that he must necessarily do this seems gratuitous. Perhaps, some of the confusion lies in associating the

82. Ninian Smart, op. cit., p. 105.
83. ibid.
84. Paul H. Hirst, in *Learning for Living*, March 1972, p. 9.
85. Ninian Smart, op. cit., p. 105.

act of teaching with the "do as I do" model of the authoritarian teacher. Or is it simply true that the gap between faith and knowledge is bridged only where the teacher transcends the informative, in which case the idea of "teaching religion" depends on the prescriptive definition that what is involved leads to acceptance through the mediation of the teacher, rather than through other means.

d — "Religious studies should help people to understand history and other cultures than our own."[86]

e — "Religious studies should emphasise the descriptive, historical side of religion, but need thereby to enter into dialogue with the parahistorical claims of religious and anti-religious outlooks."[87]

A general observation which may be made on these last two points is that religion is being thought of in the widest possible way and as a unity, but (d) should not be taken as aimed specifically at understanding "history and other cultures". These are rather the natural kind of by-product which could be expected from the educational principles implicit in "teaching now" as an approach.

The last point is quite far reaching in its implications because it provides, by its very objectivity, that kind of opportunity for dialogue which might otherwise be thought of as mainly possible only where a common faith was shared, or even a common opposition. As such, it provides an important link between different groups in a pluralist society, especially as from other aspects of the same work, the author has stressed the importance of appreciating all the dimensions of religion for a complete grasp of what it involves.

What may appear most questionable to a traditionalist who is inclined towards the "teaching that" or "teaching of religion" models, is the approach which simply contents itself with the character of religion as it actually appears in society rather than with the ideal of what it *should* be. Is such a phenomenological approach not contenting oneself with the appearances of religion rather than with the substance? What actually functions as the authority in such an approach which seems to depend for its success on the unpredictable factors of student interest, rather than on what should be known if the real nature of religious belief and practice is to be understood?

4 — *Model D: "teaching about" or "teaching of" (second sense)*

As the earlier discussion has indicated, this model is taken by some as the only type which is acceptable in a pluralist society for it satisfies

---

86. ibid., p. 106.
87. ibid.

160

some who do not wish any doctrinal instruction to take place in schools, while it also is acceptable to those who deplore the religious vacuum in education and consider that this kind of teaching is better than nothing. Without judging whether or not these attitudes are justified, the following critique is offered in comparison with the other three models considered:—

a — The purposeful activity indicated by the word 'teaching' is artifically restricted in this model to the provision of factual information. As already indicated, the kinds of restrictions it imposes are implicitly a denial of what is generally understood as 'education' as distinct from 'teaching'.

b — It seems agreed by both teachers and commentators that the emphasis is on the cognitive and intellectual. This careful insulation from the emotional and experiential—possible in the other models in various degrees—is a serious shortcoming because its omission relates to the nature of religion itself.

c — As already indicated, even this approach may transgress parental rights by appearing to commend a kind of relativistic attitude towards religion.

d — The model is ambiguous, if not self-defeating in its very aims. If the teacher contents himself simply with descriptive work, it is difficult to accept that he is engaged in a fully educational activity when he sets arbitrary limits of inquiry just at the point where religion stops being history, anthropology and so on, and becomes itself. If, on the other hand, he makes use of the descriptive and objective to raise more fundamental questions about the reality of the religious in life, he is contradicting the whole point of the model.

e — What the model does include — some teaching of religion, in an objective way, safeguarding from positive indoctrination, implicitly commends religious tolerance by promoting understanding but it is difficult to see that in doing this — noteworthy though it is — it is a specifically religious form of activity or even likely to lead to religious commitment or activity. Perhaps, all that this implies for some is that religion can have only a very limited place in formal education, but the implication that the activity is of value only in terms of aims external to its own processes, is its own condemnation if it is to merit the description of religious education in the senses in which the term has been used throughout this chapter.

CONCLUSION

In what has been a long and necessarily involved chapter, it is obvious that the concept of religious education, as with that of catechesis, can only be designated indicating its core and its limits, as has been attempted here.

In this work as a whole, this leads us now to consider the nature of the relationship between the concept of religious education and that of catechesis as it was analysed in Chapter 4.

Chapter Six

THE CONCEPT OF CATECHESIS AND THE CONCEPT OF RELIGIOUS EDUCATION

INTRODUCTION

It is evident that the concept of catechesis and that of religious education have very much in common, both as regards their subject matter and their methods, as well as their common involvement with those of school age in the community, even though neither concept should be restricted to this aspect alone. Moreover, modern writings and official publications of Roman Catholic authorities, such as the General Catechetical Directory[1] and the Renewal of the Education of the Faith[2], make use of the term 'religious education' interchangeably with catechesis in their English texts of works written originally in another language.

We have already noted, however, in the preceding chapter, that there can be very different views of religious education depending on whether one begins from the basis of education or from that of religion, and these divergences are of considerable importance. The lines of convergence between catechesis and religious education are in themselves indicative of an important line of development to be studied in this chapter, but the failure to separate the terms may account for much of the serious controversy of the past decade with regard to catechetical practices, texts and schemes of work, suspicion of catechetical centres and colleges of education, in the Roman Catholic church generally.

Our concern in this chapter can be expressed simply. Are the concepts of catechesis and religious education the same, are they separable in any way which is important, or are they mutually exclusive? Depending on the answer to these questions, we must then ask what are the implications of these answers, both as regards the direction of catechesis towards religious education, as well as that of religious education towards catechesis.

To make these kinds of comparison, we shall begin by setting out in schematic form the concept of catechesis based on the 'education of faith' model of Chapter 4. As the core of this concept was thought to be faith as attested by various criteria, each of which made some explicit or implicit assumption about faith, we shall make use mainly

---

1. **General Catechetical Directory**, Catholic Truth Society, London, 1971.

2. **The Renewal of the Education of Faith** (Australian Episcopal Conference), E. J. Dwyer, Sydney, 1970.

163

of the same points to provide us with some basic areas of comparison with the four models of religious education which were drawn up at the end of Chapter 5. These points of comparison will then be:

1 — A general statement of *Aims*;
2 — The *Content* and its sources;
3 — The *Roles* of the *Teacher/Catechists;*
4 — The *Role* expected of the *Participants;*
5 — General *Guiding Principles;*
6 — A general statement on *Method;*
7 — The specific attitude taken towards *Human Development;*
8 — The importance or not of special *Language;*
9 — The kind of ideal *Achievement*.

With special reference to the English context, the models of religious education will be specified as much as possible in terms of the actual statements or general meaning conveyed according to the following sources:

1 — the 'teaching that' model in terms of the traditional post 1944 Agreed Syllabus approach;[3]
2 — the 'education in' model in terms taken largely from the 1968 'Learning for Life' syllabus of the Inner London Education Authority;[4]
3 — the 'teaching how' model from Working Paper No. 36 of the Project on Religious Education from the University of Lancaster;[5]
4 — the 'teaching about' model from various sources and experiences but especially from the "Religion and Public Education" symposium edited Sizer, and mainly based on the problem of religious education in the United States.[6]

There are a number of preliminary comments to be made about this diagram, its limitations and its strengths. First of all, for the purposes of this discussion it will be generally assumed that the models refer principally to their usage in schools with pupils of upper primary to mid-secondary age i.e. roughly from 10 years — 16 years. Secondly, it is important to underline that the 'education of the faith' model is based on an assumption which is not tenable in the other models; this is stated as a point of separation, because if the 'faith' model may appear

---

3. i.e. in the general attitude and terminology of such works.
4. i.e. in the actual terms used by the syllabus.
5. Also in the actual language, as far as possible, of the Working Paper. Schools Council Working Paper No. 36, **Religious Education in Secondary Schools**. Evans/Methuen Educational, London, 1971.
6. cf. Chapter 5.

on this presentation at least, to have more likelihood of producing 'believers' rather than 'knowers', it presumes to do so by not having to face the problem of religious pluralism or the secular setting in which the other models are forced to operate. Whether, from a Roman Catholic view, this separation should be so, or more basically, whether it can always be made, are separate but extremely important questions, which need separate treatment outside this context. Thirdly, and most importantly, the obvious breadth of the ideals proposed particularly in the 'education in' and 'teaching how' models must not be assumed to be implicitly contained in the catechesis model, any more than it can be presumed that the former models necessarily lead to *religious faith* as distinct from *human knowledge* and insight. Fourthly, the variety of the models presented here indicates something more than the absence of a religious consensus which might result in a standard model. The very conditions which are responsible for this diversity in a pluralist society have one thing in common: they all uphold values which are themselves in the last analysis, religious, based as they are on (1) respect for the liberty of the individual as regards his religion and its practices and (2) respect for religion which is something enforceable only at the expense of destroying what it enforces.

Lastly, it is a practical point of some importance to acknowledge that, if the model of 'the education of the faith' is not necessarily the most commonly used approach in Roman Catholic schools in many countries, it does, on the analysis of the past three chapters, represent the one most in tune with modern theological, educational, philosophical and sociological thinking on the concept of catechesis as a whole. This means, however, that the question which must concern us may be expressed as, follows:

Can the aims of catechesis be satisfied (ideally) by the aims of the other models considered in this diagram, or by any one other of these models?

This question, and the others already indicated, will occupy us after we have considered the diagram itself and its implications.

1. Comparison diagram according to nine criteria.

See Foldout.

2. Commentary on Comparison Table

The first comment is with regard to the titles of the various models. With the exception of the third, that based on the 'Learning for Life' syllabus, it seems generally noticeable that the models are all viewed from the nature of the main activity of the teachers, rather than from that of the pupils. This is not to affirm that all the models are 'teacher-dominated' or any such term; it is simply to make the observation that there is a strong

165

sense of authoritative transmission when religious education is mentioned. Is this simply a relic of the authoritative aspects of the 'teaching that' model, something intrinsic to the nature of the transmission of religious belief, or something which underlines religion as dealing with matters of ultimate concern and consequently, requiring the greatest care and responsibility from those concerned with it?

(a) *Aim:*

There seem to be three categories under this heading. The 'education of the faith' model, in using the verb "to develop" stresses a continuity which may be stronger or weaker in different circumstances. Implicitly it includes preparation for specifically religious actions such as the reception of the sacraments of Penance, Eucharist and Confirmation during school years, so that its emphasis is not simply one of increased knowledge, but also of invitation to participation more fully in the life of the church. In a Roman Catholic sense of the words, the terms denoting 'grace'—sanctifying and actual—will be used to speak of the benefits of the reception of these sacraments in proper dispositions, and of the means whereby particular difficulties may be countered with a Christian response. There will also be use of the term 'the Faith' as the description of the corpus of doctrinal and moral beliefs which has to be learned and practised.

This latter aspect will receive most of the emphasis of the second model, the 'teaching that', although one might observe that there is a marked and worthwhile distinction between regarding morality as consequent upon one's deep realization of the dignity of being a Christian (which is ideally the way in which morality is viewed in the first model), and that which sees morality primarily as obedience to a set of moral precepts promulgated by Christianity on the basis of Mosaic and natural law.

The London and Lancaster models implicitly envisage the possibility of faith as a point of attainment from the kind of approach they commend. But in themselves they simply provide the approach and the experience which may result in such a step. It is certainly difficult to envisage any more human preparation which could be undertaken, if the aims of 'responsible decisions' and 'awareness' and 'understanding' have been achieved; but, of course, under the circumstances of the county or state school in the pluralist society, anything further will have to be as a result of the decisions of the individual pupils themselves.

The fifth approach,* which has been discussed in the previous chapter, is by its approach limited to the factual, so that the question of faith does not arise.

(b) *Content*

As the question of the content of catechesis has been treated explicitly

---

*i.e. the "teaching about" model.

	MODERN CATECHESIS	TRADITIONAL AGREED SYLLABUS (post 1944 Butler Act in U.K.)	"LEARNING FOR LIFE" (1968)
	"The education of (the) faith"	"teaching that"	"education in"
Aim	To develop the faith received in Baptism at the various stages of life.	Instruction in common elements of Christianity of those who are or are presumed to be Christians; to provide the basis for a moral code.	Development of adults who will continue to reflect seriously on the fundamental problems of human existence and to arrive at the decisions life calls for responsibly.
Content	The word of God received through various ways: Bible, Liturgy, doctrinal teaching and the witness of Christians, under the guidance of the teaching Church.	Instruction in the Christian religion especially through the Bible as the main source of Christian truths and morality. Statutory act of worship.	Reasoned teaching of Christian doctrine and explanation of its beliefs. The Bible as the sacred book of the Christian Church. Other religions.
Role of Teacher/ Catechist	A fellow believer entrusted with a mission in the Church; fidelity to God and fidelity to man in the instruction of others.	To teach a world-view in which God is acknowledged as Creator by all 'sensible' people, and the source of moral commands; avoidance of any controversial topics.	To consider the needs of his class and to work out in the spirit of the syllabus and with its help, schemes of work which will most benefit his pupils.
Role of Participants	A dialogue of faith in which the revelation of God is understood, deepened and applied through the recognition of an ongoing revelation through the events of life.	All are presumed to be Christians or if not, should be so. Doctrinal and moral ideas are largely accepted through the Bible and the teacher's authority as a representative of the Christian church.	Enquiry is genuine, search for greater understanding is always present, a coming together of minds and a pooling of thoughts and evidence is always desired. School worship—religious and moral purpose as act of community.
Guiding Principles	Faith is to be developed in relation to life-situations i.e. the education required is the human preparation for accepting and living according to one's faith and the Faith of the Church.	Knowledge and understanding of the obligations of the Christian life to be learned through the reading and study of the Bible; the Christian life explicitly and implicitly commended.	Religion considered in light of current religious beliefs and attitudes in this country in relation to many cultures represented by pupils of immigrants.
Method	According to age and capacity of those involved; some didactic teaching, discovery methods, discussion, etc. With adolescents, much open-ended discussion. Camps, etc.	Didactic teaching generally in formal class setting. Variety in Biblical teaching according to age groups and preparation for exams. Bible also for its cultural and literary value.	Experiments, e.g. integrated studies welcomed. Atmosphere of school, integrity, tolerance and honesty in presentation of controversial topics. Witness of actions as well as words; Expertise of teachers.
Human Development	Faith in God is developed through faith in the human other. Human development is important in itself and as a means of being more open to catechesis.	Knowledge of the Bible and life lived according to its spirit develops man as he should be as creature made in God's likeness. Bible has important cultural and literary value.	Concerned with the whole person and it involves helping children grow into mature and responsible people. Religious understanding indispensable in development of a mature and complete adult.
Language	Education of (the) faith is not tied in an exclusive fashion to theological expressions, nor to oral and written formulae. Whatever means will ensure better communication are accepted: audio-visual, symbol, etc. Faith will have certain traditional expressions but understanding is more important than mechanical use.	Special terms of Bible and of religion in general are encouraged as sign of knowledge and understanding.	At every stage in children's mental development teachers must ask what are the religious ideas that they can grasp, and what language can become meaningful to them.
Achievement	Growth in faith leading to further knowledge and love of God, Ratification of personal faith as a life-task.	Adherence to a religious way of life and formal church attendance as the only solid basis for living.	To help pupils to understand the principles upon which actions are based, and the need to weigh up circumstances, not only to arrive at right decisions, but also to develop the strength of character to do what they know is right.

NEUTRALITY APPROACH

"teaching how"

"teaching about"

ss of religious issues; awareness of
ribution of religion to human cul·
e capacity to understand beliefs.
ctices; challenge of religious belief
consequences.

An objective appraisal of what religion
involves by attention to knowledge and
understanding from factual and descriptive
approaches.

ional search for meaning and the
study of the phenomena of re-
The importance of six dimensions
on.

World religions, comparative religions; the
Bible as a literary and cultural source; beliefs described factually.

zue with experience and a dialogue
g religions, with mutual interpreta-
reinforcement. No exclusion of a
d approach which is open.

To present matters with objectivity; to
avoid any semblance of indoctrination. Resource leader with group but uncommitted
(i.e. in any obvious way).

experience of the faith of in-
and groups by use of the tools
irship. Needs, interests and abili-
upils as basis for attaining worth-
ucational objectives in this field.
worship.

Understanding and appreciation of religious
heritage and of what religion means to its
adherents. Objective study and discussion
of issues which originate in religion. No
acts of worship.

ly of religion must transcend the
informative. The promotion of
iding in this area by educational
nd complete respect for freedom
s.

Religion as part of life's significance for
many; an objective appraisal; in a non-
confessional way and without any supposition of need for commitment.

related to psychological capacity
, social, problems encountered, and
f subject matter and types of learned to it. Different starting points
i dimensions of religion.

Any means of presentation which respects
the guiding principles above: films, and
audio-visual material greatly favoured as
leaving the teacher neutral.

en understanding and to develop
skills rather than to provide in-
i. Implicit and explicit aspects of
necessary for full human develop-

Religion as a cultural force in history of
mankind. Some attention to importance of
experience in religious history, e.g. great
religious leaders.

ppropriate stages, pupils should be
d to the methods of inquiry and
uage and thought forms that are
inquiry and criticism of religious
In the study of religion and the
is of religion they will naturally
d use the appropriate terminology
uage but this is simply as part of
pline of the subject itself.

Explanation of religious terminology,
Biblical terms and so on, from an objective
position i.e. from rational inspection and
definition.

pupils insight and understanding
istianity and the religious attitude
commitment must be left to their
choice.

Knowledge and some factual understanding
of the main religious traditions to be encountered in a pluralist society.

in Chapter 4 as well as in other sections, it suffices here to note that the four sources on which it relies principally, have a wider connotation than the classroom although they may all be found in their various aspects of Roman Catholic living there as well. The 'teaching that' model presumes on the faith of those involved but in a less comprehensive way, so that there are obvious difficulties especially with a narrow Biblical approach of a fundamentalist kind to middle and upper school pupils. There are similar difficulties inherent in the statutory act of worship, because of the practical difficulties consequent on presuming on a united and believing community without any basis except the authority of the school.

The remaining three models stress objectivity without presuming on the faith of those involved. The Lancaster scheme envisages something much more than an "outside looking-in" position, however, by stressing the investigation of religion in terms of its six dimensions, thereby involving not simply a cognitive or intellectual appraisal, but also wider forms of understanding resulting from personal experience, vicarious experience and the testimony and witness of believers.

(c) *Role of Teacher/Catechist*

The use of the term teacher/catechist is intended to cater both for the fact that over the range of these five models, not all teachers are 'catechists', whereas in the Roman Catholic school most catechists are also teachers. Three points should be noticed:

i — As we have indicated throughout this work, the fundamental assumption is that catechesis can only take place where believer speaks with fellow believers. This is of such importance that we shall note it here in order to return to the point in much more detail in the next main section.

ii — The position of the teacher in the fifth model has already been treated in the previous chapter, so that nothing needs to be added here.

iii — As so much of the quality of teaching is considered to be built around the quality of personal relationships, it is probably true that in the third and fourth models, the personal faith of the teacher will be one of the strongest influences on his pupils. The inclusion of the 'committed but open' approach of the Lancaster model is particularly realistic in this regard when it is considered how much 'non-specialist' teaching of religion takes place precisely because of the personal willingness of a teacher to do what will otherwise be not done or perhaps badly done. The force of personal commitment is obviously strong but quite different from the situation in the second model, where there is some danger of the manner of approach actually being in conflict with the ideals because of the

167

remoteness of the authoritarian teacher and his tendency to rely on 'do as I say' rather than imply 'do as I do.'

(d) *Role of Participants*

This aspect is so closely related to the preceding one that each model is obviously influenced by this inter-relation. As regards catechesis, the dialogue of faith can only exist where the teacher is a believer, something which, as noted already, must occupy us as a separate question, because of the common presumption that the pupils also are all believers. Attention should also be directed to the equally important aspect of the dialogue that takes place between pupil and pupil, as well as to the wider question as to what constitutes a faith community.

Of the other models, the London and Lancaster models posit ideals similar to that of the 'teaching about' but there is broader scope in the other models, both by their provision for worship together as a community, as well as their attempts to rely on a more open inquiry than seemed possible in our discussion of the 'neutrality' approach. Both the London and Lancaster models provide for the use of many different techniques to involve the participation of the group. The Lancaster suggestion of 'empathic experience of the faith of individuals and groups' is of marked educational importance. In practice, it comes close to the strength of the catechesis model precisely because it can put in front of pupils, people who are themselves witnesses to the value of their own religious traditions, a much more important experience of incarnated ideas and ideals, than their objective appraisal in the fifth model.

The assumptions of the traditional model (as with the approach of the traditional catechetical model inspected in Chapter 4) are such that experience shows that unless such ideas are supported by the home and family, this kind of authoritative approach has little chance of leading towards personal faith as distinct from the social experience of faith. The very presumption of faith with many adolescent pupils in these circumstances, seems sufficient to alienate them.

(e) *Guiding principles*

Each of the models naturally shows a close link between its aim and its guiding principles. As regards catechesis, the key word which deserves attention is that of the use of 'education' in the expression 'the education of the faith', for it includes both an ideal and the means towards attaining that ideal i.e. the faith is to be developed according to the human capacity of the recipient to accept it personally and act with it. Centred on life-situations, this means that it is the reverse of the various "filling up" models discussed in Chapter 2.

If the catechesis model shows up the inadequacies of the traditional, so too the Lancaster, in insisting that 'the study of religion must transcend

168

the merely informative',[7] shows a much deeper appreciation of the significance of religion than either the third or the fifth models. Moreover, in
imposing its own restraints and respecting the freedom of pupils, it fosters
the kind of human development proposed by the ideal of the first model.

(f) *Method*

What the diagram shows is that with the exception of the reliance of
the traditional model on an authoritative approach, there is very little
difference between the various models. The increase of the use of
discussion methods has been a most important change in this regard,
although this supposes that there are many different kinds of discussion
techniques. In particular, there has been much attention in recent years
to the informality of the 'camp', the 'week-end', the whole variety of
informal situations some of which were noted in the Babin article, in the
schema of Chapter 2 or in the discussion of the Constitution on the
Liturgy in Chapter 3.

Two important developments in the whole field of method should be
noted. The use of integrated studies and humanities projects has already
been the subject of a working paper and a number of articles, and more
recently, a book. These are important developments in curriculum but, as
with the study of comparative religion, one cannot but point out that such
studies require a considerable maturity in the students before their real
value can be perceived. Synthesis, after all, is the result of mature
appraisal, and should come after some acquaintance with separate
elements. Does integrated studies, in particular, run the risk of reversing
what is a basic learning sequence?

(g) *Human development*

All of the models are concerned with this. Ideally speaking, the
catechesis model proposes a most lofty ideal which, with its faith assumptions, can presume to go much farther than even the highest ideals of the
third and fourth models, because of the unity between its view of man and
its specific task. As the previous chapters have shown, such an ideal
depends very much on the kind of incarnational theology and its related
movements, traced earlier. It is important to note for this reason (as
shown already in Chapter 4) that in thus attempting to steer a clear course
between transcendence and immanence while losing sight of neither, such
a model is not necessarily acceptable to traditionalist groups in the Roman
Catholic church. As the pre-catechesis discussions of earlier chapters and
the appendix have reminded us, there is an important line to be observed
here between what are ends in themselves and what are only means.

The actual way in which the catechesis ideal may be realised is
clearly indicated in the emphasis of the third and fourth models on

---

7. Schools Council Working Paper 36, op. cit., p. 38.

169

cognitive skills and understanding, as well as on the clear assumption of religious development, not as an 'extra', but as an integral part of human development.

The second model may begin with similar assumptions about the nature of man and the way he is to achieve his destiny, but this approach is traditionally suspicious of the value of the human. As with the fifth model, the second remains at some remove from the more central position occupied by the human in the other models.

As has been indicated earlier, there are wider theological considerations here especially those concerned with revelation and the role of the church.

(h) *Language*

There is a common assumption in each of the models that the actual language used in religious education is entitled to its uniqueness to the extent that it describes concepts and ideas which are peculiar to it. If the expression of the catechesis model is more lengthy, it is to emphasise the great importance of freedom from technicalities for their own sake. The reduction of the traditional catechism model in Chapter 2 has already indicated the generally unsatisfactory aspects of exact formulae, memorised and recapitulated at will, as the standard of orthodoxy. This does not deny the importance of the exact expression of exact concepts, nor the importance of clear expression of beliefs, but sees the understanding and practice of religious beliefs as only peripherally served by over-attention to language outside of the knowledge and experience of pupils. In all of this, there is, of course, an obvious gradation in relation to the growing ability of pupils to express themselves and to understand more abstract terminology, but it is presumed that the first emphasis is on understanding. Moreover, in an age in which the young are growing up (even in underdeveloped countries in many cases) with most of their information and entertainment received through visual media, the presence of religion in the audio-visual sphere is of the greatest importance.

The challenge of language and its relevance is only part of the broader educational challenge in models 3 and 4, with their close attention to the very different needs of different age groups.

What is at stake here is the important issue, as seen by many of the more articulate young, that modern Christianity speaks of one reality, not of a kind of division into sacred and secular. This does not do away with the necessity of a special language and terminology for those special aspects of reality with which religion is concerned, but rather emphasises the necessity to be able to express these concepts in language found 'meaningful' to the man of to-day. We should not overlook in all this the importance of symbols, particularly in aspects of sacramental life and worship or its equivalent in other traditions.

170

(i) *Achievements*

Positing the ideal in each case, the achievements of each model are closely related to all the points already made. What is common to them all, however, is that in the final resort, the degree of acceptance and personal commitment must come from the individual pupil himself. Such a viewpoint sees religious education as having its own terminal stages, but the relationship between chronological and personal factors of self-commitment can only be one of likelihood, not certainty.

3. Are the concepts separable?

The foregoing analysis leaves us in no doubt that the concepts of religious education and of catechesis are clearly separable. But we must ask whether the nature of the separation is any different from the separation already made between each of the models of religious education already considered. In other words, is catechesis only a special model of religious education? There seem to be two points to be made here:

1 — Catechesis belongs to the general category of activities which we call loosely, religious education, but, as Gabriel Moran points out, this is not to be equated with the whole of Christian life of which it is only one part.

"To say that the aim of catechizing is 'encounter with Christ,' 'total commitment,' 'formation of the whole man' or a variety of other formulas, sounds very impressive but it confuses the whole of Christianity with the limited functions of religious education. In practice, this seems bound to result in one of two things. On the one hand this leads to the denial that understanding is a legitimate end in itself, an end for which teaching is peculiarly suited and for which schools exist ... The other alternative is that the schools and teachers really set about doing these things, namely to *make* Christians, to *form* students' freedom, to *enable* students to encounter Jesus. On the surface, these schools would appear to have considerable success, but their long-term results would be the most disastrous of all."[8]

2 — But the difference between catechesis and the other models considered here is more than one of *degree;* it is a difference of *kind.* The other models of religious education in a pluralist society, as has been noted in the preliminary remarks, are specific means devised to cope with the realities imposed by that society. In other words, they are not in a position to decide the issue from first principles but only from the particular situation which they must serve. What is intended—but not necessarily attained by each of these models—is mainly a form of cognitive

---

8. Gabriel Moran, **God Still Speaks**, Burns and Oates, London, 1967, p. 77.

and intellectual approach, which, as distinct from indoctrination or conditioning, leaves the individual not only free to choose but also informed about the area in which he may choose. The next step is faith—but on this there must not be any presumption.

Now, all of this is important in itself and in what it safeguards as we have already noted, but it is of a different order from catechesis. The model of 'the education of the faith' posits both education and faith, and it does so as part of a process in which the interaction of education and faith is all part of the one reality. Eventually, its invitation is to the confirmation and personal ratification of faith which transcends logic and knowledge, but which must have these as its platform if it is to be as fully informed as the measure of human development requires it to be. It could not be satisfied simply with the ideal achievement of the other models of religious education; it must transcend them.

But in discussing this faith as set out in the comparison table and in the more detailed comments above, we must stress that there is a world of difference between the ideal and the actual in this regard. The starting point of catechesis still describes only a more or less justifiable assumption, a potential to be developed. In which case, we may ask whether or not the catechetical model so analysed in Chapter 2 or the traditional model of our recent comparison, did not begin from the same assumption? This requires us to look at the 'actual' as compared with the 'ideal'.

4. The assumption of faith in catechesis.

As has already been indicated in the discussion of the role of the teacher in (c) above, the fundamental assumption of catechesis is that it is an activity which takes place when believers, with fellow believers, deepen their personal faith by their common dialogue, activity, and worship as members of the church. That this is the core of catechesis has been clearly pointed to throughout this work.

But the question which must be faced now may be expressed thus: May this common faith be judged to be present in every educational situation which comes within the concept of 'the education of the faith?'[9]

Let us first emphasise that we are concerned principally with the *de facto* situations of much school catechesis as distinct from catechesis in a completely free situation i.e. where attendance is up to the pupils themselves. In the magisterial model based on the catechism, it is obvious that such an assumption was made, and as the analysis of the model in

---

9. It is important to note that the whole distinction we have made throughout between personal faith and its corporate expression, is implied by the French expression *l'éducation de la foi* which may mean 'the education of the faith' or simply 'education of faith.'

Chapters 1 and 2 has shown, in circumstances where it was supported by the traditions of a small and rather separate community, faith could be assumed, at least in its external forms and practices. In other words, the faith assumption was often inseparable from sociological factors, and it would be fair to say that sometimes it came closer to the notion of "the Faith" rather than to the growth and development of personal faith, always keeping in mind that from our position, it is virtually impossible to separate the two.

Two of the articles examined in Chapter 4, those of Babin in particular and of Colomb in more general terms, pointed to the great difficulties associated with the catechesis of 14–16 year olds. From Babin's analysis and suggested remedies,[10] we might consider his suggestion that in addition to the 'fallow period' postulated by many as necessary after the intensive instruction preceding *La Profession de La Foi,* there were the important reasons stemming from the failure in communication, the poor image of the church with the young, and the loss of personal confidence experienced by teachers when confronted with the hostility and diffidence of the young. If we accept these reasons—and experience suggests that they are not limited to the French situation—the question must be asked whether this is the kind of situation in which the 'education of the faith' takes place, or is expected to? Or, expressed differently, can faith be assumed in such a situation? The following points reflect on some answers to this question.

1 — At a fundamental level, if we accept Babin's 'cultural development' (which is to be in no way directly connected with catechesis), as a necessary prelude before we can engage with the adolescent in his 'quest for faith' then we cannot begin with an assumption of faith! Babin himself expressly rules out the idea of this 'cultural development' as a kind of 'bait' for catechesis, a point we have noted previously in considering pre-catechesis. Obviously, a successful cultural development period may help the young person to attain a greater objectivity which enables him to separate his growing up problems from specific problems associated with personal faith or adherence to the faith and practices of the church. In this sense, it might be thought that there is a general understanding of faith which is played down until the kind of distinction just made can be perceived by the individual.

2 — If one can assume faith, on what is such an assumption based? In principle, four reasons might be thought to justify this assumption in the case of the Roman Catholic school:

a — the specific aim of the school which led to its foundation and financial support by the Roman Catholic community as a place where the Catholic faith would be learned;

---

10. cf. discussion of Babin's ideas in Chapter 4.

b — the explicit transfer of the parental mandate to have their children so instructed by the school;

c — the presence of a staff, themselves Roman Catholics, who undertake to share in the catechetical work of the school.

d — the fact that the students themselves are all baptized Roman Catholics, who have (via their parents presumably) chosen to attend this school.

Even if one accepts the first two of these reasons (and some schools in which there is a shortage of places realistically require parents enrolling children to bring a certificate from their parish priest to prove they are known as 'practising'), the third point would certainly seem to raise serious practical difficulties over the criteria used to make such a judgement. In other words, in practical terms, a teacher in such a school may be nominally a Catholic by birth, training and so on, but as to whether or not he actually has a strong personal faith or chooses to make others aware of it in catechetical work, are all different questions which will receive different answers in very different situations.*

But, all of this aside, it is the last assumption which is our main concern viz. that there is a community of faith because all present are baptized Roman Catholics. It may be true to say that there is an unexpressed consensus as regards 'the Faith' but this is different from the personal faith of the individuals in the group, for the following reasons:

i — The study of religion is a compulsory aspect of the school's life and while there are schools which offer options, particularly in the upper forms, these are choices within the overall obligation to attend. This is obviously a different situation from the out of school situation where attendance is voluntary. Our point here is not so much to raise the question of the school's jurisdiction in what it makes compulsory and what voluntary, but rather to point out that the first condition for a community of faith would seem to be the voluntary association of the members.

ii — Although possessing the technical qualifications of the *habitus fidei* received in Baptism, the adolescent may, in reality, not be a practising member of the church if one applies the usually taken criteria of regular attendance at Mass and the Sacraments. This is not the same thing as being an unbeliever; perhaps we might describe his position as being that of 'uncommitted' or 'suspended belief'. Such a position may well be made explicit by the adolescent in his attitude or formal affirmations of his position, in the compulsory catechetical situation. May the teacher then proceed as though he has a community of faith as the model requires? If he does, it is hard to

---

*The point is made in view of the decreased numbers of men and women of religious orders taking responsibility for this work.

see that the relationship of the teacher to the group and of the members to one another, is a truthful one.

Does the teacher then accept the situation as one of simply rational inspection thereby changing the status of the model to one of the others considered in the comparison? But to move to this form of merely rational appraisal is a betrayed of that dual fidelity to God and man and his acceptance of a mission in the church, for the whole content of faith is such that it transcends human knowledge and logical certainty, and proceeds by a decisive action which goes beyond these, the act of faith.

This very practical dilemma needs to be related to the specific circumstances in which it occurs, but the following general directions seem to be justified in retaining the 'faith context':

1 — 'Faith according to the mode of the recipient' must be always dependent on the degree of receptivity of the subject. If the adolescent has not yet been able to personalise his faith, i.e. separate it from the idea of obedience to something imposed from without, this is, perhaps, another way of saying that he has not yet made the major transition towards the personal acceptance and responsibility (autonomy?) which are ideally the characteristics of the adult. From a psychological viewpoint the role-playing and acting out which usually occur in the peer-group interaction, are the necessary stages of human development. A more mature faith may be achieved only by the separation from the childhood situations which are either habitual or even socially conditioned in a mild way. Of course, it may be too neat and categorical to treat adolescents in this either/ or way. The fact is that they are simply adolescents, and this is sufficient description: they are at an important stage of *becoming* rather than at a final one of attainment.

2 — Faith as a personal ratification of one's baptismal promises may well be regarded as *progressive* i.e. not based on dramatic decision but on a continuing fidelity and at the same time, *terminal,* only in the sense that certain stages of development are achieved. Hence the emphasis of writers such as Babin and Moran on the importance of an adult-centred catechesis because the personal development attained by the recipients and their adult status, makes the assumption demanded by the model of 'the education of the faith' possible in a way which can only be remotely approached by the 'education in' and the 'teaching how' models.

3 — The opportunities for progressive affirmations of faith (not in any dramatic way but in small ways) may arise naturally in the less formal situations of 'cultural development' and 'week-end camps' and so on, by the provision of opportunities which are left as free as possible. This does not excuse the catechist from extending both personal and group invitations e.g. to liturgical celebration and so

175

on. After all, the invitation to faith comes from a human being who is quite clear in his own balanced approach that any invitation admits the possibility of being refused.

4 — The 'open' approaches of the London and Lancaster models may well be ideal ways of conducting the 'quest for faith' of which Babin speaks, because (a) they presume the minimum degree of obligation on the pupils while at the same time respect the official mandate of the Christian school discussed in Chapter 5 and (b) they underline the progressive stages in this direction as dependent in the last resort on the participants themselves.

5. Some implications for catechesis

The preceding discussion seems to have indicated that if, in practical terms, too easy an assumption of a common faith may leave the catechesis 'dialogue' at the social level of 'the Faith' with the consequent danger of rejection at a later age, it is no solution at all and indeed a betrayal of his position by the catechist, to make no attempt to discover or arouse the personal faith of those baptized. This means that we may trace four general principles which should be applied if the distinct contribution of catechesis is to be availed of to the greatest extent.

1 — Even where an explicit common faith may not be readily assumed, the presence and attitude of the believing teacher, his attention to an approach of 'cultural development' which may later become a 'quest for faith' can still provide the opportunity and the Christian presence which may help towards creating the possibility for an act of faith. As indicated in the discussion above, such an attitude expresses a constant invitation, a possible basis of a temporary unity in the provision of circumstances which make the likelihood of further acts of personal faith more likely to be achieved.

2 — Such an attitude demands of the teacher/catechist an understanding of his own faith and a responsibility for others which is not discharged simply by providing information, indoctrinating, or so occupying or entertaining pupils that the level of the relationship remains at the objective level. Of course, activities may be the necessary basis for a confident, faith relationship. In practical terms, for example, the undoubted advantages of a syllabus such as the Joint Matriculation Board Revised Syllabus in Religious Studies,[11] with its breadth and ecumenical balance, would not of itself, satisfy the demands of catechesis at this level, unless the teacher takes a responsible view of his duties to treat controversial matters at some point from a specifically Roman Catholic view. This is not the

---

11. Joint Matriculation Board Syllabus for Religious Studies (Advanced). Specimen Questions May, 1972, SQ/RS 74 A.

same thing as treating them from *only* such a view. But the demands of 'the education of the faith' model require attention to both words, education and faith.

3 — As already indicated, open discussion and attention to the broad sense of education does not mean starting from an assumed neutral position. There can be objective appraisal of a document, for example, the Papal encyclical on Birth Control *Humanae Vitae*,[12] but the teacher qua teacher and the practising Catholic are not necessarily placed in conflicting roles. A teacher worthy of the name asks for informed discussion on the basis of knowledge and information, not on uninformed opinion, but premature declarations of 'orthodoxy' or 'heresy' must not be used in any argument stopping way which pre-empts the whole question to one of obedience rather than faith. There is, indeed, an obedience of faith but it follows such an inquiry; otherwise, it has no meaning in ordinary human terms. In other words, the question of open inquiry may eventually lead to the necessity for a statement of what the Roman Catholic church holds as regards the topic. But such an invocation of the teaching authority, or *magisterium,* of the church should not be invoked from outside the experience of the group, simply as authority; it must rather be welcomed as the statement of the beliefs which are shared by this faith community as part of its wider communion with Christ and the church. Faith, indeed, but faith buttressed and supported by inquiry and knowledge before the questions of 'the Faith' and loyalty and obedience are invoked. Otherwise, it seems to be unavoidable that what is 'rejected' or simply not accepted by the pupil, may well be not so much a question of loss or denial of faith as rather one of lack of understanding.

4 — The catechetical relationship, as the 'teaching how' model stresses of itself, must also transcend the informative. From the point of view of the catechist, it is important to stress that pastoral aspect of the relationship, which, although part of the ideal teaching relationship, has particular significance in catechesis. There are important things to be shared together on an equal footing: the word of God read and discussed, inter-personal relationships and their effects, participation as equals in worship, the moral quality of lives lived out as a positive affirmation of what it is to be God's pilgrim people, redeemed in Christ. If catechesis does not necessarily attain this ideal, it is at least an ideal which must be postulated.

---

12. This document is cited because of the unprecedented public discussion by Roman Catholics which it occasioned.

PART THREE

Chapter Seven

SOME PERSPECTIVES TOWARDS THE FUTURE

INTRODUCTION

It has been fundamental to this work that changes in language are an indication of a changed way of viewing reality. Such a change in Roman Catholic writing on the teaching of religion can be seen in the widespread adoption in English of the term 'religious education' for what has been traditionally known under various names (as noted in Chapter 2), such as Christian Doctrine, Christian Knowledge or Religious Knowledge, Divinity, Catechism and Catechetics. Where the term 're-ligious education' occurs in 19th century Papal statements or in the re-ports of regional conferences of bishops at the time of the Public Education Acts in the English-speaking world, it is easy to see that in context, it refers either to the more general term 'Christian education' or to the idea of 'religious instruction' along the lines of that historical model referred to and inspected in Chapters 1 and 2. But increasingly since the end of World War 2, the term 'religious education' has been adopted for those situations which were usually described under the general umbrella of the English derivatives of 'catechesis.'

What this seems to indicate is that teachers sensitive to the climate of their religion classes in schools have increasingly found it difficult to continue to make that assumption of faith which has been signalised as the basis for catechesis. Why they should have felt this has been sug-gested in previous discussions, especially Chapter 4 (2. a & e) and Chapter 6 (4). It should be recognised that the failure or unwillingness to make this assumption of faith with pupils may equally be the result of the weakness of faith of the teacher/catechist himself, but this is not the situation being noted here. Rather, we are concerned with those teachers who have responded to the reality of the situation they have found in their classes viz. that too easy an assumption of a faith-context with many pupils in secondary schools is false to the reality of the situation that teachers and pupils know. Hence, there has arisen an emphasis on the importance of preparing the human recipient of the *habitus fidei* in Baptism for that human development which might make the personal act of faith or that progressive commitment to faith more likely. In Australia, this same note has been sounded by the attention to what have become known as programmes of Christian Living, especi-ally in the middle and upper forms of the secondary school. Such programmes, as well as texts written with this attention e.g. the 'Come Alive' series in Australia, have often been attacked as indicating an

178

abdication of the responsibility of the catechist to spread the Christian message. But the authors and teachers of such programmes have often been aware, instinctively perhaps rather than consciously, of that basic separation between catechesis and religious education which has been argued throughout this book. Much of their activity has been based on a first-hand acquaintance with, and an awareness of, the reality of their situation, so that they have worked at what we might call building 'platforms towards faith', i.e. preparing the human recipient for the actualization of his potential for faith. In this sense, education in religion itself may well provide the platform or occasion for the explicitly catechetical, but the fine balancing point is attained only through respect for the equilibrium expressed in Colomb's "Fidelity to God; fidelity to man."

The complementary aspect of this movement in the English county schools is indicated in the clearer recognition by the Durham Report that the task of the school is 'religious education' rather than 'religious instruction' as laid down by the 1944 Butler Act. As is usual, such an 'official' recognition, follows rather than precedes the practice of good teachers who had been moving in that direction, as the breadth and understanding of the models based on the 1968 "Learning for Life" Inner London Education Authority programmes and the Lancaster University scheme of 1971 clearly indicates. What is important about this direction is that teachers were dissatisfied with approaches which, because of the restriction of an Agreed Syllabus, often resulted in an exaggerated or functional Biblicism without trying to speak to the potential faith of the hearers. A commitment to, or an assumption of, faith in the situation of the county school could not be presumed because of the restrictions of the pluralist society, but this did not mean that there should not be a better human preparation, which, through the educational engagement of both teacher and pupils, could lead the individual under the grace of God, towards the possibility of some kind of faith-commitment.

Now, to look more closely at what seem to be complementary movements, this chapter looks first at an extended comparison between the catechetical model of "the education of (the) faith' in comparison with the principles of the "teaching *how*" model already looked at in the comparison diagram of Chapter 6, as set out in Working Paper No. 36 of the Schools Council.[1] In so doing, it indicates a number of possible 'platforms towards faith' provided by the possibility of 'religious education' in an educational context. The concluding part of the chapter and of this book raises a number of important questions which should be the serious concern of all those interested in religious education.

---

1. Schools Council Working Paper No. 36, **Religious Education in Secondary School**, Evans/Methuen Educational, London, 1971.

1. Some lines of convergence between catechesis and the principles of Working Paper No. 36.

It is important to specify the nature of the comparison attempted in this section. It is not an evaluation of Working Paper 36 "Religious education in secondary schools" in terms of the project with which it was concerned, nor an appraisal of the project from the viewpoint of the Roman Catholic schools involved in the project as such, but rather a theoretical consideration of some possible relationships between the concept of catechesis viewed as 'the education of (the) faith' and the assumptions and working details of the Lancaster project. The comparison will occupy us from four main aspects of the Working Paper:

1 — The phenomenological approach.
2 — The study of other religions.
3 — The 'open-ended' approach.
4 — The role of the teacher/catechist.

1 — *The phenomenological approach.*

What is understood by the phenomenological approach has been already dealt with in essence in establishing the basis for the 'teaching how' model of the four models assembled at the end of Chapter 5. The working paper itself provides us with a convenient summary of what it calls the 'phenomenological' or 'undogmatic approach,' in the sense in which the term is being used here:

"This sees the aim of religious education as the promotion of understanding. It uses the tools of scholarship in order to enter into an empathic experience of the faith of individuals and groups. It does not seek to promote any one religious viewpoint but it recognizes that the study of religion must transcend the merely informative."[2]

Perhaps the first question to be settled is whether or not there is a certain incompatibility between catechesis, either under the 'old' model of Chapter 2 or the one called 'education of faith' and the aims of this phenomenological approach which, as analysed by the Working Paper, is not 'confessional'. And catechesis, by its nature, is confessional.

A simple way out of the problem may be to suggest that catechesis is quite free to take any things which are acceptable, provided that they are not in any way contrary to Roman Catholic teaching, so that the relationship between catechesis and this approach, is basically one of selectivity: provided that the Roman Catholic position is safeguarded, anything may be used. Such an approach seems to lack real understanding, however, both of catechesis and the Lancaster approach. The key issue is undoubtedly the 'confessional' or 'faith' aspect, but what we wish to do here, is to see the degree of convergence between the approach

2. Working Paper 36, op. cit., p. 21.

stressing understanding, empathy and experience of religion viewed in a multi-dimensional fashion, and that of catechesis as at some stage culminating in a dialogue of believers. Our working hypothesis is that catechesis may logically crown the phenomenological approach which, by its nature, prepares for and remains open to faith.

The value of the phenomenological approach with secondary school pupils is that it does meet the challenge of trying to teach religion in an open fashion. From another viewpoint, it may be said to take the challenge of the pluralist society to indoctrination or to any privileged form of access, and to use what has tended to be regarded as a limitation, as a source of possible strength. In other words, it has avoided the weaknesses of the neutralist or objective position set out earlier, by defining its role as an educational role rather than as an instructional one. What this means in practice, however, is more far reaching than the simple substitution of one term for another. The question of teaching 'for commitment' or 'to produce believers' which we have noted in some of the 'neo-confessional' models is something outside of the phenomenological approach—that belongs to the decision of the individual. In this sense, the educational task in religion is similar to the educational task in other spheres, that is, something not concluded by the attainment of knowledge or the end of schooling, but rather something continued as a life task.

Now it is precisely in this regard that the catechesis model and the Working Paper model converge in at least a procedural manner, particularly if one considers the remarks made in Chapter 4 and Chapter 6 with regard to that 14-16 years of age attitude characterised earlier as one of 'uncommitted or suspended belief.' It was stressed by Babin that a formal "quest for faith" had eventually to be instituted by the initiative of the catechist after the period of cultural development, because it was only after this stage of human development that the adolescent was judged ready for this personal "quest for faith."[3]

The phenomenological approach happens to offer an excellent example of what Babin would accept at his stage of "cultural development" for:

a — it is open in its approach and begins from the realities to be encountered in everyday life; '

b — it involves those concerned in the realistic appreciation of religion as it is encountered in life: different churches, activities, social life, personal experiences, the experiences of others and so on;

c — in being 'empathic' and 'experiential' it invites the co-operation of the adolescent, confronts him with examples of committed

---

3. cf. discussion in Chapter 4 (a).

people who present ideals in a living form as it were, and shows doctrinal matters not as abstractions, but as ideals for living.

What is beneficial about this is its attention to the importance of offering the young person some comparative standards without necessarily requiring him to accept them himself i.e. there are at the least, cognitive gains. As so many studies of adolescents reveal, such an approach affords norms as well as points of discussion outside of the adolescent himself, and to this extent, provides criteria of self-evaluation which are thought to be so important as a standard of comparison, and an encouragement to personal action. As regards religion itself, it is impossible to range across the history of religion without encountering outstanding examples of people whose lives witnessed to their lofty conception of the importance of their beliefs as the principle for their personal actions, but at a stage when the characteristic uncertainty of adolescence expresses itself in diffidence, if not in non-conformity, the very examples of commitment encountered in this fashion, can be a powerful help towards maturity. Responsibility, after all, although it is probably learned only by being responsible, can be appraised vicariously.

How does all this refer to catechesis? In the explanation of the core of the model as personal faith, while stressing at the same time the dynamic and creative tension between the poles of immanence and transcendence, the value of human development for its own sake was also emphasised. Moreover, it was stressed in Chapter 6(4) that the assumption of a community of faith in the school situation was not necessarily justified, unless the four criteria listed were shown to be applicable* in the conditions. Hence, the emphasis was on the invitation to faith e.g. via the liturgy, by Christian witness and so on, but these were also to be regarded as the progressive acts which could become the direction of the faith of the subject, particularly through the sympathy, respect for the freedom of the pupil, and the committed approach of the teacher himself. In these senses, both approaches stop short of the expectation of faith in the subject, but both invite; respect for the liberty of the individual to respond, leaves the result to him.

Now, to such an approach with Roman Catholic children, may not the parents or the official representatives of the church reply that they entrust their children to the Roman Catholic school to have them taught their 'Catholic faith' and not to be confused by being given the impression that one religion is quite as good as the next, or that it is all a question of your own choice. Such an objection, similar to the Plowden Committee's "Children should not be confused by being taught to doubt before faith is established"[4] is an important warning for the catechist to

---

*i.e. applicable in more than a nominal or superficial sense.

4. *Children and Their Primary Schools*: **Report of the Central Advisory Council for Education** (England), H.M.S.O. 1967, Vol. 1, par. 572, p. 207.

heed, but it is not necessarily appropriate in the circumstances for the following reasons:

i—As the discussion has particular references to secondary schools, and indeed to the middle forms of such schools, it may be assumed that the pupils have already, for a certain number of years, been instructed and raised in the Catholic faith. Far from intending to create doubt in any way about this, the phenomenological approach appraises the religious pluralism of society in its religious and secular differences—something which is already there, and inevitably, at one stage or another, the subject of comparison and serious questioning as the adolescent perceives the role of his own church, is baffled by differing standards of morality, and sometimes wonders whether such differences are fundamental or simply accidental. This is no more than a necessary task of sociological adaptation to begin with; it will be done, no matter what the school does. The open approach of the Working Paper will do it so much better, particularly under the guidance of a sympathetic and committed teacher.

ii—Such an appraisal is, as we have seen, a particular aspect of that 'cultural development' which, we believe with Babin, must precede the 'quest for faith'. It should not remain as an alternative to faith, but as a phase of personal education which makes the human conditions for faith more likely, always conceding that the leap to faith requires something more than this human preparation viz. God's grace.

iii—In this appraisal of alternatives, as we have seen earlier, an important opportunity is provided for the adolescent because it helps him to understand and separate better the various social manifestations of faith—church, worship, belief—everything indeed contained in the idea of 'the Faith' as we have distinguished it so often in this work. With the grace of God and the prompting of the catechist, it is possible ideally at least, that the adolescent may perceive how his personal act of faith requires social expression and support through worship with his fellow believers, so that the separate concepts of 'the Faith' outside of himself becomes complemented by the personal decision from within.

iv—The choice is not between 'teaching the faith' in an authoritative way (as though this inevitably meant that it was successful, and that failure to live up to its requirements was the fault of the individual) and not teaching it at all, but rather between the authoritative approach and the one commended here which concentrates on the preparation of the human recipient for faith. What better preparation could be imagined than the following ideals of awareness:

183

"Of religious issues, implicit and explicit; of the contribution of religion to human culture; the capacity to understand beliefs; to understand practices; of the challenge of religious belief; of the practical consequences of religious belief."[5]

2 — *The study of other religions.*

The perspective adopted towards other religions from the recent traditional Catholic position has already been indicated in questions (c) and (d) of the final section of Chapter 4, simply to indicate the complexities and general principles involved in facing such questions. The view which has dominated much thinking in this area even in the first moves towards the study of other religions, has usually had a similar kind of position viz. they were to be appraised in terms of Christianity, and if we were more interested in them, of late, it was because of a certain functional necessity i.e. they were often the religions of immigrant groups in the community and we thought it necessary to learn something about them as part of our general tolerance and acceptance. Thus, for example, the "Suggestions for Religious Education" in the West Riding Agreed Syllabus of 1968 has a single page entitled "Jewish children and their religion" and another called "Immigrant Children and their Religion."[6] The first stresses that as "Jewish and Christian children are neighbours both in and out of school... It is important that each should understand the other..."[7] For the second instance "Children from immigrant homes need sympathetic understanding, and English children need to be helped to appreciate these different beliefs and ways of worship."[8] It is evident that the emphasis has become much more marked since then, as the Working Paper comments on the non-Christian religions and the religious needs of minority groups:

"For years many pupils have asked for an introduction to other religions, and every opinion poll that has provided an opening for this kind of comment has shown that a significant proportion of the general public would like to see religious education in schools broadened in this way. The arrival of non-Christian religious groups in Britain reinforces a case that has already been argued on educational grounds."[9]

Gabriel Moran writes of a similar feeling in the United States:

"Many young people who are taught the Christian religion will not accept it to-day. It is not so much that they reject it as they cannot understand it without comparing it to alternatives. There is a

5. Working Paper 36, op. cit., pp. 44-45.
6. *Suggestions for Religious Education*: **West Riding Agreed Syllabus**, County Council Education Department, 1969.
7. op. cit., p. 104.
8. ibid., p. 105.
9. Working Paper 36, op. cit., p. 61.

184

widespread demand for courses in religions other than Christianity. This demand is a simple and legitimate one springing from the desire to know, understand and appreciate other religious options before excluding them."[10]

As we have already noted in Chapter 5, Ninian Smart considers that "religious studies should provide a service in helping people to understand history and other cultures than our own. It can thus play a vital role in breaking the limits of European cultural tribalism." As regards content and method they "should emphasise the descriptive, historical side of religion, but need thereby to enter into dialogue with the parahistorical claims of religious and anti-religious outlooks."[11]

From the 'official' Roman Catholic viewpoint of Vatican II as we have already noted in chapter 3, such aims are commended enthusiastically; but at a very practical level, the kind of question which is often voiced in the staff rooms of a number of Roman Catholic secondary schools, is likely to have one or more of the following emphases:[12]

— If the claims of Roman Catholicism are true, and if it is a missionary religion, should we not be more interested in advancing its claims to be heard rather than confusing children with a wide range of apparent alternatives?

— As it is evident that some pupils do not practise their religion and are bored by lessons on it, the teaching of other religions either increases the boredom, or also encourages them to regard the whole thing as simply depending on your own viewpoint—in other words, it means that you increase doubt instead of offering them the certainly of our Faith.

— A study of other religions is beneficial mainly because it helps to point up the superior nature of the Christian religion over all others.

— A study of other Christian religions shows how the Roman Catholic religion is the one true religion and all others have broken away from it.

This is a matter of serious concern for the teacher/catechist as such 'objections' reflect concerns which, for all of their seeming narrowness of understanding if taken individually, underline that religion is a matter of ultimate concern, so that the faith is sometimes difficult to distinguish from a particular way of expressing it. But what are the particular relations between such a study and our model of catechesis?

---

10. Gabriel Moran, **Design for Religion**, p. 117.

11. Ninian Smart, **Secular Education and the Logic of Religion**, Faber Heslington Lectures, University of York, 1966, Faber and Faber, London, 1968, p. 106.

12. Such comments are typical of those made by teachers — and even more by parents — since some Roman Catholic schools have begun studies in World Religions and in Comparative Religion, as my experience in visiting schools during 1970-72 proved.

Four points need to be considered.

a — Viewing a number of churches in terms of their various common traditions as well as their significant differences, can be an important form of appraisal of the fragmentation of the Christian tradition. Besides providing some kind of description of the religious history of a region, the experience of religious pluralism at this stage helps the adolescent to understand the tradition in which he has been raised. It is sometimes a source of wonder to Roman Catholics of this age that important prayers e.g. the Apostles' Creed, the Nicene Creed, the *Gloria in excelsis* and so on, are part of a widely shared religious tradition. In a broader sense, the kind of teaching and pupil activity envisaged in some of the work-units pp. 50-51 of the Working Paper appear to offer important ideas on the study of themes which are found in most religious traditions, as for example, the following one on Enlightenment:

> "Enlightenment: how inspiration or guidance is said to come. For example, angels in Luke, dreams in Matthew, a voice from Heaven at the baptism and temptation of Jesus and the conversion of Paul, a voice from the burning bush to Moses, a voice in the Temple to Isaiah, the Quaker 'inner light', advice of experts or friends, common sense, etc. Enlightenment in Hinduism, Buddhism, Taoism, etc. i.e. investigation of the experiential dimension of religion, discovering a further form of language used by religion—symbolism, sampling the doctrinal element of Eastern religions, etc."[13]

b — Such an approach has its own value for ecumenism, even if it is only at first in a descriptive fashion. Much ecumenism is taking place at levels of acceptance and sharing e.g. the experience of Easter at Taizé, while at the more scholarly level, there are important documents such as the recent Anglican Roman Catholic joint statements on Eucharist and on Ministry. Ecumenism seems to come more naturally, certainly more spontaneously and enthusiastically, with many of the young people who do not have the same long-standing prejudices of the past to overcome.

c — Gabriel Moran, whose "Design for Religion" was sub-titled "Toward Ecumenical Education" saw the term 'ecumenism' as having two distinct meanings viz. the study of the religions of one mankind in which Christianity should not be automatically given a normative role, and secondly, "Ecumenical education is one concerned with the world man lives in. To write about ecumenical education is to write about all education or to advocate a particular way of carrying out all education."[14]

---

13. Working Paper, 36, op. cit., p. 51.
14. Gabriel Moran, **Design for Religion**, op. cit., p. 27.

At first sight, this concept seems closer to the Lancaster scheme than it is to the idea of catechesis we have advocated, but in view of Moran's thesis in this book (which is basically that surveyed in the summary of "Catechetics R.I.P.")[15] the two directions are not so different after all. Perhaps, it would be true to say that it is only the catechist who is not concerned with the limitations imposed by the nature of the county school, who can take in this broader vision of which Moran speaks, because he can appreciate the nature and never ending character of the 'quest for faith'

d — The point is clearer when we consider a later statement of Moran's from the same book:

"The thesis maintained throughout this book is that Christianity is an invitation to human intelligence and freedom to re-create the world...I am not denying the painful realities of some of the church's past nor am I making exorbitant claims about Christianity's present. I am asserting that if Christian faith has a future it will arise from a way of looking at the world that stimulates response, creativity and passionate involvement. Any education that encourages such attitudes is an education that is already on the way to a point where Christian faith can be accepted."[16]

This is an eloquent statement of the complementary role played by catechesis following the openness of the Lancaster approach, and of the preparation for the reception of faith—the possibility of receiving faith—which this kind of approach prepares for so well.

3 — The 'open-ended' approach.

The comparison made in the first part of this chapter as regards models of religious education shows that, on grounds similar to those on which the religious freedom of the individual is based, there is less attention to the aim of producing a "committed believer." This is not because the ideal is no longer regarded as a worthwhile one, as rather that the catechist/teacher can provide the knowledge, the rational argument and so on, but the decision must be left to the grace of God and the individual's response if there is to be genuine faith. Accepting this attitude as particularly the limited mandate of the county school, how does the catechist in the Roman Catholic school, especially in terms of his "competence and mission" in the church, view this open-ended approach, especially statements such as "openness to the possibility of alternatives is not the only condition for objectivity in religious education. Criticism is required too?"[17]

---

15. cf. Chapter 4, 1(b).
16. Gabriel Moran, op. cit., p. 97.
17. Working Paper 36, op. cit., p. 26.

Three main points can be made on this issue.

a — It seems important that the catechist observes his marked duty to be faithful to God and to man by endeavouring to lead his classes towards personal belief. As we shall see in the next section, the catechist tries to do this by his own example. More importantly, he should try to show—theoretically and experientially—what it is for a person to be a believer. This would involve the intellectual and the rational basis for faith, with the correct stress, however, on showing that while faith is neither un-rational nor irrational, it is not simply a conclusion forced by logic. This may be shown very well by the example of different people, of varying ages, backgrounds and occupations, who show such faith in practice. There must be objectivity in the attention paid to personal motivation as well as to the mysterious element which accompanies all faith, but the task of the catechist is much more than simply providing the necessary background. More than this, he must endeavour to extend the invitation to personal faith, that commitment we have already described as personal ratification of one's baptismal promises.

b — If it is argued that such an attitude is not open-ended because it tends towards commitment in religious faith, the criticism must be accepted. But as was pointed out earlier in the discussion of objectivity and neutrality, objectivity and open-endedness are not ends in themselves but means of avoiding something else, in this case, the infringement of personal liberty. Under the conditions of the audience in the county school, such an approach is a necessary *first* condition, but on exactly the same kind of argument, the nature of the catechist's audience is a group of believers, at least in the sociological sense of their having been baptized as Roman Catholics. With the provisos already noted in the first part of the chapter, the catechist does have a right of invitation (to put it at its mildest) which may be said to complement the logical direction of the phenomenological approach in general.

c — In this approach, which is perhaps best described simply as educational, the teacher proceeds in a similar fashion to the way he would in aesthetics and such subjects. This means that he does not fail to conceal his enthusiasms, but he is concerned that his students are aware that he does not advocate a non-critical acceptance. Where the teaching and guidance of the church is required, the catechist tries to ensure that it is heard, but it is seen as offering of guidance with an authority which compels the obedience of free men, who at the end point of an investigation, remember that faith ultimately transcends reason.

188

4 — *Role of the teacher.*

As we have already indicated in our preliminary comments on the nature of the models of religious education, a key role in religious education is that of the teacher. The Working Paper contains an excellent chapter called "The Christian as R.E. teacher", the basis of which is acknowledged as a lecture of R. C. Morgan called "Education and/or proclamation."[18] A number of aspects of this are considered important in relation to the role of the catechist as compared with that of the teacher.

a — There is a relationship between the role of the Christian as teacher and as witness, although the distinction between these roles may be considered very important. While accepting the point, there seems more and more evidence of the greater importance of the role of witness. Such is the thesis of a remarkable book, published in Italian: *La catechesi come testimonianza* or "Catechesis as witness",[19] in which the author, argues that in an age more concerned with pragmatism, existential truth, anti-intellectualism and the decline of essentialist transmission of truth along with classical metaphysics, the function of witness—its structure, dimensions, laws, modes of expression etc. all need to be reconsidered. In practical matters, the child looks for a criterion of the truth, the adolescent for an embodiment of the Christian ideal, the young man for an authentic resolution of the doctrine-life dichotomy.[20]

b — As the Working Paper acknowledges, there are practical difficulties in ensuring that teachers who take religious education in the county schools have the requisite training and competence. From the above considerations, even more is required, especially with this age group of adolescents. As regards catechesis, two points which suggest themselves are:

i — As we have indicated already, the teacher/catechist in the Roman Catholic school should be ideally a believer and an embodiment of the Christian ideal. But it is rare for headmasters of such schools to have sufficient applications for positions, let alone the necessary insight when appointing staff, to ensure that all these conditions are fulfilled. Moreover, when in most Roman Catholic schools, staff are appointed in terms of their major subjects, it is a matter of fact that many who are called upon to take on religion teaching are regarded as qualified mainly in terms of their standing as 'practising' Catholics. This is as it should be in many ways, and it must not be denied that many such teachers—non-specialist technically—are the most successful teachers of religion, especially where they are prepared to allow their successful relationships via their ordinary

---

18. ibid., note 11, p. 104.
19. Flavio Pajer, f.s.c. **La catechesi come testimonianza. Fondamenti di una catechesi rinnovata**, Series Torino, Leumann, 1969.
20. Paraphrase from a review in **Lumen Vitae**, Vol. XXVII, No. 3, 1972, p. 518.

subjects to carry over into their teaching of religion. But there are also serious problems associated with this rather haphazard arrangement. Putting to one side, the instances where, due no doubt to other shortcomings in the school, there is no religious education department as such, and teachers are more or less left to work out their own syllabuses and procedures, there is the equally serious or perhaps more serious point, that teachers in such circumstances may well feel that their freedom has been infringed by their being asked to take religious education. As a result, they are not prepared to act a role of Christian witness but confine themselves to a completely objective role of presenting factual information. Even if this content is the teaching of the Church or readings from the texts of Vatican II, such a way of proceeding is hardly worthy of the title Religious education; at the best it is instruction, and it hardly needs to be said, it is a long way removed from the ideal of catechesis proposed throughout this work.[21]

ii — The young teachers, and of course even more, their elders, were often given a far more traditional kind of catechetical training themselves in their school years and, compared with their professional training in other subjects, have often had little opportunity to be trained in terms of the kind of developments indicated by the schema of Chapter 1. The evidence for this is written large in many schools, as for example by the absence of a religious department or even a co-ordinator, or in other cases, to the lack of comprehension by other staff, of what someone who has endeavoured to keep up with modern developments in catechetics is trying to do. The correspondence in the Roman Catholic press in many English-speaking countries over the past three years has had a number of incidents which have become national controversies. There is nothing at all wrong with this—indeed it may show a very healthy state of affairs in that issues in this area do matter to everyone—but there is a marked polarization over this kind of discussion which, with due regard to either side, fails to appreciate the effective balance of both 'education' on 'faith' and of 'faith' on 'education' as this model requires.

c — Just as the Working Paper emphasises what a disaster it would be for the school to concentrate on factual knowledge and leave the rest for the church, or else "present Christianity as straight, rational knowledge," so too in catechesis, the same applies, as noted already, over an automatic assumption of a faith context existing between catechist and pupils.[22] As noted above, too easy an assumption of every Catholic teacher as a believer, prepared to witness to the Christian ideal by the quality of

---

21. Perhaps this is the point at which an unjustified complacency about catechesis in Roman Catholic schools is least justified.

22. cf. especially "The assumption of faith in catechesis", in Chapter 6:4.

his own life, is a matter of concern for all those interested in the future of such schools. Without setting out a complete treatment of the important role of the catechist and his willingness to be involved in catechesis and not simply religious instruction, the following norms are suggested as minimal:

i — Living according to Christian ideals.

ii — Willing to share what he values most highly in dialogue with his pupils, i.e. a genuine dialogue of faith.

iii — Willing to teach for "a vision of Christianity not yet discovered" as one author puts it, reminding us subsequently of what a non-conformist pupil Francis of Assisi might have appeared to be, and under what number of present school regulations his propensities might have been curtailed:

iv — Being careful neither to limit young people to his own experience and his own expectations, nor to isolate his work in the education of the faith from the formative factors in the lives of the pupils. And when we have said this, we have again underlined the advantages of an open and dialogical approach.

There is a completeness about such a vision which is open to the catechist much more than it is to the county school teacher, but as the Working Paper has shown in its principles, such a faith context is prepared for in all kinds of ways. Teachers/catechists, as we have seen, may not necessarily assume it of pupils simply because they are in the Roman Catholic school; but it would be a tragedy if pupils realised that such a faith context could not be assumed with their own teachers.

CONCLUSION

There seems every justification for saying that there are strong lines of convergence between the catechetical model 'the education of (the) faith' and the principles of Working Paper No. 36, despite some of the important differences noted.

This is not simply to limit the value of the Working Paper to its function as a possible platform towards catechesis but rather to applaud the breadth of an approach to the teaching and learning of religion, which values the importance of addressing the man of today in terms of his own surroundings, of affording a vision which, at one and the same time, is open to man and the immanent but also to God and the transcendent, and to a practical involvement with ecumenism which leads in the direction of a unity of faith. When we have said all this, we have described an education which leads towards faith; we have described at least an important prelude to the 'education of faith'.

191

2.   Some perennial questions.

If the preceding discussion has endorsed the wide range of possibilities towards the development of faith through religious education, there still seem to be two major areas in which questions need continually to be asked if the dynamic evolution which should characterise religious, no less than general, education is to be maintained.   The first area includes that of religious education and the possibility of catechesis in schools begun expressly as religious foundations, as well as the more general kind of schools where religious education of some kind is possible, or where the original grouping of the school is extended through camp situations, week-ends and similar activities.   The second area is that of religious education apart from a school context.

With regard to the specifically religious foundations, the following observations and questions seem important.   The same questions, with appropriate modifications imposed by the limitations of state or county schools already discussed in the opening part of Chapter 5, should be asked of all forms of religious education in a school context, especially for middle and upper secondary forms.

1 — Can there be a genuine dialogue of faith if the initiative for such dialogue comes only from the authoritative organisation of the school? In practical terms, if the main grounds for the dialogue of faith are text and source materials coming only from outside the group e.g. official doctrinal teaching, texts prescribed by the hierarchy etc., what view of Church, of Revelation, of Christ's Incarnation in the world, is implicitly passed on?   The point here is not one of undervaluing the importance of such texts or sources when used imaginatively and creatively with groups, but rather to point up how easy it is to confuse the importance of the texts with an authoritative model of transmission to ensure that they (supposedly) are known.   In addition to the analysis made earlier with regard to the pedagogical inadequacies of such a model Chapter 2 (4), it may help if we apply to such a procedure the remarks made by Paulo Freire on what he terms the 'banking concept' of education:

"1.   The teacher teaches and the students are taught.
2.   The teacher knows everything and the students know nothing.
3.   The teacher thinks and the students are thought about.
4.   The teacher talks and the students listen—meekly.
5.   The teacher disciplines and the students are disciplined.
6.   The teacher chooses and enforces his choice, and the students comply.
7.   The teacher acts and the students have the illusion of acting through the action of the teacher.
8.   The teacher chooses the programme content, and the students

(who were not consulted) adapt to it.

9. The teacher confuses the authority of knowledge with his own professional authority, which he sets in opposition to the freedom of the students.

10. The teacher is the subject of the learning process, while the pupils are mere objects."[23]

This is a delicate matter. There is a tension between the freedom of the pupils and the demands of truth as seen by the teacher. Probably it has always been this way, but the point being underlined here is that it is important to perceive the possibly conflicting elements which reduce the dialogue to a monologue, whether it comes from the authority of the teacher wishing to ensure that the objective truth is heard or the limitations and intolerance of the group to anything except personal experience. It is the debate which has already been noted in the discussion of 'indoctrination' in the third section of Chapter 5. There does not seem to be any 'blanket' solution to the problem, but to keep asking question (1) may ensure the establishment of the kind of educational climate where such polarization is unknown, or where the tension between conflicting interests becomes creative for the whole group.

2 — Conceding the basic rights of parents with regard to the education of their children, how does the school attempt to reconcile the, at times, conflicting rights between children, their parents and their teachers?

As this question has occupied us at different points of this work, notably in Chapter 5, one main point only will be made. The school is generally in the best position to mediate between pupil and parent precisely because it is often the response to the wider vision stimulated by the educational process which appears to alienate children from their parents. This is no less true in matters religious. Indeed, in terms of the analysis of the opening chapter, it might be thought that the major failure of the modern catechetical movement (and the same thing would apply to the other Christian Churches especially with regard to understanding modern scholarship on the Bible), was precisely in its failure to involve parents. From a positive viewpoint, it would seem to be an important duty for the school to provide 'mediating occasions' where, particularly with middle and upper secondary pupils, parents, children and teachers could enjoy a common experience of learning and sharing.

3 — Does the school recognise the complexity of 'language' in its attempt to build 'platforms towards faith'?

23. **Pedagogy of the Oppressed**, Penguin Education, Middlesex, England, 1972, pp. 46-47.

The Appendix of this book illustrates the richness and variety of terminology which has come from the original term 'catechesis.' Language, for the school, must not be confined to words nor to exact theological terminology, important though the latter may be in certain situations. The school's attitude towards religion and the religious view of life generally, will be conveyed through various kinds of language: its concern for the freedom of the individual, its genuine moral concerns (i.e. in the direction of justice and charity), and its own self-image with regard to the religious as an essential dimension of living. The enlarged vision of religion implied in a consideration of its fundamental dimensions demands forms of language which extend beyond words to attitudes to living.[24]

When we come to consider religious education outside of a school context, there is one major question which must be asked: What provision is made for the continuing religious education of adults or for the necessary 'initation-instruction-worship' sequence noted in Chapter 1 for those who do not receive any religious education in school?

The question may be sub-divided into many different areas depending on the age-group under consideration. For example, the *de facto* situation in many English-speaking countries is that increasingly, Catholic children do not attend Catholic schools.[25] Are the provisions made for the religious education of such children actually handicapped by the attention given to those who do attend such schools, so that there are neither the resources nor the personnel to cope with this situation? For many Christian Churches, does the principle of the Sunday school work effectively only for children prior to their early teens, so that there is little opportunity for them to receive a more adult vision of their faith unless they are raised in a believing and worshipping family?

There have been many different attempts to cope with the kind of situations envisaged by these questions which are only a few of those which could be asked. What may yet be increasingly important about this whole field of questions, is that the general western experience with the de-schooling movements and the increasing contestation of many aspects of the school by pupils themselves, may help us to appreciate the important, but limited contribution of the school. If the development of a more conscious attitude towards 'continuing' or 'permanent education' is one of the important educational currents of our time, this should be no less so as regards religious education. We have had occasion to notice to what

24. cf. Ninian Smart's analysis of the six dimensions of religion referred to in several places in this work, especially Chapter 1, note 4.

25. cf. **The Future of Catholic Education in England and Wales**, Catholic Renewal Movement, London, 1971, p. 31, par. 53 & p. 33, par. 57. Also, *Report of the Catholic Education Office to the Melbourne Catholic Education Board*, October, 13th, 1971.

extent certain aspects of religious education in the past have been limited by the desire to avoid proselytising or indoctrination of the young; perhaps, the opportunity to work with an older and more mature age-group offers the richest possibilities for religious education. Perhaps the ultimate direction is towards those small groups of believers which characterised the early Christian church, where everything in the life of the community was adjusted to the encouragement and development of a deeper knowledge of the faith and a life style most in keeping with it, yet set firmly in the reality of to-day's world.

CONCLUSION

In an elaborately developed analogy, Joseph Colomb[26] compares the work of the catechist (and hence, of the religious educator in the fullest sense of the term) with that of a master pianist who not only acts as an intermediary between the written notes of Mozart or Bach or Beethoven, but who, in the process of so doing, recreates for himself and his listeners something of beauty. The potential beauty of the music lies in the score itself but it must be brought to life. This, the pianist does, not simply by the technical competence of his playing but even more by his shaping, phrasing and general interpretation, so that there is something of himself in addition to the original vision of the composer.

This is an analogy which touches at many points the work of the religious educator who attempts to prepare the way for, and hopefully to participate in, that dialogue of believers represented by the Christian concept of catechesis.

26. Joseph Colomb, **Le service de l'évangile**, tome 2, p. 710.

195

CATECHESIS AND SOME RELATED TERMS.

The general enrichment of the concept of catechesis as the original term has found its way into the principal European languages via its Latin usage, indicates both the breadth of the original term as well as the necessity for interpretation of the term according to the special circumstances in which it is being studied. In any survey of the modern catechetical movement, it seems particularly important to recognise that the enrichment indicated by the variety of terminology associated with catechesis needs to be seen as related to the dynamic aspect of the concept itself. At the same time, there are serious ambiguities unless some important distinctions are recognised. Catechesis as one form of the pastoral ministry of the Church is related to terms such as evangelization, kerygma and preaching, pre-catechesis and pre-evangelization, but needs also to be distinguished from such terms because of its special character. This is also important in considering the range of meanings associated with the common derivatives of 'catechize', 'catechism', 'catechist', 'catechetics' and 'catechetical.'

1.   Catechesis; Evangelization; Kerygma; Preaching.

Each of the above terms is associated with a common element in that they all presume someone telling others of personal belief in Christ and His message so that the manner of telling and the personal conviction of the one who speaks carry their own force. This is the clear sense of 'catechesis' as discussed explicitly in Chapter 2.[1]

But this is also the force of "evangelization" and "kerygma." The former term derived from the Latin *evangelizare* (and *evangelium* = Gospel) is most easily translated by the word "to preach" and of course is often complemented by the noun "the Gospel." 'Kerygma', from the Greek word *keryx* signifying 'a herald' or 'one who proclaims' brings us straight back to something already noted in 'catechesis'.[2] The English word "preaching" because of its later (Christian) origin places this same idea in a more advanced context by signifying a role in the community, a place and an audience, and again, a special kind of authority which flows from the subject matter itself rather than from the authority of the preacher. It becomes difficult to speak at any length of the pastoral ministry of the Church without encountering one or another of these words. For example, the Vatican II document *Ad Gentes* which deals with the Missionary Activity of the Church says:

---

1. cf. Chapter 2, footnotes 1-5.
2. ibid.

"The specific purpose of this missionary activity is *evangelization* (my emphasis) and the planting of the Church among those peoples and groups where the faith has not yet taken root...
The chief means of this implantation is the *preaching* (my emphasis) of the gospel of Jesus Christ."[3]

In defining "Preaching" in "Concise Theological Dictionary", Rahner and Vorgrimler write (my emphasis added):

"In the broad sense, *preaching* is the *proclamation* of God's word by those whom the Church has commissioned in Christ's name. It is not mere instruction about facts... but the *proclamation* of God's eternal Plan (*gospel*)—hidden in itself—carried into effect when God attaches an efficacious grace to the word that is preached..."[4]

In the same reference, Kerygma is described as:

"a NT term which in modern use means the word that is *preached* to the Christian community or individual in the name of God, by lawful commission of God and the Church, as the very word of God and Christ..."[5]

What is common to each of these terms despite their linguistic and historical differences is that they indicate the common model for the transmission of the faith. Man hears the word of God spoken to him by his fellow man, but the tone and the authority of the utterance flow from the message itself, not from the eloquence of the speaker. This model, the *Fides ex auditu* model, is expressed in simple terms by St. Paul:

"So faith comes from what is preached, and what is preached comes from the word of Christ."[6]

Within this common area, however, it is possible to make some important distinctions.

1 — Evangelization is particularly that first preaching of the word to those who either have not heard it previously or who do not yet believe. It aims at conversion and hopes to obtain from those it approaches, a free response, their initial act of faith. It is therefore particularly addressed to adults or at least to those who are old enough to take a responsible personal decision.

2 — The particular content and spirit of this proclamation, indeed the very form of the message of salvation, is what has been brought back

---

3. W. M. Abbott (ed.), **The Documents of Vatican II**, Geoffrey Chapman, London, 1966, par. 6, p. 591.

4. Herder/Burns and Oates, London, 1965, p. 371.

5. ibid., pp. 249-250.

6. Romans 10:17.

to our attention by modern exegesis "which has made it plain that the Epistles and Gospels took shape from a nucleus of primitive teaching common to all the apostles, including Saint Paul."[7] This is what is known by kerygma. Colomb expresses the particular quality of Kerygma as follows:

"It is of the order of knowledge; it is the proclamatory element, the limited content of the living Word and as such, it produces from the human hearer a response. In the Gospel and the Acts of the Apostles and in the course of "missionary history, it often appears accompanied by signs which show forth the power of the Spirit."[8]

Kerygma in relation to the catechetical movement of modern times has been dealt with in Chapter 1.

3 — In present day practice, Preaching in its precise sense (i.e. apart from the metaphorical uses of the term such as "preaching" implying a superior attitude assumed for an occasion and of course, the missionary sense of "preaching the Gospel"), is usually applied to teaching and instruction given in a formal—often liturgical—setting, to adults or believers already initiated into the Church. Even within this classification, however, allowance would need to be made for the particular distinction between 'sermon' and 'homily', the latter perhaps tending to be based on Scripture and in this sense exhortatory and devotional, the former more doctrinal in content.

4 — It is evident from the foregoing that the particular function of 'catechesis' in comparison with these other pastoral forms, is its dual role of instruction and initiation, particularly in the post-Reformation era, where it has been particularly concerned with the task of preparing children baptized as infants, for the reception of the sacraments of Eucharist, Penance and Confirmation, often through association with a school context. It has also extended itself to the preparation of adult converts for their reception of Baptism, and in the recommendations in this regard of Vatican II, catechesis is seen as the main function of the restored catechumenate.[9]

For an expression of these differences in relation to one another, the following statement of D.S. Amalorpavadass in the 1971 Catechetical

---

7. Domenico Grasso, *The Core of Missionary Preaching* in **Teaching All Nations** edited by Hofinger, Herder Books, New York, 1961, p. 39. This statement acknowledges reference to C. H. Dodd's **The Apostolic Preaching and its Development** so that it is not meant to purport that the preaching of the Apostles and Paul was exactly the same.

8. Joseph Colomb, **Le service de l'évangile**, tome 1, Desclée, Paris, p. 4, footnote 1. (my translation)

9. *Editio typica*, published 6th January 1971. Noted in **Liturgy Newspaper**, Vol. 3 No. 4, 1972.

Congress in Rome is an excellent guide and summary: "Evangelization is a primary and fundamental ministry of the Word: the two constitutive elements of it are kerygma and sign: kerygma is the oral and verbal announcement or the heralding of the Gospel of Jesus Christ by unfolding the creative and dynamic potentialities of God's Word. But this must be accompanied by and testified by signs (whether physical or moral miracles) or the unique sign of the Resurrection of Christ or the universal and infallible signs of fraternal charity and humble service. It is addressed to the non-Christians or non-converts in view of calling them to faith and conversion. The announcement of the Word, is therefore, made in a global, dynamic and interpellating manner.

Whereas Catechesis is a second or subsequent ministry of the Word: it also transmits God's Word, but it is done in an enlightening and educative way. It is addressed only to Christians or converts or those who have made the first act of faith as a response to evangelization. It is done in view of awakening, nourishing and educating their faith and of deepening and completing their initial conversion. Between these two ministries of the Word, there is a capital event, namely initial conversion and first act of faith."[10]

It is tempting to simplify all this by simply reserving catechesis to a role of supplying for children (or convert adults) a series of basic teachings on the doctrinal aspects of the faith they already have either through baptism or their expressed desire to receive it.

This clear distinction between the closely related processes of Evangelization and Catechesis by the important first act of faith is possible to sustain only in the kind of discussion which supposes both processes as applied to adults, because talk of a "first act of faith" is quite a different thing when applied to adults, as compared to the *habitus fidei* received by an infant at baptism.[11]

Posset notes that for Domenico Grasso, "kerygma is 'to convert', catechesis is 'to initiate the new believer into the mystery of Christ;' Nebrada's distinction is that in catechesis, faith in Christ is the point of departure; in kerygma, faith is the point of arrival."[12] These clear distinctions are obviously related to the idea of people arriving at faith as adults, in the manner of an adult catechumenate, rather than to the idea of young people coming to make an adult assent of faith after a number of years of living a nominally Christian life since their baptism as infants.

This opens up perhaps the central issue of catechetics in the past decade viz. the discussions which have marked the discussion and use of the terms 'pre-catechesis' and 'pre-evangelization', where both terms have

---

10. Subsequently published **Lumen Vitae**, Vol. XXVII, No. 2, 1972, pp. 261-2.

11. cf. footnote 6, Chapter 2.

12. Franz Posset, **American Catechetics**, St. Mary's College Press, Winona, Minesota, 1969, p. 63.

been used to refer particularly to the problems of missionary areas, as well as to those of the so-called 'de-Christianized' areas of Europe.

2. Pre-catechesis and pre-evangelization.[13]

Although the above terms did not originate with Alfonso Nebrada, their general usage and acceptance in English was undoubtedly greatly aided by his influential "Kerygma in Crisis" published in 1965.[14] Basically, Nebrada was concerned to emphasise the difference between the proclaiming of the Christian message in a traditionally Christian country—the kind of action which might be thought of as 'reminding' people of the Gospel message—and the necessity in a missionary environment of carefully preparing the way *before* such first preaching, lest, without such a preparation, the hearers were not humanly capable of perceiving what was being announced to them.

In Nebrada's justification of this kind of approach, he drew on his personal experience of endeavouring to preach Christianity in Japan, and his view of the kind of preparation necessary prior to the hearing of the kerygma was based on a rather different sense of the term 'apologetics.' His understanding of this term, and its application to his thesis is best expressed in his own words:

> "Reality forces us to nuance the kerygmatic approach and to prepare the people for it by a kind of threefold apologetics. We need to keep a proper balance 'apologetics for the sake of kerygma.' This is precisely what I call 'pre-evangelization,' namely, preparing men so that the kerygma may have meaning in this milieu or for that individual."[15]

For Nebrada, there is basically no difference between the terms 'pre-catechesis' and 'pre-evangelization' as described here: in both cases they describe work which prepares the ground for conversion. As to its actual programme, Nebrada's 'threefold apologetics' has been summarized around the following steps:

1 — helping the man of good will perceive that the values of this present life can never bring complete security;

2 — showing how man's cultural expression in his confrontation with and mastery of the world, always points to a perfection beyond actual realisation;

---

13. These terms are not offered as equivalents, but the distinction between them is best carried out with reference to context.

14. op. cit., Loyola University Press, Chicago, 1965.

15. ibid., p. 46. It is important to note that Nebrada is here proposing in a tentative manner a question which has become clearer in recent years namely, do people in mission areas need necessarily to be "Europeanised" before being evangelised? The 1971 Rome Catechetical Congress was strongly against such a procedure.

3 — awakening man to a sense of the sacred.[16]

By comparison, the notion of 'pre-catechesis' which is contained in an appendix of the proceedings of the Eichstaett conference of 1960, is far more closely tied to the idea of the catechumenate as described earlier in Chapter one. "For the instruction of those who are not yet believers, it is necessary to have a period of pre-catechesis more or less long, before the complete formulation of the doctrine is given to them. During this period, the catechist should endeavour with the help of grace, to awaken in the catechumen a desire for God, to stir up his unquenched spiritual longings, and to show how these longings find their fulfilment in the divine truth. He must help them to realise whatever is disorderly in their lives, as well as their attachment to earthly values. He should arouse in them a longing for forgiveness and a desire to give themselves to God. In this way, he will prepare them soil for the sowing of the word of God. Unless these spiritual powers are awakened in them, the catechumens will remain incapable of understanding the meaning of the Christian message."[17]

An important separation can be made between these formulations in what is really a very fundamental point. This earlier formulation seems to assume the later catechesis as the sole justification for this period of preparation; its real purpose lies outside of itself. But the Nebrada formulation, aimed as it is towards catechesis, still relies on a much more basic appreciation of the importance of the human growth and appreciation of values for their own sake, as well as their natural flowering into the acceptance of God's grace inviting them to accept the kerygma of salvation.

Further reflection on the 'pre-evangelization/pre-catechesis' discussion by well-known catechetical writers, Colomb and Moran, and further refinement of his own position by Nebrada some years after "Kerygma in Crisis", enables us to be more specific about the development of the concept in recent years.

1 — For Colomb, "pre-catechesis has for aim to remove the obstacles which prevent man from making a real encounter with the Word of God. Pre-catechesis assures first of all the physical presence of the Church." He argues from the example of the 'worker-priest' movement in de-Christianized areas of France that this physical presence of the Church should be completely integrated in the community it serves, as a human psychological presence offering "sympathy, attention and welcome, and dialogue." As we have already noted, "this human dialogue is already valuable in itself, and the values experienced in a world sociologically distant from the Church are some-

16. Thus J. P. Labelle, quoted by Posset, op. cit., 6. 63.
17. Teaching All Nations, Appendix B.P. 401-402 op. cit.

times implicitly Christian to begin with or at least establish a mentality much closer to Christianity than might seem to be the case."[18] With these conditions in mind, it hardly matters where pre-catechesis ends and formal catechesis begins, for the important thing is that such individual and group presence, provide their own witness at the level of an existential reality, even if not at the level of formal Christian practices.

2 — Nebrada's development of thought may be seen in a key paper on "Fundamental Catechesis" provided for the Medellin Conference of 1968, in which he applies his ideas particularly to catechesis in the school situation. The leading ideas of the paper as regards 'pre-catechesis' and adolescents are paraphrased as follows: Our expectations in the catechesis of adolescents are to provide "the transit from a more or less 'notional' (idea of faith) to a 'real' assent . . . Our young people 'know by heart (often to the point of sheer boredom!)' all the external details of the history of salvation. But all too often this knowledge, far from connecting them with the salvific stream, seems to stand as an obstacle in the way to their grasping the meaning of these saving events."

Two important directions follow from this:

a — Our expectations that our adolescents will, as a matter of course, "ratify their baptismal promises . . . dangerously under-estimates the decisive and mysterious role of the two partners in the dialogue of salvation—God (his grace) and man (his freedom) —and is perhaps the main reason why dubious positions are taken which may eventually prove fatal."

b — Without daring to rashly conclude that our adolescents do not have faith, it would be wise to proceed in part at least "as if they did not believe." Such an approach will obviously help those who are not yet at the level of faith and even those will be confirmed in their faith who, despite apparent contradictions and uncertainties, actually believe.[19]

3 — Nebrada's first observation is substantially that made by Moran who strongly opposed an uncritical 'missionary pre-evangelization' with pupils in a Christian (or even de-Christianized environment) because, as Moran observed, "the problems are exactly opposite, that is, we suffer not from a lack of acquaintance with and a scarcity of relationships to Christianity, but from an oversaturation (without accompanying assimilation) of Christian ideas and words." An uncri-

18. Joseph Colomb, **Foundations of Catechesis Today,** part 2, translated from 'Vérité et Vie', Series 78, 1967-68, in **Our Apostolate,** Vol. 17, No. 2, p. 70-71.
19. Re-printed in **Our Apostolate,** Vol. 18, No. 2, Paraphrased pp. 117-119.

tical application of pre-evangelization techniques, can simply be a psychological preparation "to give them the real Christian message ... that is, the truths of Scripture and Christian doctrine."[20] More importantly there is substantial agreement between Moran and Nebrada as to the necessity of a sound theological basis for pre-evangelization, and such a basis can only be that of God's continuing revelation in the Christian community, such being the best counter to "jargon, gimmicks and a new rigidity of approach."[21]

4 — From a theological viewpoint, what Moran has in mind is specifically that outlined by Jacques Bournique, whose note on pre-evangelization Moran quotes:

"(1)   the world in which we live is not pure nature, man is always more than man;

(2)   there are traces of likeness to God that are not erased by sin;

(3)   'Every man is given over to his incompleteness and his intrinsic contradictions so long as he has not reached the level of Jesus Christ. On the other hand every effort to bring human life into line with true nature brings man closer to Christ, for nature is called to higher things. Pre-evangelization in this context is (1) a necessary dimension of all evangelization; (2) not necessarily first chronologically although there may be a long preliminary stage; (3) a form of evangelization which is (a) *implicit* though directed to the proclamation of salvation in Jesus Christ, (b) *partial* but conducive to global adherence to the fullness of mystery, (c) *attentive* to signs that are human realities and which lead to discovery of the plan of God."[22]

One final comment should be made. As has been indicated in Chapters 1 and 3, the theological background to the modern catechetical movement is of the greatest importance and the enlargement of meaning in some basic concepts has been indicated in the survey in Chapter 4 of the catechetical congresses of the sixties. The point is that however fine the distinctions made as regards terminology, interpretation must always pay attention to the circumstances in which the terms are used.

It is appropriate also to look at some of the main derivatives most closely related to the root word 'catechesis,' in the sense in which it was examined in Chapter 2.

---

20. **God Still Speaks**, Burns & Oates, London, 1967, pp. 142-143.
21. ibid., p. 144.
22. ibid., footnote 11, p. 146.

3. Some other terms.

The verb 'to catechize' has reminded us that catechesis is concerned essentially with persons and not simply with the objective facts of communication; in that sense it is usually more varied in its forms, unlike preaching. The "catechist" himself, usually not an ordained minister, is himself, at least ideally, an example in his own living, of the truths he teaches. Catechesis, in this very best sense, shows examples of Christian living before it reduces the faith to doctrinal summaries; such summaries are necessary but they represent a natural synthesis or reflection which follows from the acceptance and living of the Christian life. In this sense all theological formulation should ideally be informed by the spirit of the kerygma: the "catechism" is not a substitute for catechesis. The renewed attention to the "catechumenate" reminds us principally of the successive stages of prayer and instruction and probation which followed the first act of faith as a response to the kerygma. The existence of 'catechetics' is especially reminiscent of the basic role of instruction both of the young and of those who come to the Church as adults. In a particular way it has been linked with the Catholic school with its special opportunities for "catechetical" instruction but with the real danger of limiting the concept to instructional aspects. Catechesis, as the amalgam of all these features highlighted by its derivatives, has the flexibility to be adapted because it always stands apart from and above any one of its particular historical manifestations.

BIBLIOGRAPHY

Books

Abbott, Walter M. S.J. (ed.), **The Documents of Vatican II**, Geoffrey Chapman, London, 1966.

Ackland, Richard, **We Teach Them Wrong**, Gollancz, London, 1963.

A Catholic Catechism (German Catechism), Burns and Oates, London, 1957.

Alves, Colin D., **Religion and the Secondary School**, S.C.M. Press, London, 1968.

Archambault, Reginald D. (ed.), **Philosophical Analysis and Education**, Routledge and Kegan Paul, London, 1965.

A New Catechism: **Catholic Faith for Adults**, Burns & Oates, London, 1970.

Audinet, Jacques, **Forming the Faith of Adolescents**, Geoffrey Chapman, London, 1968.

Augustine, Saint. 'De Catechizandis Rudibus.' **The First Catechetical Instruction**, ed. J. P. Christopher in *Library of Ancient Christian Writers,* Longmans, Green & Co., London, 1963.

Babin, Pierre, **Crisis of Faith**, Gill & Son, Dublin, 1965.

Babin, Pierre, **Faith and the Adolescent**, Gill & Son, Dublin, 1965.

Babin, Pierre, **Options**, Burns & Oates, London, 1968.

Battersby, W. J., **De La Salle: Pioneer of Modern Education**, Longmans, Green & Co., London, 1949.

Battersby, W.J., **De La Salle: Saint and Spiritual Writer**, Longmans, Green & Co., London, 1950.

Birnie, Ian H. (ed.), **Religious Education in Integrated Studies**, SCM Press, London, 1972.

Branigan, J. J. (ed.), **The Teaching of Religion in Catholic Schools.** Edited for the Catholic Teachers' Federation of England & Wales. Macmillan & Co. Ltd., London, 1954.

Brodrick, James S.J., **Robert Bellarmine: Saint and Scholar**, Burns & Oates, London, 1961

Bull, Norman D., **Moral Judgement from Childhood to Adolescence**, Routledge and Kegan Paul, London, 1969.

Bull, Norman D., **Moral Education**, Routledge and Kegan Paul, London, 1969.

Cameron, James, **Images of Authority**, Burns & Oates, London, 1966.

Carter, G. Emmet (Bishop), **The Modern Challenge to Religious Education**, William H. Sadlier, Inc., New York, 1961.

Catechism of the Council of Trent. Translated and annotated by McHugh & Callan, B. Herder, London, 1958. (15th impression)

Catechetics Reconsidered, St. Mary's College Press, Winona, Minnesota, 1968. Readings in catechetics for high school teachers.

Catholic Catechism, Books One and Two, E. J. Dwyer, Sydney, 1963. (The Australian Catechism)

Catholic Catechism Book One Teacher's Book and Catholic Catechism Book Two Teacher's Book, E. J. Dwyer, Sydney.

Children and Their Primary Schools: A report of the Central Advisory Council for Education (England), HMSO, 1967, Vol. 1.

Christian Commitment in Education: Report of the Methodist Conference Commission on Education, Epworth Press, London, 1970.

Colomb, Joseph, Le service de l'evangile, Tomes 1 & 2, Desclée, Paris, 1968.

Coudreau, Francois P.S.S., Basic Catechetical Perspectives, Paulist Press Deus Books, New York, 1969.

Cox, Edwin, Changing Aims in Religious Education, Routledge & Kegan Paul, London, 1967.

Cox, Edwin, Sixth Form Religion, S.C.M. Press, London, 1967.

Congar, Yves O. P., Jesus Christ, Geoffrey Chapman, London, 1966.

Dodd, C. H., The Apostolic Preaching and its Development, Hodder & Stoughton, London, 1963.

Donnellan, Michael, What to Believe, Logos Books, Gill & Son, Dublin, 1968.

Drinkwater, F. H., Telling the Good News, Burns & Oates, London, 1960.

Drinkwater, F. H., Teaching the Catechism, Burns & Oates, London, 1958. editions.

Evening, Margaret, Approaches to Religious Education, Hodder & Stoughton, London, 1972.

Fogarty, Ronald (Brother), Catholic Education in Australia, 2 Vols., Melbourne University Press, Melbourne, 1959.

General Catechetical Directory, Catholic Truth Society, London, 1971.

Grasso, Domenico, Proclaiming God's Message, University of Notre Dame Press, 1965.

Greeley, A. M. and Rossi, P. H., The Education of Catholic Americans, Chicago, Aldine Publishing Company, 1966.

Goldbrunner, Josef, Teaching the Catholic Catechism, 3 Vols., Burns & Oates, London, 1963 (5th impression).

Goldman, Ronald, Religious Thinking from Childhood to Adolescence, Routledge and Kegan Paul, London, 1964.

Halverson & Cohen, A Handbook of Christian Theology, Fontana Books, London, 1966.

Heenan, John Cardinal, Teaching the Faith, Catholic Truth Society, London, 1972.

Hilliard, F. H., Religious Education 1944-1984, George Allen & Unwin, London, 1966.

Hofinger, Johannes S.J., The Art of Teaching Christian Doctrine, University of Notre Dame Press, 1962 (2nd edition).

206

Hofinger, Johannes S.J., **The ABC of Modern Catechetics**, William H. Sadlier, Inc., New York, 1962 (with William J. Reedy).

Hofinger, Johannes S.J., **Teaching All Nations: A Symposium on Modern Catechetics**, Burns & Oates, London, 1961. (Revised and partly translated by Clifford Howell, S.J.)

Humanities for the Young School Leaver: An Approach Through Religious Education. Published for the Schools' Council by Evans/Methuen Educational, 1969.

Jebb, Dom Philip (ed.), Religious Education: 8th Downside Symposium, Darton, Longman & Todd, London, 1968.

Jeffreys, M.V.C., **Truth is Not Neutral**, Religious Education Press, Oxford, 1969.

Jeffreys, M.V.C., **Religion and Morality**, Religious Education Press, Oxford, 1967.

Jeffreys, M.V.C., The Ministry of Teaching, Pitman, London, 1967.

Jungmann, Josef Andreas S.J., **Handing on the Faith: A Manual of Catechetics**, Burns & Oates, London, 1959.

Jungmann, Josef Andreas S.J., **The Good News Yesterday and Today**, William H. Sadlier, New York, 1962.

Kay, William, **Moral Development**, Allen and Unwin, London, 1968.

Lance, Derek, **Till Christ be Formed**, Darton, Longman & Todd, London, 1965.

Learning for Life: The Agreed Syllabus of Religious Education of the Inner London Education Authority, County Hall, London, S.E.1., 1968.

Ledogar, Robert (ed.), **Katigondo: Presenting the Christian Message to Africa**, Geoffrey Chapman, London, 1965.

Lee, J. M. & Rooney, P. C. (eds.), **Towards a Future for Religious Education**, Pflaum Press, Dayton, Ohio, 1970.

Lewis, Eve, **Children and their Religion,** Sheed & Ward, London, 1962.

Life and Worship: Northamptonshire Education Committee Agreed Syllabus (Senior), Jolly & Barber, Rugby, 1968.

Lonergan, Bernard S.J., **Method in Theology**, Darton, Longman & Todd, London, 1972.

Loukes, Harold, **Teenage Religion**, S.C.M. Press, London, 1961.

Loukes, Harold, **New Ground in Christian Education,** S.C.M. Press, London, 1965.

Macy, Christopher (ed.), **Let's Teach Them Right**, Pemberton Books, London, 1969.

Making All Things New: Fundamentals and Programs of a New Catechesis, Divine Word Publications, Techny, Illinois, 1966.

Mathews, H. F., **Revolution in Religious Education**, Religious Education Press, Oxford, 1966.

McBride, Alfred, **Catechetics: A Theology of Proclamation**, Bruce, Milwaukee, 1966.

Moran, Gabriel, **Theology of Revelation**, Burns & Oates, London, 1967.

Moran, Gabriel, **God Still Speaks**, Burns & Oates, London, 1967.

Moran, Gabriel, **Visions and Tactics**, Burns & Oates, London, 1968.

Moran, Gabriel, **Design for Religion**, Herder, New York, 1970.

Nebrada, Alfonso, S.J., **Kerygma in Crisis**, Loyola University Press, Chicago, 1965.

O'Collins, Gerald, S.J., **Theology and Revelation**, Mercier Press, Cork, 1968.

O'Shea, K. and Meehan, N., **A Human Apostolate**, Spectrum Books, Melbourne, 1971.

Pajer, Flavio FSC, **La catechesi come testimonianza**, Series Torino, Leumann, 1969.

Papal Teachings on Education, St. Paul Books, Boston, 1960.

Peters, R. S., **Ethics and Education**, Allen & Unwin, London, 1966.

Peters, R. S. (ed.), **The Concept of Education**, Routledge and Kegan Paul, London, 1967.

Posset, Franz, **American Catechetics: Personal and Secular,** St. Mary's College Press, Winona, Minnesota, 1969.

Rahner, K. and Vorgrimler, H., **Concise Theological Dictionary**, Herder— Burns and Oates, London, 1965.

Rahner, Karl (ed.), Ernst, Cornelius and Smyth, Kevin, **Sacramentum Mundi: An Encyclopaedia of Theology**, 6 Vols, Burns & Oates, 1968.

Readings In European Catechetics, Lumen Vitae Press, Brussels, 1962.

Ryan, M. P., **Are Parochial Schools the Answer?** Angelus Books, Guild Press, New York, 1963.

Sauvage, Michel FSC, **Catéchèse et Laicat**, Editions Ligel, Paris, 1962.

Scheffler, Israel, **The Language of Education**, Charles C. Thomas, Springfield, Illinois, 1968. (7th printing)

Scheffler, Israel (ed.), **Philosophy of Education**, Allyn & Bacon, Boston, 1966. (2nd edition)

Schillebeeckx, Edward, **Vatican II: The Real Achievement**, Sheed & Ward, London, 1966.

Schools Council Working Paper 36, **Religious Education in Secondary Schools**, Evans/Methuen Educational, London, 1971.

Sizer, Theodore (ed.), **Religion and Public Education**, Houghton Mifflin Company, Boston, 1967.

Sloyan, Gerard (ed.), **Modern Catechetics: Message and Method in Religious Formation**, Collier — Macmillan Ltd., London, 1964.

Sloyan, Gerard (ed.), **Shaping the Christian Message: Essays in Religious Education**, Deus Books, Paulist Press, Glen Rock, New Jersey, 1958. (abridged edition)

Smart, R. N., **Secular Education and the Logic of Religion: Faber Heslington Lectures, University of York, 1966,** Faber & Faber, London, 1968.

Smart, R. N., **The Religious Experience of Mankind,** Collins (Fontana), London, 1969.

Smith, J. W. D., **Religious Education in a Secular Setting,** S.C.M. Press, London, 1969.

The Fourth R: The Durham Report on Religious Education, SPCK, London, 1970.

The Future of Catholic Education in England and Wales, Catholic Renewal Movement, London, 1971.

The Newman, No. 2, May 1972. Newman Association of Great Britain, 15 Carlisle Street, London.

The Renewal of the Education of Faith, Australian Episcopal Conference, Sydney, 1970.

Towards a New Era in Religious Education, Cripac Press, Melbourne, 1972.

Tucker, Bernard, **Catholic Education in a Secular Society,** Sheed & Ward, London, 1968.

Van Caster, Marcel S.J., **The Structure of Catechetics,** Herder & Herder, New York, 1965.

Van Caster, Marcel S.J., **Themes of Catechesis,** Burns & Oates, London, 1967.

Wicker, Brian, **Culture and Liturgy,** Sheed & Ward. London, 1963.

Wicker, Brian, **Culture and Theology,** Sheed & Ward, London, 1966.

Wilson, John, **Education in Religion and the Emotions,** Heinemann Educational Books, London, 1971.

Wilson, John (with Williams, N. & Sugarman, B.), **Introduction to Moral Education,** Penguin Books, London, 1967.

Woodhall, Ralph S.J., **Theology of Incarnation,** Mercier Press, Cork, 1968.

209

ARTICLES

Amalorpavadass, D. S., *Catechesis as a Pastoral Task of the Church,* in **Lumen Vitae**, Vol. XXVII, 1972, Nr. 2, pp. 259-280.

Babin, Pierre, *J'abandonne la catéchèse?* in **Catéchistes**, No. 76, October 1968, pp. 415-428.

Baum, Gregory, *Commentary on the Constitution of the Church of Vatican Council II,* Deus Books, Paulist Press, New York, 1964. (Study Series).

Bournique, Jacques, *Note on Pre-Evangelization,* in **Teaching All Nations**, (II) January 1965, pp. 92-97.

Bournique, Jacques, *Catechetics after the Council,* in **Presenting the Christian Message to Africa**, edited by Robert Ledogar, Geoffrey Chapman, London, 1965.

Borowitz, Eugene B., *Judaism and the Secular State,* in **Religion and Public Education**, edited by Theodore Sizer, Houghton Mifflin Company, Boston 1967, pp. 265-286.

Butler, B. C. Bishop, **The Tablet**, 16th September, 1972, pp. 876-877.

Colomb, Joseph, *The Catechetical Method of St. Sulpice,* in **Shaping the Christian Message**, edited by Gerard Sloyan, Deus Books, Paulist Press, Glen Rock, New Jersey, 1958, pp. 98-118.

Colomb, Joseph, *The Use of the Bible in Teaching the Church's Faith,* in **Modern Catechetics**, edited by Gerard Sloyan, Collier-Macmillan Ltd., 1964, pp. 1-22.

Colomb, Joseph, *Catechesis Contested,* in **Lumen Vitae**, Vol. XXV, Nr. 3, pp. 369-386.

Colomb, Joseph, *Foundations of Catechesis Today,* in **Our Apostolate**, Vol. 17, Nos. 1 & 2, February, 1969, translated by Brother Peter Gilfedder from Vérité et Vie Series 78, 1967. — 68., No. 577. pp. 5 — 14 & 66 — 72.

Coudreau, Francois, *Introduction to a Pedagogy of Faith,* in **Shaping the Christian Message**, edited by Gerard Sloyan, Deus Books, Paulist Press, Glen Rock, New Jersey, 1958, pp. 135-152.

Cox, Edwin, *The Aims of Religious Education,* in **Religious Education in Integrated Studies**, edited by Birnie, SCM Press, London, 1972, pp. 26-43.

Cox, Harvey G. "The Relationship between Religion and Education" in **Religion and Public Education**, edited by Sizer, Houghton Mifflin Company, Boston, 1967, pp. 99-111.

Delcuve, George S.J., *Confirmation at the Age of Reason* in **Shaping the Christian Message**, edited by Gerard Sloyan, Deus Books, Paulist Press, Glen Rock, New Jersey, 1958, pp. 211-244.

Delooz, Pierre S.J., *Catechesis and Secularization. A Sociological Viewpoint,* in **Lumen Vitae**, Vol. XXIV, 1969, No. 2, pp. 197-211.

Erdozain, Luis S.J., *The Evolution of Catechetics,* in **Lumen Vitae**, Vol. XXV, 1970, No. 1, pp. 7-31.

Godin, Andre, S.J., *Faith and the Psychological Development of Children and Adults,* in **Faith and Commitment**, edited by Mark Link, Loyola University Press, Chicago, 1965, pp. 123-137.

Grasso, Domenico, S.J., *The Core of Missionary Preaching,* in **Teaching All Nations**, edited by Johannes Hofinger, S.J., Burns & Oates, London, 1961, pp. 39-58.

Hammans, Herbert, *Recent Roman Catholic Views on the Development of Dogma,* in **Concilium** Vol. 1, No. 3, January 1967, pp. 53-63.

Hare, R. M., *Adolescents into Adults,* in **Aims of Education**, edited by T.H.B. Hollins, Manchester University Press, 1964, pp. 47-70.

Hirst, Paul H., *Liberal Education and the Nature of Knowledge,* in **Philosophical Analysis and Education**, edited by Archambault, Routledge and Kegan Paul, London, 1965, pp. 113-140.

Hirst, Paul H., *Christian Education—A Contradiction in Terms?,* in **Learning for Living**, March 1972, pp. 7-11.

Hirst, Paul H., *Morals, Religion and the Maintained School,* in **Let's Teach Them Right**, edited by Macy, Pemberton Books, London, 1969, pp. 8-24.

Hirst, Paul H., *The Foundations of Moral Judgement,* in **Let's Teach them Right**, edited by Macy, Pemberton Books, London, 1969, pp. 123-129.

Hofinger, Johannes, S.J., *The New Australian Catechism,* in **Lumen Vitae**, Vol. XVIII., 1963, No. 3, pp. 529-540.

Hosegood, Barbara, *The Faith and Indoctrination,* in **Catholic Education in a Secular Society**, edited by Tucker, Sheed & Ward, London, 1968, pp. 167-194.

Jungmann, Josef. S.J., *Religious Education in Late Mediaeval Times,* in **Shaping the Christian Message**, edited by Gerard Sloyan, Paulist Press, Glen Rock, New Jersey, 1958, pp. 46-69.

Lance, Derek, *Roman Catholic Children and What They are Being Taught,* in **Religious Education**, edited by Jebb, Darton, Longman & Todd, London, 1968, pp. 39-56.

La Noue, George R., *The Conditions of Public School Neutrality,* in **Religion and Public Education**, edited by Sizer, Houghton Mifflin Company, Boston, 1967, pp. 22-36.

Liégé, André, *The Ministry of the Word: From Kerygma to Catechesis,* in **Readings in European Catechetics**, edited by Delcuve & Godin, Lumen Vitae Press, Brussels, 1962, pp. 21-36.

Liégé, André, **Liturgy Newspaper Vol. 3 No. 4, 1972**, published by St. Thomas More Centre for Pastoral Liturgy, 7A Henry Road, London.

Michiels, Robrecht, *Incarnation. The Relation between Faith in God and His Revelation in Christ,* in **Lumen Vitae**, Vol. XXV, 1970, No. 4, pp. 629-656.

211

McCluskey, Neil G., S.J., *The New Secularity and the Requirements of Pluralism,* in **Religion and Public Education,** edited by Theodore Sizer, Houghton Mifflin Company, Boston, 1967, pp. 231-248.

Miller, Samuel H., *Oppositions between Religion and Education,* in **Religion and Public Education,** edited by Theodore Sizer, Houghton Mifflin Company, Boston, 1967, pp. 112-124.

Moore, Dom. Sebastian OSB., *The Teaching Role of the Church,* in **Religious Education,** edited by Dom Philip Jebb, Darton, Longman & Todd, London, 1968, pp. 246-270.

Moran, Gabriel, *Catechetics R.I.P.,* in Commonwealth, 18th December, 1970, pp. 299-302.

Moran, Gabriel, *Religious Education Today,* Address to the 39th General Chapter of The Brothers of the Christian Schools in October, 1967. Printed in **Our Apostolate,** Vol. 15, No. 4, 1967, and Vol. 16, No. 1, 1968, De La Salle Training College, Castle Hill, NSW, Australia.

Moran, Gabriel, *A New Catechism. A Discussion of the Dutch Catechism.* Reprinted in **Our Apostolate,** Vol. 16, No. 1, pp. 32-35 (cf. above).

Nebrada, Alfonso S.J., *Fundamental Catechesis,* reprinted from The Medellin Papers, in **Our Apostolate,** Vol. 18, Nos. 2 & 3. De La Salle Training College, Castle Hill, NSW, Australia.

Nebrada, Alfonso S.J., *The Preparation of the Message,* in **Faith and Commitment,** edited by Mark G. Link, Loyola University Press, Chicago, 1964, pp. 186-203.

Nebrada, Alfonso S.J., *The Theological Problem of Transmission,* in **Lumen Vitae.,** Vol. XX, 1965, No. 2, pp. 309-324.

Nebrada, Alfonso S.J., *East Asian Study Week on Mission Catechetics (Bangkok),* in **Lumen Vitae.,** Vol. XVII, 1962, No. 4, pp. 717-732.

Oakeshott, Michael, *Education: The Engagement and the Frustration,* in the Proceedings of the Philosophy of Education Society of Great Britain. Talk given on January 2nd., 1971, pp. 43-76.

Olafson, Frederick, A., *Teaching ABOUT Religion: Some Reservations,* in **Religion and Public Education,** edited by Theodore Sizer, Houghton Mafflin Company, Boston, 1967, pp. 84-98.

Peters, R. S., *Moral Education — Tradition or Reason,* in **Let's Teach Them Right,** edited by Christopher Macy, Pemberton Books, London, 1968, pp. 100-110.

Peters, R. S., *Reason and Habit: The Paradox of Moral Education,* in **Philosophy and Education,** edited by Israel Scheffler, Allyn & Bacon, Boston (2nd edition), 1966, pp. 245-262.

Peters, R. S., *Education as Initiation,* in **Philosophical Analysis and Education,** edited by Reginald D. Archambault, Routledge & Kegan Paul, London, 1965, pp. 87-112.

Peters, R. S., *What is an educational process?,* in **The Concept of Education,** edited by R. S. Peters, Routledge & Kegan Paul, London, 1967, pp. 1-23.

Ranwez, Pierre S.J., *General Tendencies in Contemporary Catechetics,* in **Shaping the Christian Message**, edited by Gerard Sloyan, Deus Books, Paulist Press, Glen Rock, New Jersey, 1958, pp. 119-134.

Scheffler, Israel, *Philosophical Models of Teaching,* in **Philosophy and Education**, edited by Israel Scheffler, Allyn & Bacon, Boston, 1966 (2nd edition) pp. 99-114.

Sloyan, Gerard S., *The Relation of the Catechism to the Work of Religious Formation,* in Modern Catechetics: **Message and Method in Religious Formation**, edited by Gerard Sloyan, Collier-Macmillan, London, 1963, pp. 63-101.

Sloyan, Gerard S., *Religious Education: From Early Christianity to Mediaeval Times,* in **Shaping the Christian Message**, edited by Gerard Sloyan, Deus Books, Paulist Press, Glen Rock, New Jersey, 1958, pp. 11-45.

Smart, Ninian R., *The Comparative Study of Religion in Schools,* in **Let's Teach Them Right**, edited by Christopher Macy, Pemberton Books, London, 1968, pp. 61-69.

Theis, Margaretha, *The Dialogic Principle in a catechesis for adolescent girls,* in **Lumen Vitae.**, Vol. XXV, 1970, No. 1, pp. 69-92.

Tilman, Klemens, *Origin and Development of Modern Catechetical Methods,* in **Teaching All Nations**, edited by Johannes Hofinger, S.J., Burns & Oates, London, 1961, pp. 81-94.

Van Caster, Marcel S.J., *The Substance of the Christian Message: The Mystery of Salvation,* in **Faith and Commitment**, edited by Mark G. Link, Loyola University Press, Chicago, 1965, pp. 28-42.

Van Caster, Marcel S.J., *Towards a Christian Understanding of Experience,* in **Lumen Vitae.**, Vol. XXV, 1970, No. 4, pp. 599-616.

Van Caster, Marcel S.J., *A Catechesis for Liberation,* in **Lumen Vitae**, Vol. XXVII, 1972, No. 2, pp. 281-303.

Van Caster, Marcel S.J., *Catechesis in the Spirit of Vatican II,* in **Lumen** Vitae, Vol. XXI, 1966, No. 2, pp. 117-134.

White, Morton S., *Religion and the Higher Learning,* in Philosophy of Education, edited by Israel Scheffler, Allyn & Bacon, Boston, 1966 (2nd edition), pp. 307-326.

Wilson, John, *The Logical Basis of Moral and Religious Education,* in **Let's Teach Them Right**, edited by Christopher Macy, Pemberton Press, London, 1968, pp. 93-99.

INDEX OF SUBJECTS

Butler Act (1944), 1, 6, 17, see liftout, 179.

Baptism, of infants, 37, 132;
    — promises of, 178, 205;
    — responsibilities of, 34, 35, 175, 176.

Catechesis, biblical basis of, 33;
    — concept of, 93–118; compared with religious education 163–177;
    — core of, 93, 109, 182;
    — definitions of, 26–27;
    — distinguished from other pastoral forms, 32, 196–200;
    — ideal of in relation to education, 51–56;
    — in documents of Vatican II. 78–80;
    — of object, 18;
    — of subject, 18;
    — origin and development of, 25–29;
    — of witness, 43;
    — recipient of, 32;
    — sources of, 3, 60;
    — poles of, 93, 11–112.

Catechetics, 98, 101–102.

Catechetical mission, 35–38;
    — movement of modern times, 1–24;
    — theological influences on, 59–92;
    — educational assumptions underlying, 32–38;
    — model of teaching, 39–51, 103;
    — methods, 8.

Catechism, traditional, 4, 8, 11, 28–29, 44, 205;
    — approach, 40–47; rejection of, 94–107;
    — lesson, 2;
    — diocesan, 30;
    — teaching the, 42;
    — of Christian Doctrine, 6;
    — of the Council of Trent (Roman), 5, 29–31, 65, 93;
    — Penny Catechism, 41–42;
    — Australian, 3, 13, 14–15, 17;
    — German, 3, 13–14, 17;
    — Dutch, 27, 94.

Catechist, duties of, 35–38, 116, 204;
    — as teacher, 176, 177, 187–191.

Catechize, to, 34, 204.

Catechumenate, 26, 94, 204.

Christian education, catechesis within, 54–55;
    — Declaration on, 79–80;
    — aims of, 34–35.

216

217

Initiation, 27–29, 67, 144.

Influences, theological on catechetical movement, 59–92.

Instruction, in the Faith, 29, 32;
— in religion, 52;
— positive, 52;
— religious, 131;
— distinguished from education, 134–136.

Journals, catechetical, 1.

Kerygma, 196–200;
— in crisis, 17, 106, 200–201.

Kerygmatic movement, 90, 96.

Knower, 6, 36, 165.

Knowledge, Christian, 2–3;
— distinct forms of, 125 n. 15, 128;
— human, 165.

Language, of catechesis, 25, 104, 111;
— in different models of religious education, 166–168, 170.

Laity, Decree on the Apostolate of, 73–75.

Liturgy, Constitution on, 60, 64–68.

Liturgical, life of the Church, 10, 29.

Life-centred situations, 2–3, 18–22;
— "Leakage from the faith", 6, 56.

Liberation, theology of, 107–108;
— a catechesis for, 108.

Learning for Life Syllabus, 164–165, 167–168, 166, 179.

Magisterium, of the Church, 177.

Magisterial, approach in teaching, 2, 5, 7, 8;
— model of teaching, 7.

Man, theory of, 122.

Manner, of education, 122.

Matter, of education, 122.

Meaning, of life, 122.

Method, catechetical, 8, 30, 41–42;
— discussion, 3, 19;
— in religious teaching, see liftout, 169;
— Munich, 8, 13.

Mission, of the catechist, 35–38;
— of the Church in catechesis, 33–38.

219

Missions, Decree on, 60, 79.

Models, of religious education, 156–162.

Mobility, social, 7 n.

Motivation, 2–3, 5.

Movement, modern catechetical, 1–24;
— theological influences on, 59–91.

Message, 36.

Neutrality, approach (teaching about), see liftout, 181;
— procedural, 150–152.

Non-directivity in catechetics, 3, 23, 96, 97.

Non-Christian religions, 82–83, 116, 184–186.

Objectivity, in teaching religion, 139–142, 145–150.

Orthodoxy, 38.

Orders, religious, 38.

Paraliturgy, 15;
— paraliturgical ceremonies, 15, 67.

Parental rights, 54, 133, 149, 193.

Pedagogy, traditional of the Church, 29–32.

People, of God, 60, 67, 70–72;
— pilgrim, 3, 23, 71.

Participants, role of in catechesis, 109–110, see liftout, 168.

Preaching, 45, 197–198.

Pre-evangelization, 21, 200–203.

Pre-catechesis, 21, 200–203.

Propositional, view of Revelation, 61.

Poles of catechesis, 111–112.

Pluralism, in forms of worship, 66;
— in catechesis, 97, 183.

Pupils, experience of, 51;
— passive, 50–51.

Principles, guiding, see liftout, 168–169.

Rationality, human, 128, 144, 189.

Relationship, of participants in catechesis, 2–3, 5, 168;
— of participants in education, 137.

Religion, 121, 125–126;
— the study of other religions, see liftout, 184–187;
— and education, 120;

— from the viewpoint of education, 120, 123–129.

AUTHOR INDEX

Alves, Colin D. 154.
Amalorpavadass, D. S. 105, 198.
Audinet, Jacques 20, 47, 105; 107.

Babin, Pierre 23, 96, 97, 98, 99, 100, 103, 107, 111, 113, 114, 115,
        169, 173, 175, 176, 181, 183.
Ball, William B. 149, 153.
Baum, Gregory 72.
Bellarmine, Robert (Saint) 50.
Bonhoeffer, Dietrich 86, 87.
Bournique, Jacques 68, 105, 203.
Branigan, J. J. 56.
Bultman, R. 85, 87, 88.
Butler, B. C. (Bishop) 81.

Canisius, P. (Saint) 50.
Carter, G. Emmet (Bishop) 29, 130.
Christopher, J. P. 26.
Colomb, Joseph 10, 20, 29, 35, 96, 103, 118, 173, 179, 195, 198, 201.
Congar, Yves 84.
Coudreau, Francois 33, 37, 52.
Cox, Harvey 87, 141, 143.

Delooz, Pierre 97.
Drinkwater, F. H. 8.

Erdozain, L. 108, 112.

Freire, Paulo 192.

Goldbrunner, J. 14.
Goldman, R. 17, 41, 146, 154.
Grasso, Domenico 45, 199.

Hare, R. M. 150.
Heenan, John (Cardinal) 37, 39.
Hirst, Paul 125, 155, 156, 158, 159.
Hofinger, Johannes 10, 42, 105.

Jeffreys, M. V. C. 123, 147.
John XXIII 59.
Jungmann, J. A. 1; 10, 26, 29, 65, 89.

Knox, Ronald 12.
Kohlberg, L. 154.

Lance, Derek 40, 41.
Le Du, J. 103.
Lee, James Michael 45, 46, 49.

223

224